HOUSING AND THE MIGRATION OF LABOUR
IN ENGLAND AND WALES

Housing and the Migration of Labour in England and Wales

JAMES H. JOHNSON
JOHN SALT
PETER A. WOOD
University College London

assisted by
ROBIN FLOWERDEW
NATHALIE HADJIFOTIOU
and HILARY ROBINSON

SAXON HOUSE | LEXINGTON BOOKS

Published by
SAXON HOUSE, D.C. Heath Ltd.
Westmead, Farnborough, Hants, England

Jointly with
LEXINGTON BOOKS, D.C. Heath & Co.
Lexington Mass. U.S.A.

c C

ISBN 0 347 01024 5
Library of Congress Catalog Card Number 73-21196

Printed in Great Britain by Robert MacLehose & Co. Ltd
The University Press, Glasgow

Contents

List of figures

Preface

This book is the result of a study concerned with housing and the geographical mobility of labour, largely financed by the Joseph Rowntree Memorial Trust and undertaken in the Department of Geography at University College London. The project was an exploratory investigation, in which it was hoped to identify the key relationships between housing and labour mobility and to provide a framework for further research. The work undertaken consisted of three separate components. The first involved a survey of the literature on the housing and labour markets in Britain in an attempt to indicate the points at which housing characteristics and labour mobility might be expected to interact. The second used census information for the analysis of migration flows and for the study of the characteristics of the origin and destination areas of migrants. The third and major part of the research programme employed questionnaire surveys to assess the migration experience of individual households in four sample areas.

The work presented here is in every sense a piece of co-operative research, involving not only ourselves but also the various research assistants who have been employed on the project at various times. During the first year Mrs Nathalie Hadjifotiou, Mr Richard Herne and Miss Hilary Robinson made valuable contributions during the elaboration of the original idea for the project and played a most important part in the design of the questionnaire that was used. During the second year of the project Mrs Hadjifotiou and Miss Robinson continued as full-time research assistants and, as well as carrying the main load of organising the field survey and manipulating census data, they contributed to the writing-up process by preparing a number of working papers which are referred to in the book. At this stage, too, Mr Martin Cawood served as a part-time research assistant, largely concerned with administering the questionnaire survey, and Dr Tom Wesselkampfer gave valuable advice on computational problems. During the third year of the project the Department of Geography at University College London allocated a departmental research assistant to help with the final stage of the project: we have a particular debt to Mr Robin Flowerdew for his many valued comments on a number of aspects of the work and for his considerable assistance with the preparation of the final text of this book, particularly in drafting chapters 5 and 7.

In carrying out this study we have been assisted at various times by a great number of individuals who have freely given their help. A complete list would be impossible to compile, but three people must be singled out for special mention. Mr L.E. Waddilove gave our original idea for this project a most sympathetic reception when we approached the Joseph Rowntree Memorial Trust for financial help; and the Trust generously supported the project for two years. Professor W.R. Mead, Head of the Department of Geography at University College London, helped us in innumerable ways, not least in making space and research assistance available at critical moments in the project. Mr Ken Wass, senior technician in the Department of Geography, assisted with the financial administration of the project and gave useful advice on the maps and diagrams, which were drawn by his staff in the cartographic unit of the Department of Geography.

The credit for much in this book should be given to these various people. Its faults must remain our responsibility.

1 October 1973   James H. Johnson
Department of Geography   John Salt
University College London   Peter A. Wood

Introduction

Movements of population have been classified in many ways, reflecting the complexities of migration. A critical distinction, however, is between temporary movements connected with everyday activities and those moves which involve a change of home, with the social and economic costs that this process entails. Moves of this latter kind are particularly important since they are relatively permanent — insofar as any population movement in a modern urban society is permanent — and hence they represent a significant force behind geographical change. This book is concerned with aspects of this last type of movement: in the context of England and Wales it examines 'labour migration' — that is, those movements of population that involve changes of residence associated with changes of job.

Labour migration results in relatively long-distance relocation of skills and, thus, has an important bearing on regional contrasts in economic change. It involves a move from one community to another, making an important impact on the social life of the families and communities involved. Finally, it is likely that the pressures encouraging labour migration will become increasingly strong in the future, as current social and technological changes foster greater mobility and as the economic adjustments associated with the enlarged European Economic Community begin to take effect.

In spite of these pressures and the present high level of mobility, it is clear that major barriers to labour migration exist. The sheer money costs of moving probably prevent migration in many cases. Distance and social disruption undoubtedly deter many would-be movers for whom community and family ties are too strong to be easily broken. Lack of information about job opportunities in other areas also tends towards stability rather than movement.

Housing is often assumed to be one of the most important barriers to labour migration. An OECD seminar on manpower policy claimed that in Britain 'the principal obstacle to geographic mobility is generally agreed to be the shortage of suitable houses'.[1] A similar sentiment was expressed by the Confederation of British Industries, which commented on 'the general discouragement of movement resulting from current housing policy'.[2] According to the CBI the shortage and price structure of housing contributed

1

to high labour costs by deterring movement of skilled and trainable workers, thus aggravating labour shortage. A pool of housing at a wide range of price was regarded as an essential prerequisite of increased mobility and hence important for the sound growth of the economy. Stone has attempted to elucidate the relationships between housing and labour mobility in similar fashion: 'Many people are likely to be discouraged from moving to a new area if suitable accommodation is not at their disposal, and firms are likely to be discouraged from creating additional jobs, which can only be filled by migrant labour, if accommodation is not available for the workers'.[3] A similar observation was made for Scotland in the Toothill Report on the Scottish economy.[4]

Despite unanimity of opinion that connections exist between housing and labour mobility, the actual relationship is far from clear. Indeed Cullingworth was able to comment on the lack of any firm factual information on the importance of housing in labour mobility.[5] A popular view is that owner-occupied houses allow more labour mobility, and that publicly-owned and rent-controlled housing is associated with much less movement of population. What firm evidence there is, however, tends to be conflicting.[6] The real situation is too complicated to be expressed as a simple relationship between migration and tenure. The people who are attracted to new owner-occupied housing are largely selected by their financial prospects and family structure and would tend to be mobile anyway, whatever the nature of their housing. Similarly, the average resident in local-authority housing estates may be less inclined to move a long distance to a new job for reasons which have little to do with his house.

Differences in local housing markets, in individual housing preferences and in access to housing finance are all likely to affect the relationship between housing and mobility. Nor is labour migration all of one type: movements of population may involve people of very different socio-economic and demographic characteristics; the distances moved and the attributes of the origin and destination areas may vary. The effect of housing on mobility may differ according to all these factors.

The distribution of jobs and homes is an expression of the operation of the housing and labour markets. In the economic literature on housing the statements that are made are often concerned with the general situation, rather than with the spatial variations that are found when the national picture is disaggregated. This is perhaps less true of labour market studies, but nonetheless these often bear little relationship to the areas within which people actually search for jobs. As a result there is little written about the inter-relation of local housing and local labour markets, but it is clear that these markets are complementary and reinforcing. As Stewart has pointed out, 'power in the job market is associated with power in the housing market, while a weak job market position (low, insecure income) is often linked to a weak position in the housing market'.[7] The same association also exists in spatial terms, since the limits of local labour markets are likely to coincide with those of local housing markets.

Despite the known existence of such associations, a general criticism that can be made of housing research in Britain is that there has been a failure to explore the role of housing as one part of a complex economic and social system. In particular there is need to investigate the links between the housing market and other urban processes and phenomena. One of these phenomena is the migration of population between local labour markets; and the aim of the investigation presented in this book is to explore in greater detail than has been attempted before the relationship between the geographical mobility of labour and the housing characteristics of migrants.

The book can be divided into two sections. The first outlines the general picture of labour migration in England and Wales, using local labour market areas as a framework for study; the second describes the experiences of households which have been involved in the labour migration process.

The first chapter discusses the general context of labour migration and housing in Britain. Then, in the second chapter, a theoretical basis for the study of labour migration is developed and an attempt is made to indicate some of the likely connections between labour mobility and housing. Chapters 3 and 4 present basic factual information about housing and labour market conditions in England and Wales in the mid-1960s, using data from the 1966 Sample Census. Chapter 3 provides a description and classification of the hundred local labour market areas that can be recognised in England and Wales, discussing their migration experience and their housing and employment conditions. Chapter 4 analyses the geographical pattern of labour migration in terms of those movements of population which took place between these local labour market areas during 1965–66. Although there has been previous discussion of labour migration in Britain, this is the first attempt that has been made to plot in some detail migration flows at the optimum scale for studying this phenomenon, which is the local labour market area.

At this point the scale of analysis changes, with attention being focused on the experiences of the households actually making the decision to move home and job. Chapter 5 summarises previous studies of migration which appear relevant for the present investigation and forms a point of reference for the study of labour migrant households presented later.

Chapter 6 discusses some of the methodological problems involved in contacting labour migrant households and outlines the contents of the questionnaire used in a field study of four contrasting areas in England and Wales. Chapter 7 portrays the characteristics of the labour migrant households that were interviewed, in a manner which allows some comparison with Chapter 5. Chapter 8 examines the causes and consequences of labour migration as revealed by our survey; and Chapter 9 concentrates on the specific problems that our sample of labour migrants experienced in their search for new accommodation and in obtaining access to it.

The work that is presented in this book must remain a preliminary investigation of an important but difficult topic. What has been attempted here is to outline the spatial expression of labour migration and to codify the experiences of households which have simultaneously moved home and job on migrating into four contrasting places in England and Wales. It can justly be argued that the book raises more questions than it answers, but at least its conclusions support the proposition that the further understanding of the geographical mobility of labour and of the role of housing in the migration process demand a disaggregated mode of analysis.

Notes

[1] Organisation for Economic Co-operation and Development, *International Management Seminar on Active Manpower Policy*, Paris 1964, p. 64.

[2] Confederation of British Industry, *C.B.I. Regional Study: Regional Development and Distribution of Industry Policy*, duplicated typescript (1968), p. 11.

[3] P.A. Stone, *Urban Development in Britain; Standards, Costs and Resources 1964–2004* vol. 1 (Population Trends and Housing), Cambridge 1970, p. 280.

[4] *The Scottish Economy 1965 to 1970: a Plan for Expansion*, Cmnd 2864, HMSO, Edinburgh 1966, p. 63.

[5] J.B. Cullingworth, *Housing and Labour Mobility*, Paris 1969, p. 67.

[6] J.H. Johnson, J. Salt and P.A. Wood, 'Housing and the geographical mobility of labour in England and Wales: some theoretical considerations', in L.A. Kosinski and R.M. Prothero (eds.), *People on the Move* (in press).

[7] M. Stewart, 'Markets, choice and urban planning', *Town Planning Review* 44, 1973, p. 212.

1 Migration, Employment and Housing: the British Context

For the purposes of this study movements of population involving both a permanent change of residence and a permanent change of job will be called 'labour migration'. Unfortunately there is little firm information about the number of such moves. The 1966 Census recorded over five million residential moves in Britain during the year before the enumeration; and during the five years from 1961 to 1966 the number was 16 million, virtually one-third of the total population.[1] More significant for the present study than numbers of individuals moving is the number of households that migrate. Unfortunately there is no available source of information that tells us this. However, previous surveys of households have found that about 7 to 8 per cent move house each year.[2] The 1966 Census recorded 15·7 million households in England and Wales, and assuming that 7·5 per cent of these will move, it seems reasonable to suppose that about 1·2 million households move house each year.

But many of these moves were made for reasons unconnected with employment, and many movers must have changed homes more than once. Even less is known of the number of people who change jobs in any given year, although a Ministry of Labour estimate, made in 1966, has suggested that over 8 million people in Britain change their employer every year.[3] Again, as some individuals will have changed more than once, the figure does not represent 8 million different people, but in relation to a total labour force of 25 million it will at least bear the conclusion that a remarkable volume of job-changing does take place. Confirmation of this estimate comes from an OECD report on labour mobility, published in 1965, which suggested a labour turn-over of about 30 to 40 per cent per annum.[4]

Many of these moves of homes or jobs were independent of one another, since they took place over a limited distance, so that a move of job did not necessarily demand a change of home or *vice versa*. One-half of the residential moves recorded in the census were within the same local authority area; and similarly, Harris and Clausen's sample study showed that almost 80 per cent of residential moves were of less than 10 miles.[5] Nevertheless the absolute number of people moving longer distances is large; between 1961 and 1966, for example, gross inter-regional movement was over 2 million people and it seems reasonable to think that many of the longer moves were stimulated by job reasons. Harris and Clausen demonstrate, for example, that for migrants who moved over 10 miles, the most frequent reason for moving was because of a job, and the proportion moving for this reason increased with distance.[6]

Migration and employment in Britain

Such a large amount of migration is characteristic of a modern industrial economy like that of Great Britain where technological and ensuing industrial change necessitate redistribution of labour, both occupationally and geographically, in accordance with changes in demand. During the last half-century many of the older industries, such as mining, heavy metals and textiles, have suffered decline in their demands for labour. In contrast, new light industries, including electrical engineering and motor-vehicle manufacture, have presented increasing numbers of job opportunities. Broadly speaking, the areas of decline have been the old industrial areas of the coalfields of the north and west, while most expansion has taken place in the towns of midland and southern England. Hence there has been a regional shift in the demand for labour.

This has not been matched by a parallel regional shift in the supply of labour. Since the Second World War all the Standard Regions have experienced population growth, and in most cases natural increase was the main element in this expansion. (For Standard Regions see Fig. 1.1.) It is true that a considerable amount of inter-regional migration has taken place, in particular from areas where job numbers are declining to areas of expansion.[7] Only in East Anglia, where in recent years much in-migration has been planned overspill, and the south-west, with a large proportion of retirement movement, has migration accounted for more than half the total population growth. (Table 1.1).

Details of regional changes in population distribution and the proportions accounted for by natural change and by migration are well-documented elsewhere.[8] All the Standard Regions have been growing in population and, although there are regional variations in the rates of natural increase, these differences are not as great as regional variations in job opportunities as measured by the unemployment rate. Nor do regional rates of natural increase necessarily correspond with regional changes in

6

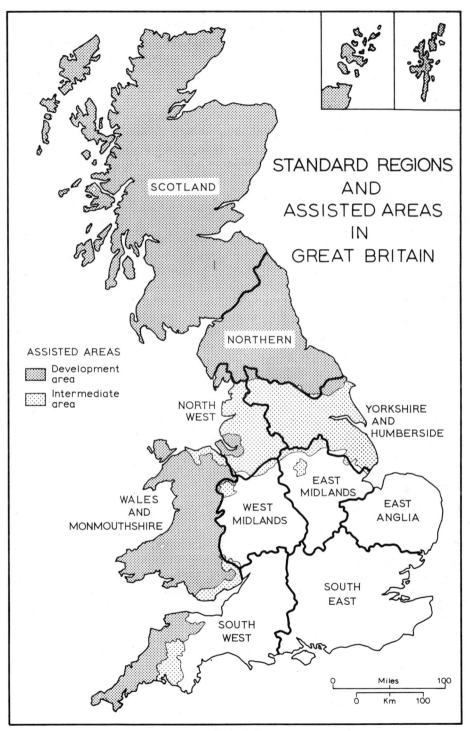

ASSISTED AREAS
Development area
Intermediate area

SCOTLAND

STANDARD REGIONS
AND
ASSISTED AREAS
IN
GREAT BRITAIN

NORTHERN

NORTH WEST

YORKSHIRE AND HUMBERSIDE

EAST MIDLANDS

EAST ANGLIA

WALES AND MONMOUTHSHIRE

WEST MIDLANDS

SOUTH EAST

SOUTH WEST

Miles
0   100
Km
0   100

Fig. 1.1

Table 1.1

Great Britain: components of population change by regions, 1951 – 69

Region	Natural increase (per cent)	Net migration (per cent)
West Midlands	13·6	2·3
East Midlands	11·8	3·3
Northern	11·0	−4·2
South-east	9·9	3·4
East Anglia	9·6	9·7
Yorkshire and Humberside	9·2	−3·1
North-west	8·2	−3·1
South-west	7·2	8·4
Wales	6·5	−1·9
Scotland	12·4	−11·3
Great Britain	10·0	—

Source: Department of Environment, *Long-term Population Distribution in Great Britain: a Study*, HMSO, 1971, pp. 15, 16

the numbers of jobs. For example, between 1951 and 1969 the rate of natural increase of 9·9 per cent in the South-east was not the highest in Britain, despite the region's economic prosperity reflected in low levels of unemployment. In contrast, Scotland and the Northern region, both areas characterised by employment decline in major industries, have had consistently high levels of fertility and, despite considerable net outward migration, they have maintained levels of natural increase above the national average.

As rates of natural increase vary between regions, so also do rates of migration. Eversley[9] has demonstrated that a comparison of regional rates of natural increase and of migration suggests three principal categories: (1) those areas which have more or less retained their natural increase; (2) those which have grown faster; and (3) those which have lost population through migration. These categories do not entirely correspond with levels of economic prosperity, certainly not with 'prosperous', 'development' and 'intermediate' areas. There is a closer relationship between migration and regional prosperity if one considers only the migration of males of working age.[10] Between 1961 and 1966, for example, the traditional high-unemployment regions of Scotland and the North had the heaviest losses of men of working age, although the prosperous South-east and West Midlands merely achieved migration balance for this group.

The principal features of population change have been described at the level of Standard Regions, and although variations exist at this scale, their range is not very great. These broad regional figures mask considerably larger sub-regional variations in both natural change and in migration. In the case of natural change some extremes do exist. In the North-west region, for example, the highly fertile Merseyside had a remarkable natural increase of 14 per cent between 1951 and 1969, compared with a natural decrease of 5·5 per cent in the Fylde. [11] In general, however, sub-regional variations in net migration exceed those in natural change. As a result, although natural increase is an important element in population change, it is migration which largely brings about local divergences from national trends. Migration has a double impact. Movement of people between areas has a direct effect on population distribution. Migration also tends to be selective: there is abundant evidence that it is young adults who move most readily. Migration therefore acts on population distribution indirectly through its effect on demographic composition, reducing fertility in areas of out-migration, increasing it in areas of in-migration. Eversley argues that, although overall changes in population distribution are not drastic when measured by the total population of Standard Regions, certain age-groups and sub-regions can be identified where serious movements occur. [12] Even if the demand for labour expanded at an even rate throughout the country, which it does not, local differences in fertility and migration imply that additional workers will be added to local labour forces at uneven rates. Policies are therefore required to ensure the relatively faster expansion of employment in the high-fertility areas to absorb the proportionally larger entry to the workforce, or some migration is necessary to redress the balance.

It is also clear that, at the broader regional level, no simple distinction can be made between regions of labour surplus and shortage. Much has been written about the so-called 'drift to the South' and the conclusion has been drawn from the use of this generic term that the principal internal currents of migration have been long-distance moves from the depressed to the prosperous areas — for example, from north-eastern to south-eastern England. To a large extent this view stems from the misconception that unemployment is high throughout the assisted areas. In fact this is not so and, especially over the last decade, unemployment in Britain has been developing a pattern of greater local variation. Thus, within the assisted areas, now covering virtually all the northern and western parts of Britain, there are adjacent local labour markets with widely differing levels of unemployment (Fig. 1.2). At the same time, within midland and south-eastern England, there are pockets of unemployment

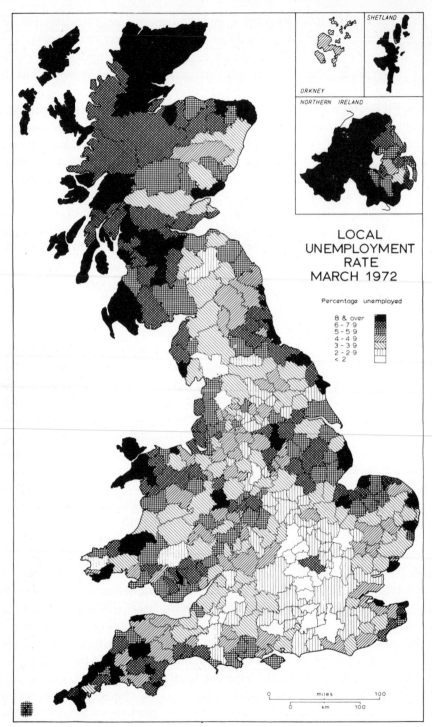

SHETLAND

ORKNEY

NORTHERN IRELAND

LOCAL
UNEMPLOYMENT
RATE
MARCH 1972

Percentage unemployed

8 & over
6 - 7.9
5 - 5.9
4 - 4.9
3 - 3.9
2 - 2.9
< 2

miles   100

km   100

Fig. 1.2

considerably above the national average. This situation indicates that spatial equilibrium in the labour market as a whole can be approached through relatively short-distance movements of labour from local areas of unemployment to nearby ones where job opportunities are more plentiful.

Furthermore, the indications are that this pattern is likely to persist in the future. Recent trends in local unemployment suggest that communities are increasingly being hit by redundancies that are caused, not by concentration of employment in structurally-declining industries, but by corporate rationalisation programmes as employers review their production patterns in the face of rapid technological change. Increasingly, unemployment is being faced not only in the nineteenth-century industrial areas concentrated on the coalfields. It is also being found in the more dispersed early twentieth-century industrial areas that grew up in the West Midlands, the South-east and elsewhere outside the older industrial zones, where plant is now getting old and restricted sites are becoming more uneconomic as a result of the adoption of new technologies.

Policies to aid labour migration

These spatial imbalances have implications for national economic and social policy and they have been a prime motivation in the somewhat disjointed series of measures adopted by Government and employers to influence the movement of population. Government measures have primarily operated through the medium of the 'work to the workers' policy, attempting to stem the flow of labour from the depressed areas, with an emphasis more recently on steering industry to growth zones within the assisted areas. Thus policies for achieving full employment in the regions have been more geared towards the geographical mobility of jobs than to the geographical mobility of labour.

These policies concerned with the distribution of industry have been complemented by attempts to assist the movement of population to those areas where it is needed. Subsidies from both national and local government are available for families moving to live and work in the new and overspill towns, through the Industrial Selection Scheme. Most of this assistance goes to aid migration out of the congested inner areas of the conurbations, especially London. Hence it does not necessarily aid migration from areas of labour surplus to those of shortage. Attempts have been made, however, to steer industry to growth zones within depressed areas, to new towns like Washington and Cwmbran, thus encouraging intra-regional movement away from small, declining communities towards those more favoured in their locations.

11

Government assistance for migration between local labour market areas, where the destination is not a new or overspill town, is limited. The Department of Employment operates three schemes for migrant households in which a range of grants and allowances is available to cover travel and housing costs, including assistance with house sale and purchase.

These are the Employment Transfer Scheme (called Resettlement Transfer Scheme until April 1972), the Key Workers Scheme and the Nucleus Labour Force Scheme. The first of these is a general scheme designed to assist unemployed workers or those likely to become redundant within six months to move away from home and take jobs in other areas beyond daily travelling distance. The other two schemes are more restricted in their application. The Key Workers Scheme is designed to assist employed workers who transfer either permanently or temporarily beyond reasonable daily travelling distance of their homes to key posts in establishments which their employers are setting up or expanding in assisted areas. The Nucleus Labour Force Scheme helps unemployed workers from areas of high unemployment to move temporarily for training at the parent factories of firms preparing to set up new plants in the workers' home areas. After training they return home to form the nucleus of employees in the new establishments.

The numbers taking advantage of these schemes have been small. Before 1972 only 7,000 to 8,000 per annum received assistance, the vast majority under the Resettlement Transfer Scheme. This small number reflects the modest level of assistance made available. However, in March 1972 the Government announced an increase from £1·4 million to £5 million in the money available for mobility assistance, the increase to become operational almost immediately.[13] More aid was given to individual migrant households and the changes had an abrupt effect. During the first year of operation, grants totalling £4·4 million were paid to help people move away from home and take jobs in other areas. Between April 1972 and March 1973 18,557 people were paid grants, exceeding by over 2,000 the number estimated when the scheme was brought in. Over 80 per cent of these movements originated in the assisted areas, with Scotland (5,511), the Northern region (3,001) and the North-west (2,706) being the principal origins. [14]

Two points of special significance arise from these figures. First, the introduction of a higher level of assistance has more than doubled the number of migrants in Government-supported schemes in just one year. Although we cannot know how many of these people would have moved anyway, the statistics support the conclusion that there are many potential migrants, who have hitherto lacked the resources to move, but will do

12

so if supported by a modest Government investment. This contention is given added weight by the fact that many more people than expected actually took advantage of the schemes.

Second, there is an important geographical gap in the operation of these aids to mobility. The Employment Transfer Scheme is primarily available for unemployed workers who have no immediate prospects of jobs in their home areas. In practice most aid has gone to workers moving within or from the assisted areas, but, apart from the special case of the Industrial Selection Scheme, there has been little help for migrants wanting to move within or from the 'prosperous' areas. Yet we know there are substantial currents of migration within these areas and also from them to the assisted areas.

Despite the increases in Government sponsorship of migration, a large proportion of the total migration flows within the country attracts little or no Government aid under employment mobility schemes. This does not mean that these moves are completely unaided, since at least some of them are sponsored by individual employers, although there is a marked absence of statistical information on the scale of this sponsorship. The growth of corporate organisation, with spatially-dispersed production and administrative units, frequently leads to the transference of labour within a firm from one location to another. In such cases the costs of migration are usually borne by the company. Executive and, occasionally, skilled manual grades are the groups most affected by these moves. Many firms are also willing to pay removal expenses for new recruits to the higher echelons of management. Unfortunately, a large sector of the labour force is not covered by the company umbrella. The National Coal Board stands almost alone in assisting the movement of workers of all grades from pits which are closing to areas where coal production is expanding: between 1962 and 1970 over 14,000 miners were moved between coalfields under official NCB schemes. For the most part, however, manual and lower-paid clerical workers, perhaps the most vulnerable to the employment changes wrought by modern technology, rarely benefit from the geographical labour mobility policies of firms. With little financial aid for migration available from either Government or employers, these sectors are highly immobile. The sheer money costs of moving, in terms of fares and removal expenses of various kinds, will probably prevent movement even if the deterrents of housing problems, social disruption, family ties and lack of information can be overcome.

The housing context in England and Wales

Data for the study of the housing market in England and Wales are grossly inadequate, especially at the regional and local level. [15] Hence regional and urban analyses of housing have been regarded as geographically-restricted versions of national analysis, although national data are inadequate for use at smaller scales. Despite this shortage of data, there is a great volume of literature on the housing market, most of little or no relevance for the present study. Much of what has been written is concerned with policy and with the estimation of housing need, both present and future. At first sight this would seem to be important in assessing whether housing shortage exists and acts as a deterrent to migration, but there is still no really satisfactory estimate of the degree to which need is met at the national level, let alone in local housing markets. To some extent deficiency stems from the lack of any commonly-held view of what constitutes an acceptable standard of housing provision. It also results from the various tax and social policies which distort the housing market, making it impossible to assess the real demand.

Attempts have been made to measure surpluses and shortages of housing. The simplest way is to use census information to compare number of dwellings with number of households, but the validity of the resulting balance is questionable. Cullingworth has pointed out that, where accommodation is shared, the census definition of a household may underestimate the number of potential households. Instead he uses the 'household unit', an omnibus term which includes 'households without families and all families in family-type households'. [16] The 1961 Census recorded 14,646,000 dwellings in England and Wales and 14,621,000 households, an excess of dwellings of 25,000. The number of household units, however, was 15,043,000, giving a deficit of dwellings of 397,000. Cullingworth himself admitted that such figures give only a crude estimate of housing excess or deficit; much depends, for example, on the proportion of households that share of necessity but would in fact prefer separate accommodation.

Such numerical comparisons of totals oversimplify the very complex situation that exists in reality with the national housing market being divided up into series of spatial sub-markets, each including different types of accommodation. It is quite possible that in some areas there are shortages of some types of accommodation and surpluses of others.

The characteristics of housing

In order to understand the nature of possible shortages and surpluses of housing in England and Wales, three of its fundamental characteristics need to be considered: durability, immobility and high capital cost.

The significance of durability is that a high proportion of the supply of housing stock is represented by the existing stock. Table 1.2 shows that well over half the national housing stock predates the Second World War, and over a third was built before 1918.

The immobility of housing is an even more important characteristic for the present study. Since a high proportion of aggregate stock is not of recent construction, its location pattern reflects past distributions of population and economic opportunity. Hence, if growth in employment is not evenly distributed between labour and housing markets, those areas which are growing fastest are more likely to experience greater housing demand relative to supply and in-migrants are likely to find more difficulty in obtaining a house. Conversely, areas of economic decline may experience less demand and potential out-migrants, if they own their own houses, may have difficulty selling them. In fact, the situation in England and Wales in recent years has rarely been so clear cut. Most areas, even in the older industrial regions, have been increasing their population and household numbers and, therefore, their demand for housing, while slum clearance programmes have reduced the number of what might have become surplus houses.

The third characteristic of housing, its high capital cost, means that in England and Wales few people have the resources to buy housing outright. As a result the majority of households must pay for housing services as they receive them. Thus, the availability of long-term credit is of critical importance in making the demand for housing effective. The need to phase housing payments with income receipts is particularly crucial for

Table 1.2
Percentage of dwellings of different ages, December 1971

	Pre-1891	1891 – 1918	1919 – 44	Post-1944
England	20	15	25	40
Wales	27	20	16	37
Great Britain	20	16	24	40

Source: Derived from *Social Trends* 3, 1972, p. 137

low-income groups who have little possibility of saving much money and for whom credit is less readily available.

Additions to housing stock

In the short-term the housing stock in an area can be increased by sharing and sub-letting, but with rising expectations increasing demand can only be satisfied by building more houses. Fig. 1.3 shows house completions in England and Wales between 1950 and 1970. Low output in the late 1950s and early 1960s was succeeded by rapid increase from 1963 to 1968, followed by two years of marked recession.

These fluctuations in the level of total building were accompanied by similar and often divergent trends in the public and private sectors. Broadly speaking, during the 1950s output in the private sector rose rapidly and consistently, but the 1960s were years of instability, with peaks in 1964 and 1968 and then two years of rapid decline. The public sector dominated housebuilding in the early postwar years, but declined markedly between 1954 and 1963. The recovery in the mid-1960s was influenced by programmes of building in the new towns; as in the private sector, the end of the 1960s was a period of falling output.

Two points of particular relevance for this study arise. First, because new housing forms only 2 per cent of existing stock, it is often said that its significance is not great. All new housing, however, is occupied by migrants. Allowing for fluctuations in completion rates, moves into new housing represent about a quarter of total household moves each year. Thus, the importance of new building for migration far exceeds its relative importance in the total housing stock. It follows that the substantial fluctuations in the supply of new stock must have a considerable impact on the amount of migration that can take place. Second, rates of building in the public sector for most of the period from the middle 1950s to the present have been relatively low. Hence, housing supply in this sector has not been rising very rapidly, a feature that becomes even clearer if the large number of houses built in the new towns is omitted.

It has been shown that a remarkably uniform regional pattern of housebuilding occurred during the 1960s, in that each Standard Region's share of the total number of houses completed in Britain was almost exactly proportional to its share of total stock of dwellings in 1961.[17] The only exceptions were in certain sub-regions, such as Greater London, where 'suburban' movement had been taking place. The evidence thus suggests that, measured by Standard Regions, new housebuilding was not related to population change. Although the total housing stock expanded at equal rates in each region, there were marked differences between public and private sectors. Broadly speaking, those regions (Northern, Yorkshire and Humberside, Greater London, Scotland) with more houses in the public sector in 1966 had proportionately more dwellings completed in that

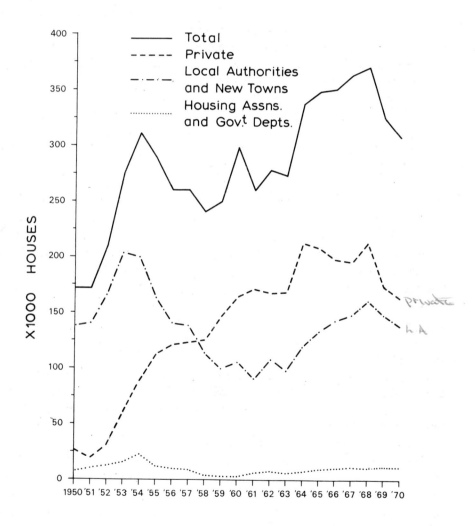

Fig. 1.3 Houses completed in England and Wales, 1950–70.

sector during the late 1960s. Conversely, areas with a higher proportion of owner-occupiers in 1966 (North-west, South-east excluding Greater London, South-west, Wales) failed to expand their public sector relative to their private sector. During the later 1960s there was an increase in the range of regional variation in tenure. Thus, although owner-occupation increased in all regions, those regions where owner-occupation rates were already high had a more rapid increase in that sector.

Housing tenure groups

As Table 1.3 shows, the 17 million dwellings in England and Wales can be divided into three main tenure groups and one residual group. By the end of 1970 over half the nation's stock was in owner-occupation. A further 28 per cent was rented from local authorities or new town corporations, and about 15 per cent from private landlords. These three groups thus accounted for 95 per cent of the stock.

The situation is not static. Between 1966 and 1970 total dwellings increased by about 1 million. [18] The greatest gains were by the owner-occupied and public-rented sectors, both of which increased their numbers and share of dwellings, with the biggest increases both absolutely and relatively in the owner-occupied sector. These increases were at the expense of the private-rented sector, the share of which dropped from 19 per cent to 15 per cent, with a fall in numbers of almost half a million. The residual 'other' category maintained its number of dwellings but its share of an increasing total fell slightly.

Owner-occupation

These different tenure groups have different access citeria which affect the overall demand for particular types of housing. Table 1.3 shows that owner-occupation is the most common form of tenure. Most owner-occupiers buy their houses with the help of mortgages, the arrangements of which vary widely. [19] There are three main sources of mortgage finance: building societies, local authorities and insurance companies. Of these the building societies are easily the most important: in 1969 they accounted for 472,000 advances, compared with 19,000 from local authorities and 40,000 from insurance companies. [20] Furthermore, their importance as lenders has increased in recent years. In 1962 they accounted for 75 per cent of the total amount advanced for house purchase in the UK, compared with 11 per cent by local authorities and 14 per cent by insur-

Table 1.3

Stock of dwellings by tenure: England and Wales

Tenure	December 1966		December 1967		December 1968		December 1969		December 1970	
	'000s	%	'000s	%	'000s	%	'000s	%	'000s	%
Local authority and new town renting	4,250	26·7	4,390	27·1	4,520	27·4	4,650	27·8	4,785	28·3
Owner-occupation	7,830	49·0	8,060	49·8	8,330	50·6	8,540	51·1	8,730	51·6
Private renting	3,040	19·1	2,920	17·9	2,790	16·9	2,690	16·1	2,582	15·2
Other	830	5·2	840	5·2	850	5·1	840	5·0	838	4·9
All tenures	15,950	100·0	16,210	100·0	16,490	100·0	16,720	100·0	16,935	100·0

Source: Department of the Environment, Handbooks of Statistics (annual)

ance companies. In 1970 building societies provided 88 per cent of the total amount advanced, local authorities 7 per cent and insurance companies 5 per cent. [21]

It is clear, therefore, that access to building society credit is the prime requirement of most house purchasers. Normally the building society is willing to grant up to three times a person's annual income for a period from 20 to 30 years, although precise details vary. Considerations other than income level are weighed by building societies in deciding whether to grant mortgages: for example, the quality of the house, the likely length of working life and job security. Local authorities and insurance companies use broadly the same criteria as building societies in deciding whether to grant mortgage loans. Mortgages with low deposits and long repayment periods are more difficult to obtain for older houses and for flats. Older people usually have to accept shorter repayment periods or smaller loans and, therefore, need larger deposits or higher incomes in order to buy houses. In a family situation, the wife's earnings are rarely given much weight since frequently the continuity of that income is in doubt. Barbolet's study of mortgages granted by building societies for low-priced houses in metropolitan Kent suggests that, in marginal cases involving low-income clients, earnings were not the chief determinant of either the amount given or to whom mortgages were awarded. [22] The aim of Barbolet's study was to see if constraints on housing allocation differ between manual and non-manual workers. It was found that the average ratio of mortgage to income and the average ratio of house price to income was greater for non-manual workers than for manual workers. However, the average income of the non-manual group was never as great as the average income of the total sample chosen. Barbolet concluded that, despite their lower incomes, non-manual workers obtained mortgages more easily than manual workers. Thus they were able to compete for the same price segment of the housing market as higher-income manual workers.

Despite these other considerations, the income of the head of the household normally sets a ceiling on the amount a building society is willing to lend. Because house prices vary greatly between regions, [24] the income required to buy a house varies likewise. Using 1969 figures, Richardson, Vipond and Walker quote the case of a 100 per cent mortgage over 25 years at a rate of interest of 8½ per cent. In order to buy the average-priced house in his region a person in the South-east would need to earn £700 more than a person in the Yorkshire and Humberside region if the loan were three times more than his income, and £800 more if it were 2½ times his income. [24] There are, therefore, many people whose income is high enough to buy a house in some parts of the country but

not in others. This situation may sometimes prevent migration and sometimes encourage it. If the income of the head of a household is below the
necessary threshold to buy a home in a new area, that household may
decline to move there. Another household, living in rented accommodation in a high-price area but wishing to buy, may decide to move out
because there is no chance of buying a home where they are. Unfortunately, the lack of any information on house prices at a scale smaller than the
Standard Region prevents recognition of those local housing markets
where it is most difficult to buy.

Local authority renting

Probably only about 20 per cent of those households that are not owner-
occupiers could afford a mortgage, although this estimate has to be very
tentative. [25] Thus, for the most part, other forms of tenure exist for those
who cannot afford to be owner-occupiers. Nearly 30 per cent of households in England and Wales currently rent from local authorities. Unlike
the other tenure groups, local authority housing is a highly-standardised
product with 90 per cent of new council dwellings having two or three
bedrooms. Apart from slum clearance and other public projects, where
local authorities have a duty to rehouse those affected, each authority is
autonomous in its selection of tenants. Most operate a points system,
which reflects a prospective tenant's need and suitability. Such factors as
state of present accommodation, health, and number of children are taken
into account; and usually there is a local residential qualification. 'Access
to a council house is, therefore, likely to be positively related to the
individual's immobility and negatively related to his present housing conditions'. [26] In fact, the systems of allocation which operate are diverse,
since the criteria of selection built into the points system vary between
different local authorities, largely in relation to the length of the local
waiting list. In practice local authority housing allocation systems and the
weightings given to various criteria are almost never made public, [27] perhaps partially to allow for discretionary actions, but the residential qualification is often the most significant criterion for the labour migrant seeking council housing.

Waiting lists in the large cities are often long, and considerable delays
are usually experienced before suitable council accommodation can be
obtained. This suggests there are implications for labour migration resulting from the local administration of publicly-provided housing. Indeed,
Cullingworth has suggested that local authority allocation procedures
threaten to impose a new Law of Settlement because they allow for

movement and choice only within the locality. [28] Hence council house allocation policies are generally adequate to meet local demand but not the demands of migrants.

Provision for migrants is sometimes tied to employment in particular firms, for example in the housing of 'key workers'. [29] Exchange of council houses between tenants is one way of implementing migration between local authorities, but this requires the agreement of both local authorities, since it circumvents the local demands indicated by the waiting lists.

Private renting

Private renting, in contrast with owner-occupation and council housing, forms a declining sector of the housing market. About 15 to 20 per cent of private tenancies are for furnished accommodation, the remainder almost evenly divided between controlled tenancies and regulated tenancies for unfurnished accommodation. Controlled rents are lower than other rents and the tenancy can be passed on within the family by direct inheritance. [30] The low rents of controlled tenancies, and frequently also of regulated tenancies with long leases, act as a disincentive to migration. This, combined with the steady fall in numbers of unfurnished private-rented dwellings, means that the furnished sector is often the one most easily available to new tenants, including migrants.

Despite its generally poor physical quality, the private-rented sector is the only one with a large number of very small dwellings, such as one- and two-roomed flats. This is most important since 46 per cent of households consist of one or two persons. Thus the private-rented sector is not unattractive for many young households, particularly single persons and those couples without children. At the other end of the life-cycle it also has its attractions, since, unless households have bought their own houses by middle age, their income expectations will probably be insufficient for them ever to reach that favoured sector.

When a household intending to rent a home moves into an area, it is likely to seek private-rented accommodation, since it is unlikely to qualify for local authority accommodation. As a result, it will have to negotiate at current market rates rather than past market prices. The Camden study, for example, showed that for each dwelling category in the private-rented sector, rents were consistently higher for those who had moved in the two years prior to the study than those who had moved earlier, reflecting not only the rate of inflation but also increases in the real cost of housing. [31]

The Camden study also shows that private-rented accommodation prices are highly erratic for similar situations, probably due to information inadequacies in a situation of grossly excess demand. In such a situation diverse income groups compete for similar housing, forcing low income households to pay out considerable proportions of their incomes for poor quality accommodation which is frequently too small for them. If these are high labour demand areas, migrants, particularly those with families, may be most reluctant to move to where jobs are plentiful since they are likely to have to make sacrifices in their housing situation.

Other tenures

Although the three tenure groups described above account for about 95 per cent of dwellings, the small 'other' category merits some attention in the context of the present study. This is because it includes rent-free housing which is often tied to particular employments; agricultural cottages and police houses are two examples that come easily to mind. Because of the close relationship between much of this accommodation and employment, a change of job will invariably mean a change of residence. Therefore, this tenure category is likely to be associated with proportionately more labour migration than the others.

Conclusion

It is clear that, in a modern economy like that of Great Britain, technological change leads to the existence of areas of growth, where new industries find favourable locations, and also of decline, where they do not. Hence there is a need, on the grounds of labour supply and demand alone, for some labour to move from areas of decline to areas of growth, if national expansion is not to be curtailed. Undoubtedly much of the movement that goes on is a response to this need, but labour also moves for reasons that may have little to do with a desire to leave an area of high unemployment or to reside in an area of plentiful jobs and lucrative pay. As a result, labour mobility also takes place between areas that are alike in the level and type of employment they offer.

From this review of the main trends in migration and employment in Britain and of the principal characteristics of housing, two points of particular relevance for this study emerge. First, it is apparent that, in spite of the substantial amount of migration that takes place in Britain, there is no well-defined national policy for aiding it. Instead there exists a series of *ad hoc* policies, largely unstructured and at best only loosely related to each other. Operated as they are by both public and private bodies, they are only insensitively related to the needs of potential migrants and of the national economy. Such aid as is provided for migration goes only to some sectors of the labour force and does not apply equally in all parts of the country. The barriers to migration are thus likely to be more easily surmountable by some groups than by others.

Second, housing cannot be regarded as a single phenomenon, the shortage of which can easily be measured. Of all its complex characteristics, perhaps the most significant for our study is the emergence of a mixture of tenure types, each with its own set of institutions and each having its own criteria for access. These criteria are broadly the same in all parts of England and Wales, differences being mainly ones of degree. Hence the migration propensity of different groups in the labour force needs to be related to the access they have to the types of housing available.

Notes

[1] Census of Population, *Sample Census 1966, England and Wales: Migration Summary Tables*, Part I, Table 1, HMSO, London 1969.

[2] D.V. Donnison, C. Cockburn and T. Corlett, *Housing since the Rent Act*, Occasional Papers on Social Administration, no. 3, Welwyn 1961; J.B. Cullingworth, *English Housing Trends*, Occasional Papers on Social Administration, no. 13, London 1965; M. Woolf, *The Housing Survey in England and Wales 1964*, HMSO, London 1967.

[3] *Ministry of Labour Gazette* 74, 1966, p. 379.

[4] OECD, *Wages and Labour Mobility*, Paris 1965, p. 51.

[5] A.I. Harris and R. Clausen, *Labour Mobility in Great Britain: 1953–1963*, HMSO, London 1967, p. 12.

[6] Ibid., p. 17.

[7] D.E.C. Eversley, 'Population changes and regional policies since the war' *Regional Studies* 5, 1971, pp. 211–28; Department of the Environment, *Long Term Population Distribution in Great Britain – A Study*, report by an inter-departmental study group, HMSO, London 1971.

[8] See for example, Eversley, op. cit., and Department of the Environment, op. cit.

[9] Eversley, op. cit., p. 216.

[10] Ibid., p. 216.

[11] Ibid., p. 217.

[12] Ibid., p. 219.

[13] *Department of Employment Gazette* 80, 1972, pp. 354–5.

[14] *Department of Employment Gazette* 81, 1973, p. 664.

[15] R.K. Wilkinson and S. Gulliver, 'The economics of housing: a survey' *Social and Economic Administration* 5, 1971, pp. 84–5; J.B. Cullingworth, 'Housing Analysis' in S.C. Orr and J.B. Cullingworth (eds.) *Regional and Urban Studies*, London 1969, p. 154.

[16] Cullingworth, op. cit., p. 159.

[17] H.W. Richardson, J. Vipond and J.B. Walker, *The Finance of House Purchase*, Housing Research Foundation, London 1972, pp. 22–4.

[18] In this context it should be noted that about 75,000 were lost per annum through slum clearance.

[19] For a detailed account of finance for house purchase, see Richardson, Vipond and Walker, op. cit.

[20] Ibid., p. 16.

[21] Ibid., p. 16.

[22] R.H. Barbolet, 'Housing classes and the socio-ecological system' Centre for Environmental Studies *University Working Paper* 4, 1969.

[23] Regular information on regional house prices is provided by the Nationwide Building Society, *Occasional Bulletins*.

[24] Richardson, Vipond and Walker, op. cit., p. 32.

[25] Ibid., p. 34.

[26] Ibid., p. 13.

[27] E. Burney, *Housing on Trial: a Study of Immigrants and Local Government*, London 1967.

[28] J.B. Cullingworth, *Housing and Labour Mobility*, OECD, Paris 1969, p. 30.

[29] Ministry of Housing and Local Government, *Council Housing – Purposes, Procedures and Priorities*, 9th Report, The Housing Management Sub-Committee, Central Housing Advisory Committee, HMSO, London 1969.

[30] But if passed on more than once it becomes a regulated rent tenancy.

[31] Centre for Urban Studies, *Housing in Camden*, London 1967.

2 A Framework for the Study of Labour Migration and Housing Characteristics

An essential preliminary for any research into the geographical mobility of labour and the housing characteristics of migrants is the construction of a theoretical framework to serve as a basis for empirical investigation. Much of the evidence at present available is derived from general household surveys in which only a small proportion of the respondents were migrants.[1] There have been no studies directly concerned with the housing characteristics of migrants, nor is there any clear view of the key relationships between housing and labour mobility. This chapter presents a tentative outline of an appropriate framework for further study by weaving together some of the relevant strands that appear in the separate literatures on labour migration and housing to form a coherent pattern which has particular reference to conditions in England and Wales.

Barriers to movement between occupations

We have defined labour migration as involving the simultaneous change of employment and of home. The most important job change is normally that undertaken by the head of the household, but other working members of the household are also likely to be involved in changes of employment because of the changed location of their home. This type of migration includes as well the non-employed adults and children who form part of the migrant households. Population movements of this particular kind are assumed for simplicity to be motivated largely by the attraction of a new job or, at least, to be conditional upon the availability of suitable employment in the destination area. Hence they can be interpreted as part of the labour-market mechanism which matches the supply and demand for particular occupation groups, each with its own short-term elasticity of supply. These elasticities are low for occupational categories which involve long periods of training and are high for unskilled and semi-skilled jobs. Thus the occupational structure of the workforce is determined by 'barriers' to movement between different occupational categories, largely based upon training and formal requirements for admission to certain occupations. These barriers are relatively fixed, in so far as education, training and skill determine the subsequent role of an individual in the labour force.[2]

Second only to the degree of training required, perhaps the next most important barrier to the ready attraction of suitable numbers of workers to a point of employment demand is the geographical location of this demand in relation to sources of supply. Conversely, from the point of view of the individual worker, the location of his residence also limits his choice of job. The locations of job opportunities and of places of residence are mutually linked in space by the commuting 'tolerances' of workers. Given the location of work-places in centralised nodes, the area over which housing opportunities will be sought by a household depends on its members' tolerance to commuting. In the same way, given the location of residence, the workers in a household seek employment opportunities over an area defined in terms of commuting tolerance.

It may well be easier for many workers to move to a similar job in a different local labour market area (thus producing labour migration) than to change their occupations or skill groups in the same local labour market. Hence, from the point of view of increasing the flexibility of the national economy through providing appropriate labour supply conditions, a knowledge of the constraints on the locational readjustment of the labour force is as important as an understanding of the educational and training requirements of the workforce. Access to housing probably forms one of a number of key factors in determining the mobility of workers between different geographically-defined labour market areas. In theory, at least, housing takes on particular relevance in the study of labour migration because it is regarded as a necessity by virtually all households and normally demands a substantial proportion of a household's earnings. As a result, housing is likely to be an important item in the calculations of all households proposing to migrate.

Occupational and spatial mobility

The close interdependence of occupational and spatial barriers in the free allocation of workers to jobs has been emphasised, since one cannot be considered without reference to the other. Because of this there are probably strong contrasts in the motivation and behaviour of labour migrants from different occupational groups and from different types of places

28

(classified by their location and their socio-economic attributes).

The interdependence of occupational and spatial mobility can be illustrated by considering the factors influencing potential labour migrants. People are attached to particular locations partly because they have a job there, but also because economic costs of movement elsewhere (assessed in the broadest terms) may be too great in relation to the likely returns they can perceive. There is little systematic information about the costs of moving, but a recent survey suggested that in Britain an owner-occupier selling a £6,000 house and buying a £7,000 one would be likely to pay over £300 in solicitor's and estate agent's fees, while similar charges for someone selling a £12,000 house and buying a £14,000 property would be over £500.[3]

As well as assessing the gains to be made by moving to a new job in a different area, the cost of housing there and the expense of moving, many potential migrants will be faced with considerable social 'costs' in moving since they may be attached to the particular facilities offered by their present house, they may enjoy their social contacts in an area and they may value local amenities. Thus, even if there are definite job opportunities elsewhere, in theory potential labour migrants make a calculation of the comparative net advantage to be derived from either staying in an environment which they know or moving to an alternative which will be a relatively long distance away, and where they are unlikely to have detailed information about the housing market.

It may be doubted if, in reality, potential migrants attempt anything approaching a rigorous calculation, since they have imperfect knowledge about the possibilities of obtaining comparable housing and social facilities elsewhere. Even with good sources of information the problem is considerable. The physical stock of houses is heterogeneous, it varies considerably in price, and it can be paid for under a variety of tenure arrangements. The accessibility of an individual home is also difficult to appraise, since it is the base for a whole household's pattern of activities, not simply the employment of the principal wage-earner. Furthermore, the dwelling is set in the midst of a local context of social desirability and environmental quality, with the result that identical dwellings in different locations can be regarded as different goods, commanding different prices. Perfect substitutability between two dwellings in different areas is virtually impossible to imagine, providing problems in comparison not only for the labour migrant himself, but also for the researcher.

Information about certain kinds of job opportunities may also be localised in character, so that potential migrants may be unaware of employment possibilities in other places. In addition to this, many types of jobs are fairly ubiquitously available (at least in a condition of rising demand) and people in these occupations have little stimulus to move to another town. High-level managerial and professional employment, on the other hand, is often found only in large cities, while some highly-skilled manual or technical workers may be able to find suitable work only in certain specialised industrial regions. Generally speaking, large urban-industrial centres should offer greater opportunities than smaller centres for all types of worker to change employment without having to migrate elsewhere. One would expect, in the light of this, that labour migration rates would be less from big cities, and there is some evidence that this in fact is so.[4]

In extreme cases the various factors influencing the mobility of a particular socio-economic group tend to combine to produce a pull in one particular direction. More highly-educated workers, for example, are less attached to particular places by social ties. They are better informed about employment opportunities and the jobs that they seek are, in any case, often advertised nationally. Their jobs are such that changing an employer will often require a relatively long-distance move; but financially they are able to undertake such moves readily, since they are deemed to be credit-worthy by building societies and insurance companies. Alternatively, their paths of promotion within an individual large firm will demand the periodic relocation of their homes, in which circumstances it is likely that at least some of the financial (if not the social) costs of moving will be borne by their employers. Thus, to complement the relative scarcity and inelasticity of supply of these skilled occupational groups, a higher level of geographical mobility is usually found among them.

Unskilled workers, on the other hand, are usually recruited locally and scan much more restricted horizons for job opportunities (except where single men and women may migrate over long distances early in their working lives). Because the kinds of jobs they fill are often available in a wide range of locations, they tend not to be involved in long-distance migration between jobs. Their lower incomes make the financial costs of moving a more significant item of expenditure. They depend on council housing or on cheap rented accommodation, to which access would be difficult in a new area. Last but not least, until migration is first undertaken, the households in traditional working-class communities are enmeshed in a social network characterised by high connectivity but limited geographical extent, features which are normally associated with low levels of out-migration.[5] Thus, in extreme cases, their housing, their sources of information, the pattern of location of suitable jobs and their social

30

networks all combine to reduce their propensity to migrate.

From a practical point of view it may be argued that the forces encouraging or discouraging mobility in these extreme cases are so strong that little can be done to bring about change (if this were thought desirable). There remain, however, 'intermediate' occupational groups, which emerge as of particular interest as a result of this theoretical discussion of housing and labour mobility, since less is known about them and their behaviour is more open to influence by government decisions. This group is very large: the 1966 Census shows that 48 per cent of the population of England and Wales falls into socio-economic groups which might be classified in this way.[6] These comprise skilled manual, technical, 'middle' managerial, lower-paid professional and trained clerical workers — groups displaying a great variety of characteristics, though they have been studied regrettably little in the sociological literature. There is reason to think that shortages of such workers form a key problem in the modern labour market situation in Britain, although this applies more to some groups, for example skilled manual workers, than to others. Following our line of reasoning, it may be suggested that in general these workers are occupationally 'fixed' by their training, and that on this basis their geographical mobility might be expected to be relatively high.

Because of their lower incomes and because they are less frequently aided by employers, these intermediate groups are likely to find housing availability particularly critical in changing jobs over long distances, in comparison with the easier problem facing relatively well-off professional and higher managerial workers. If they occupy council houses, they probably experience considerable difficulties in exchanging a council house in one local authority area for a similar house elsewhere, particularly when moving to areas of high labour demand and housing shortage. Again, in both the owner-occupied and private-rented sectors of the housing market, prices in high labour-demand areas tend to be above those in the other regions from which the 'middle-group' workers might be expected to be recruited, thus providing a similar check to movement.

An indication of this situation is given in Harris and Clausen's survey of migration, which found that although there was a fairly close correlation between higher educational qualification and greater *actual* mobility, this was not necessarily so in the case of *willingness* to move.[7] It was those with intermediate qualifications, such as the Ordinary National Certificate and General Certificate of Education (Ordinary Level), who were most willing to move, rather than the more highly qualified. This suggests that many people in the intermediate groups wish to move but are frustrated in their desire to do so.

The problem of geographical scale

It has been long recognised that aggregate migration flows accord quite closely with a 'gravity' model in which the interaction of two population centres is related to their populations and to the distance between them.[8] This basic model has been elaborated by measuring distance and population in various ways and by varying the functional form of the relationships. Derivatives of the basic gravity model have given a good fit with the available empirical evidence, confirming the general conclusion that most migration may be expected to take place between large cities and also over short distances, although the model itself gives no insights into why this should be so. The model provides a good general description of migration behaviour, but it has been argued that in practice it suffers from its undiscriminating nature,[9] since it works best when providing a statement of expected movement at an aggregate level, involving migration at all scales and for all purposes.

The present study requires more selective and disaggregated examination of migration, although the distance over which potential labour migrants are planning to move is of critical importance in their decision to change their residences as well as their jobs. An important problem needing attention here is that of indicating the appropriate geographical scale at which migration might most reasonably be studied in order to highlight the geographical mobility of labour and, if possible, its association with housing.

Housing is most obviously associated with population movements at the intra-urban scale, since much of the mobility of population within individual cities is a product of changes in housing requirements at different stages in the family life-cycle and of changes in status and income which also encourage moves from one type of residential area to another.[10] The literature on this topic is expanding rapidly, with particular reference to conditions in United States cities. This growth of American interest in intra-urban population movements has been particularly encouraged by the analysis of social areas in cities and, more recently, by studies of urban 'factorial ecology',[11] since the selective movement of population within an urban area provides a missing explanatory basis for such studies.

Intra-urban movement of population has been a largely neglected theme in Britain, possibly because of the relatively greater importance of local authority housing and the administrative constraints that this feature imposes on the development of a pattern of social areas which fits American models.[12] In any case there is good reason for thinking that at this scale moves of home are largely independent of job changes. Although sometimes a change of job may imply a change of status or of income, which might well encourage a change of home, the resultant moves are not an inescapable concomitant of a change of job. Or again, in large cities the inconvenience or the costs of the journey to work may induce a move of home in association with a change of job; but those moves of home that are connected with job changes are so intermixed with and dominated by moves caused by other factors, that the intra-urban scale does not provide a particularly useful point of entry to the problems under consideration in this study.

Most British work on population migration has focused on the 'inter-regional' scale, often using the somewhat arbitrary boundaries designed for economic planning purposes. [13] The level of statistical 'explanation' achieved by these studies has been disappointingly small; and the reason for this lack of resolution is probably the highly aggregated nature of the statistical data being processed.

Migration takes place for a variety of reasons besides strictly economic ones, and the wide range of motives of migrants tends often to be lost in multivariate analysis. Equally important, the boundaries of the economic regions do not reflect the geographical realities of population movement. An unknown proportion of migrants are merely undertaking relatively short-distance movements which by chance happen to cross one of these arbitrary boundaries. Other moves between quite distinct communities, but within the major regions, are completely missed by these large statistical units, although moves of this kind may well involve as great a social and economic wrench as inter-regional migration. The inter-regional scale does not yield the level of detail that will shed light on movement between geographically-defined communities, and hence it does not appear to offer a useful scale at which to examine the social and economic context within which migration takes place.

Given the emphasis of this study, the most logical scale at which to study migration is one which stresses movement from one town or city to another, since at this scale a movement of home normally implies a change of employment for the principal wage-earner in a household. Unfortunately, the administrative areas for which urban statistics are presented in the census are not necessarily appropriate units with which to undertake such an analysis, because they have boundaries which bear little relationship to the realities of journeys to work. The key unit, then, is not just an individual urban settlement, but the local labour market of which it forms the central core. As a result, the difficult problem arises of recognising actual local labour market areas, since although these may exist in theory there are many technical difficulties in delimiting them in reality.

The concept of the local labour market

The labour market in any country consists of a complex of local sub-markets, each centred on a concentration of employment opportunities and characterised by flows of information about the availability of workers and their qualities, and about vacant jobs and their conditions of employment. The areal extent of each market is then defined by its coverage of interested parties and the efficiency of its operation; the local labour market becomes the area around an employment centre in which, in an aggregate manner, competition for labour normally takes place. Around such an employment centre there will also be an aggregate local housing market in which the employees of that centre compete for housing. At this aggregate level the local housing market and the local labour market will be similar in extent.

There are marked differences in the size of area over which different occupational groups will search for jobs and from which employers will expect to recruit certain types of workers. Not all workers confine their job search to the local area, nor do all employers necessarily expect to recruit from the immediate vicinity of their firms. Highly specialist workers usually seek jobs within their occupations rather than purely locally, using specialised information channels such as professional journals. For these people the extent of the labour market may be national or even international; but for the majority of the labour force, and for most employers, information flows about the labour market are local. Information is gleaned from friends and from other employers, and vacant jobs are advertised in the local press or filled through the public employment service. Hence, the bulk of workers seek and expect to find work within a fairly restricted area.

It is possible, therefore, to imagine a series of unique, short-run supply curves for particular labour types in individual labour markets. For any centre of employment the short-run elasticity of supply for certain occupations will depend on the availability of suitably-trained workers within a reasonable distance. Where barriers to movement between occupational groups exist, as in the case of highly-skilled occupations needing specialist qualifications, it is not possible to increase supply by local substitution of lower-skilled workers. In this case, migration into the local area is needed to increase supply. Conversely, if short-run substitution between occupation groups in the local labour market is high, as with most lower skilled groups, then demands can more easily be satisfied locally and there is less need for geographical mobility of labour into the area.

The tolerance of an individual worker to commuting determines the area over which he will offer his services to an employment centre. This tolerance varies between workers, because the complex bundle of costs, disutilities and benefits associated with a particular journey to work is not perceived and evaluated equally by individual workers, and, therefore, cannot easily be measured objectively. Because of this, attempts to define local labour market areas have tended to be rather vague. Kerr, for example, maintains that it is not possible to define the local labour market precisely, arguing that it is 'merely an area of indistinct geographical and occupational limits within which certain workers customarily seek to offer their services and certain employers to hire them'. [14] Others have suggested definitions that vary slightly in detail, though the principal characteristic of them is that of an area in which most workers can respond to job opportunities and change their jobs without changing their residences. [15] Goodman has attempted to make the concept more precise: he argues that the two essential requirements of a local labour market are self-containment and internal cohesiveness. [16] A local labour market should be largely self-contained, with little journey-to-work movement across its boundaries. It should also have an internally active and unified structure with a high degree of intra-market movement. This latter criterion is similar in practice to Thompson's suggestion of an area-effect component in the local wage: he suggests that the presence of enterprises paying high wages tends to raise the level of local wages as a result of intra-urban competition for workers. [17]

In Britain it would be difficult to satisfy Goodman's criteria. The urbanised nature of much of the country means that there is substantial overlap between some labour market areas defined on a journey-to-work basis, especially in the London area. The criterion of an internally-unified structure is also difficult to satisfy, although there is some empirical evidence of an area-effect on the local wage. For example, at Ellesmere Port in the 1950s and 1960s the presence of large, high-paying firms in the oil, petro-chemical, paper and car industries created a local area where pay rates were substantially above the general regional average. [18] Such a situation is probably quite rare: Goodman maintains that there is considerable variation in earnings within individual occupational groups in many local areas. As a result it is normally impossible to define local labour market areas satisfactorily in terms of their wage rates.

Although the areal extent of a local labour market in terms of journey-to-work lengths may vary between occupational groups, practical methods of delimitation are normally based on the requirement that a certain proportion of an area's economically-active population should commute to a specified employment centre. In practice, zones of influence, defined by the distance travelled by commuters into employment centres, overlap. Hence, local labour markets do not easily correspond with community boundaries. Larger centres tend to have concentrations of job opportunities for specialised high-income personnel. Transport networks are centred upon these kinds of employment node to provide swift but quite expensive accessibility for these highly-paid workers. Thus, large employment centres usually have extensive zones of influence within which there are several component labour markets; for example, one centred on the main concentration of office employment, another on the principal industrial zone, each attracting different types of labour with different commuting tolerances. The existence of several labour markets in a metropolitan context forms the basis of Cullingworth's criticism of the idea of the local labour market, when he argued that the concept is no longer useful because of increased personal mobility and the willingness of people to travel greater distances in order to obtain a satisfactory residential environment. [19] But away from Greater London and, to a lesser extent, the West Midlands, the concept still seems to have validity, particularly if attention is focused on the bulk of employees, rather than the most affluent professional workers. For example, in a study that was primarily concerned with manual workers, MacKay and his associates found that the bulk of the employees with whom they were concerned had journeys to work of less than five miles. [20] Hence, this particular study was able to use a fairly restricted definition of local labour market areas. However, if one is concerned with the whole of the labour force, as is the present study, then a broader definition has to be adopted which takes account of the possible differences in commuting tolerance between occupation groups. The local labour market area then becomes an aggregation of the various labour market areas of individual workers, with the aim of fitting together as many of these as possible, knowing that the result will not be meaningful for all.

If the difficult problem of delimiting local labour markets on a comparable and useful basis throughout England and Wales is left on one side (and this is a matter to which it will be necessary to return in the next chapter) it remains true that the local labour market area provides the scale at which the interaction of housing characteristics and the geographical mobility of labour can be most reasonably studied. Whatever the validity of the local labour market concept, the area over which an individual household seeks employment without moving home is clearly related to the journey-to-work distances which the members of that household find acceptable.

36

Notes

[1] See, for example, D.V. Donnison, C. Cockburn and T. Corlett, *Housing since the Rent Act*, Occasional Papers on Social Administration, no. 3, Welwyn 1961; P.G. Gray and R. Russell, *The Housing Situation in 1960*, HMSO, London 1962; J.B. Cullingworth, *English Housing Trends*, Occasional Papers on Social Administration, no. 13, London 1965; and M. Woolf, *The Housing Survey in England and Wales: 1964*, HMSO, London 1967.

[2] L.C. Hunter and G.L. Reid, *Urban Worker Mobility*, OECD, Paris 1968, p. 14; see also R. Herne, 'Housing and labour mobility: some theoretical considerations' Housing and Labour Mobility Study, Department of Geography, University College London, *Working Paper* no. 6, 1972.

[3] The Consumers' Association, 'The cost of moving home' *Which?*, June 1973, pp. 174–6.

[4] See below, Chapter 4.

[5] A recent survey of the literature in this field is J. Connell, 'Social networks in urban society' in B.D. Clark and M.B. Gleave (compilers), *Social Patterns in Cities*, Institute of British Geographers, Special Publication no. 5, 1973, pp. 41–52.

[6] Here the 'intermediate' groups are taken as socio-economic groups numbers 5 to 9, as defined in the 1966 census; see Table 7.11.

[7] A.I. Harris and R. Clausen, *Labour Mobility in Great Britain: 1953–1963*, HMSO, London 1967, p. 26.

[8] The simplest form of the model is as follows:

$$M_{ij} = K \ \frac{P_i P_j}{D_{ij}{}^e}$$

where M_{ij} is the movement between two centres i and j, P_i and P_j are the populations of the centres, D_{ij} is the distance between them and K and e are constants.

[9] See, for example, the comments of A.J. Fielding, 'Internal migration in England and Wales' Centre for Environmental Studies *University Working Paper* 14, 1971, p. 22.

[10] For a summary of the literature, see R.J. Johnston, *Urban Residential Patterns*, London 1971, especially Chapter 5.

[11] A summary and critique of these studies is provided by B.J.L. Berry (ed.) 'Comparative Factorial Ecology' *Economic Geography* 47, no. 2 (Supplement), 1971, pp. 209–367.

[12] One not completely satisfactory study using census information is R.J. Johnston, 'Population movements and metropolitan expansion: Lon-

don, 1960–61' *Transactions, Institute of British Geographers* no. 46, 1969, pp. 69–91; see also D.T. Herbert, 'Residential mobility and preference: a study of Swansea', in B.D. Clark and M.B. Gleave (compilers), *Social Patterns in Cities*, Institute of British Geographers, Special Publication no. 5, 1973, pp. 103–21.

[13]   For example, R.A. Hart, 'A model of inter-regional migration in England and Wales' *Regional Studies* 4, 1970, pp. 279–96.

[14]   C. Kerr, 'The balkanization of labor markets', in E.W. Bakke (ed.), *Labor Mobility and Economic Opportunity*, New York 1954, p. 93.

[15]   See, for example, the discussion in J.F.B. Goodman, 'The definition and analysis of local labour markets: some empirical problems' *British Journal of Industrial Relations* 8, 1970, pp. 179–95; see also Hunter and Reid, op. cit., pp. 41–2.

[16]   Goodman, op. cit., p. 184.

[17]   W.R Thompson, *A Preface to Urban Economics*, Baltimore 1965, p. 72.

[18]   J. Salt, 'The impact of the Ford and Vauxhall plants on the employment situation of Merseyside, 1962–1965' *Tijdschrift voor Economische en Sociale Geografie* 58, 1967, p. 256.

[19]   J.B. Cullingworth, *Housing and Labour Mobility*, OECD, Paris 1969, p. 14.

[20]   D.I. MacKay, D. Boddy, J. Brack, J.A. Dieck and N. Jones, *Labour Markets under Different Employment Conditions*, London 1971.

3 The Characteristics of Labour Market Areas

The general background to patterns of migration, employment and housing was discussed in Chapter 1, although little was said about spatial variations at a level below that of the Standard Region. It has been argued, however, that the choice of scale for analysis is critical in the study of labour migration, especially in distinguishing labour migration from other forms of migration. The local labour market, based on aggregated daily journeys to an employment centre, appears to be the most effective areal unit for examining patterns of labour migration and for studying their relationship with characteristics of housing.

A necessary preliminary to this analysis is the empirical delimitation of local labour markets for England and Wales, and a background investigation of the pattern of migration in them, together with a review of their housing and employment conditions. Because of the diversity of these conditions, the labour market areas are then classified in order to indicate more clearly the differences and similarities among them. The classification, by suggesting 'types' of labour market areas, is of interest in itself, but it will also provide an areal framework for use in selecting sample labour market areas for more detailed study.

Delimitation of local labour markets

The problems involved in defining local labour markets based on journey-to-work patterns have been discussed in Chapter 2. A delimitation of such areas for England and Wales has already been carried out by Political and Economic Planning,[1] and in order to avoid unnecessary duplication of work the applicability of PEP's results for the present study was examined.

The PEP investigation was 'an attempt to regionalise the country on the basis of the linkages that exist between places of residence and places of work'. Although related to the concept of the Standard Metropolitan Statistical Area in the USA, commuting patterns were linked to centres of economic activity and not simply to population centres. Data used were from the 1961 Census. The 'Central Labour Area' was based on an employment density of over 12·5 persons per hectare in any local authority, or an actual workforce of over 20,000. Contiguous local authorities were included in the hinterlands of such centres where the analysis of commuter flows indicated that over 15 per cent of the resident economically-active population commuted daily to the 'labour core'. To avoid the overlapping of labour-market boundaries, local authorities with 15 per cent or more of the workforce commuting to two or more 'labour cores' were allocated to the core receiving the largest share of commuters.

The resulting 100 labour markets, called Standard Metropolitan Labour Areas (SMLAs), are concentrated in the main urban-industrial zone in England and Wales, extending from the south-east into Lancashire and Yorkshire, and with smaller groups in the north and north-east, south Wales and the south-west (Fig. 3.1). In 1966, 77·1 per cent of the total population of England and Wales lived in the SMLAs, a proportion that had changed little over the previous 35 years. The size of the areas ranges considerably, from London with a 1966 population of 8,890,270, to Stafford with 70,870.

The usefulness of these labour markets for the present investigation may be affected by three limitations:

1   The 15 per cent threshold of out-commuting is arbitrary, and the need to avoid overlapping of boundaries distorts the pattern of flows into closely competing labour centres.
2   The contiguity constraint may also distort the delimitation of the housing and labour markets relevant to a labour core, particularly around the largest conurbations.
3   The journey-to-work data are derived from the 1961 Census, and significant alterations in the pattern of flows may have occurred in the intervening period.

Any further attempt to create a pattern of local labour markets for England and Wales is unlikely to overcome the first two problems. The 15 per cent threshold level was that chosen in the USA for the delimitation of Standard Metropolitan Statistical Areas and any decision on the cut-off point must be arbitrary. Despite the resulting distorted pattern, a contiguity constraint is necessary if any generalised distribution of local labour markets is to be obtained. The lack of information on journey-to-work patterns after 1961 is of greater significance. However, a random sample of SMLAs was redefined using 1966 data and no significant changes were found. It was decided therefore that the time and costs of reworking the method using 1966 Census data would outweigh any gain from using slightly less out-of-date material. As the Standard Metropolitan Labour Areas devised by PEP appear adequate areal units for analysing inter-labour market movement, they were adopted as the unit for study.

Choice of indices for the classification of SMLAs

It might be expected that there would be diversity in the characteristics of SMLAs, reflecting differences in their location and size. Unfortunately, the amount of published material available for the comprehensive analysis of those characteristics of interest for the present study, especially migration, housing and employment, is limited by the choice of the SMLA as the appropriate unit of analysis. Owing to the lack of coincidence between SMLAs and such statistical units as Economic Regions, Board of Trade research areas and Employment Exchange areas, data based on these units cannot be used without considerable error. Statistics published for individual local authority areas, however, can be aggregated to give information about SMLAs, the most easily accessible and comprehensive source being the 1966 Census. The major limitation of using census data is the time that has elapsed since 1966, but the census does represent the only comprehensive source of data on migration at the local authority level, and until the relevant 1971 Census figures are published there is no possibility of indicating changes since 1966.

The 1966 Census contained more information on migration than any of its predecessors, providing data at the local authority level about the volume and direction of flows. By aggregating the flows for local authorities, the pattern of gross migration for the periods 1961–66 and 1965–66 can be ascertained for SMLAs. Unfortunately, the characteristics of the migrants involved in these flows (for example, their age, marital status, family composition, and socio-economic group) cannot be determined for SMLAs from the census. The value of local labour market areas for the discussion of migration patterns must therefore be restricted to an analysis of the volume and direction of flows.

Although data on the nature of the actual movers are limited, information is available on some characteristics of SMLAs that might have relevance to patterns of migration. It has already been suggested that the household's decision whether or not to move may be discussed in terms of a net advantage calculation. The perception of net advantage by any individual household may be influenced by the conditions of housing and employment existing in both origin and destination SMLAs. Some attempt to measure the range of these conditions would therefore appear appropriate.

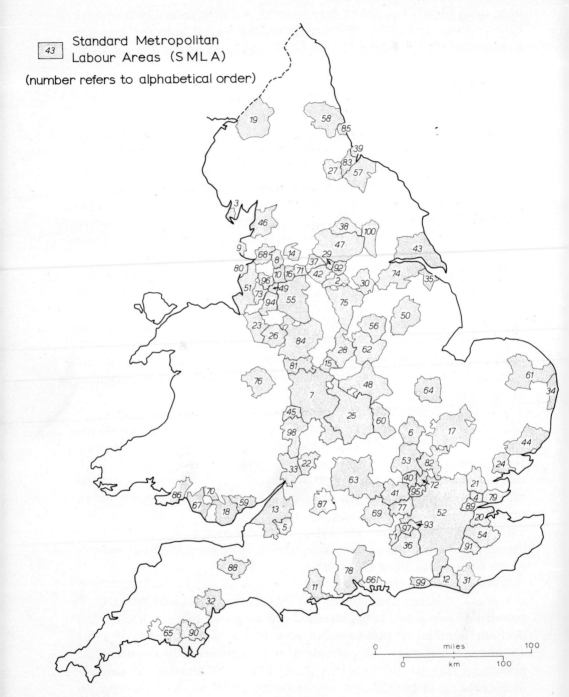

Standard Metropolitan
Labour Areas (SMLA)

(number refers to alphabetical order)

Fig. 3.1

Figure 3.1: Key

SMLA Identification (names based on major labour core)

1	Aldershot	51	Liverpool
2	Barnsley	52	London
3	Barrow-in-Furness	53	Luton
4	Basildon	54	Maidstone
5	Bath	55	Manchester
6	Bedford	56	Mansfield
7	Birmingham	57	Middlesbrough
8	Blackburn	58	Newcastle-upon-Tyne
9	Blackpool	59	Newport
10	Bolton	60	Northampton
11	Bournemouth	61	Norwich
12	Brighton	62	Nottingham
13	Bristol	63	Oxford
14	Burnley	64	Peterborough
15	Burton-on-Trent	65	Plymouth
16	Bury	66	Portsmouth
17	Cambridge	67	Port Talbot
18	Cardiff	68	Preston
19	Carlisle	69	Reading
20	Chatham	70	Rhondda
21	Chelmsford	71	Rochdale
22	Cheltenham	72	St. Albans
23	Chester	73	St. Helens
24	Colchester	74	Scunthorpe
25	Coventry	75	Sheffield
26	Crewe	76	Shrewsbury
27	Darlington	77	Slough
28	Derby	78	Southampton
29	Dewsbury	79	Southend
30	Doncaster	80	Southport
31	Eastbourne	81	Stafford
32	Exeter	82	Stevenage
33	Gloucester	83	Stockton-on-Tees
34	Great Yarmouth	84	Stoke-on-Trent
35	Grimsby	85	Sunderland
36	Guildford	86	Swansea
37	Halifax	87	Swindon
38	Harrogate	88	Taunton
39	West Hartlepool	89	Thurrock
40	Hemel Hempstead	90	Torquay
41	High Wycombe	91	Tunbridge Wells
42	Huddersfield	92	Wakefield
43	Hull	93	Walton and Weybridge
44	Ipswich	94	Warrington
45	Kidderminster	95	Watford
46	Lancaster	96	Wigan
47	Leeds	97	Woking
48	Leicester	98	Worcester
49	Leigh	99	Worthing
50	Lincoln	100	York

In order to synthesise the information available, a classification was attempted. An immediate problem here was presented by the selection of SMLA characteristics for the classification process. Given the emphasis of this study, it seemed appropriate to concentrate on both housing and labour market conditions, particularly those which previous research had suggested might be of importance in understanding migration flows between areas. Thirty-two appropriate variables were available, but these gave an uneven representation of housing, migration and labour market conditions. As a result, a balanced selection of 11 variables was made, and these statistics were transformed into a comparable form, each being given equal weight.

The choice of variables to be included resulted from three decisions. First, to avoid bias, each aspect of SMLA conditions should be as nearly equally represented as possible. Second, where possible, the various aspects of SMLA conditions should be represented by variables having the greatest variation between areas, to aid in the identification of dissimilar areas. Finally, the variables chosen should be those indicated by previous research to be most closely linked with migration patterns.

Amalgamation of census variables to combine several related aspects in one measure allowed more information to be included in the 11 variables chosen.[2] The indices chosen were:

A. *Migration*	Gross in-migration	Percentage of total residential population (1966) which moved into each SMLA 1965–66.
	Gross out-migration	Percentage of total residential population (1966) which moved out of each SMLA 1965–66.
	Net migration	Migration balance 1965–66 as a percentage of total residential population in 1966.
B. *Housing market*	Additions to stock	Change in the number of dwellings 1961–66 as a percentage of total dwellings in 1961.
	Overcrowding	Percentage of total households living at over 1·5 persons per room in 1966.
	Local authority/owner-occupier ratio	Local authority tenants as a percentage of total of local authority tenants and owner-occupiers (1966).

	Private-rented sector	Percentage of total households in private-rented accommodation (1966).
C. *Labour market*	Employment growth	Change in the workforce 1961–66 as a percentage of total workforce (1961).
	Unemployment	Percentage of economically active males 'out of employment' in 1966.
	Executive and professional workers	Percentage of economically active males in socio-economic groups 1, 2, 3 and 4 (1966).
	Manual workers	Percentage of economically active males in socio-economic groups 9, 10 and 11 (1966).

The migration characteristics of SMLAs

The existence of regional variations in migration rates has already been alluded to in Chapter 1, where it was also pointed out that the use of such terms as 'drift to the south' oversimplifies a rather complex spatial pattern. Analysis of the migration characteristics of SMLAs makes this more explicit.

As a preliminary to migration analysis, it is helpful to review briefly the main changes in total residential population so that migration, as one component of change, can be related to population change as a whole. Fig. 3.2 shows the percentage change in the residential population of SMLAs between 1961 and 1966. The range of variation is surprisingly uniform, although both increases and decreases did occur. Areas of decrease were of two types: (1) older industrial areas, for example, some Lancashire towns, Tyneside and Rhondda, where the staple industries of cotton textiles, shipbuilding and coal have undergone decline; and (2) conurbation centres, such as London and Manchester, surrounded by other urban areas and running short of land for further building. The largest increases, over 15 per cent, were all in south-east England, beyond London's Green Belt. The most important areas for growth were the SMLAs immediately to the west and east of London. Away from the capital's influence only Swindon, St. Helens and Leicester had increases of over 10 per cent.

This pattern of residential population change bears much resemblance to the pattern of net migration, shown in Fig. 3.3 as a proportion of total residential population. Most SMLAs increased their populations by migra-

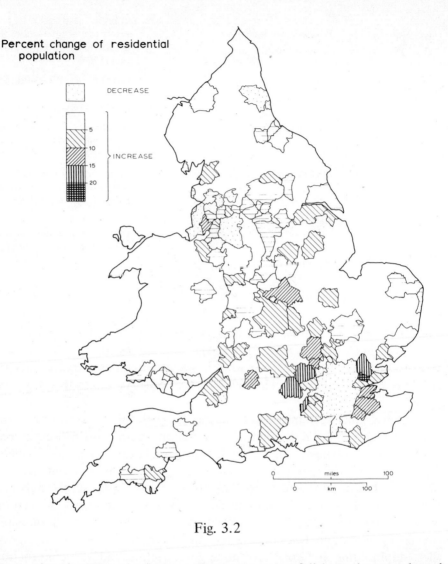

Percent change of residential
population

DECREASE

5
10 } INCREASE
15
20

Fig. 3.2

tion; only 10 had net decreases. These decreases fell into the same broad
groups as residential population change. One included the conurbation
centres of London, Liverpool, Manchester and Sheffield, from which suburban movement has taken place, often in planned overspill schemes. The
second category consisted of some of the older industrial areas, like
Rhondda, Barnsley, Burnley and Sunderland, where severe structural decline has occurred in major industries. Although areas of decrease in total
residential population and net out-migration usually coincided, there were
some exceptions. Cardiff, for example, increased its total population but
had net out-migration. In contrast, Newcastle had a decrease in total

46

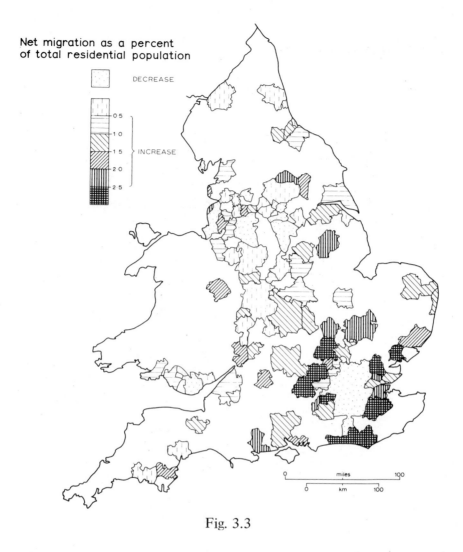

Net migration as a percent
of total residential population

DECREASE

0·5
1·0
1·5 } INCREASE
2·0
2·5

miles 100
km 100

Fig. 3.3

population but also a gain from net migration. To some extent these anomalies may be a product of measuring the indices over different time periods (residential population change related to 1961–66 and net migration to 1965–66), but they also probably reflect different local conditions.

The largest migration increases were clearly in south-eastern England, especially in the outer parts of the London ring. There can be no doubt that to a considerable degree these increases result from suburban movement, including planned overspill, out of the capital. South-eastern England, in fact, displays a wide range of net migration conditions, but,

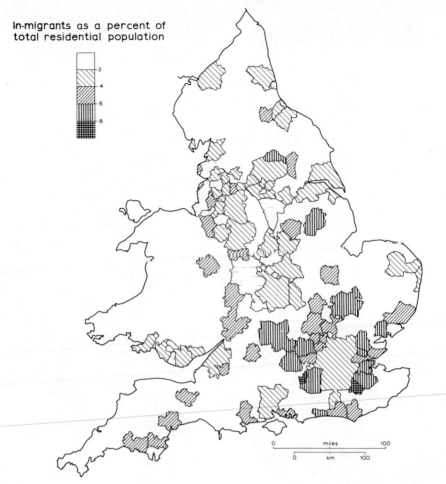

In-migrants as a percent of
total residential population

2
4
6
8

Fig. 3.4   Gross in-migration 1965–66, as a percentage of total residential
population, 1966.

although the range is more marked than in other parts of the country, conditions elsewhere are also not by any means uniform. Areas with higher-than-average gains by migration include retirement areas such as Brighton, Worthing, and Eastbourne in the south, and Southport and Harrogate in the north. Also in this category are some of the more elegant residential cities, like Lincoln, Shrewsbury and Gloucester, which attract migrants from surrounding rural areas.

Statistics of net migration hide much larger gross movements of population, as Fig. 3.4 and 3.5 make apparent. High in-migration (Fig. 3.4) is especially concentrated in the ring of SMLAs around London, with Aldershot having the highest rate (9·3 per cent), no doubt reflecting its special

Out-migrants as a percent of
total residential population

2
4
6
8

Miles
0   100
Km
0   100

Fig. 3.5   Gross out-migration 1965—66, as a percentage of total residential
population, 1966.

function as military centre. North of the Severn—Wash axis, only Lincoln
and Harrogate had more than 6 per cent in-migration. Retirement areas on
the south coast, as well as Blackpool and Southport, emerge as might be
expected, as areas of fairly high in-migration. The pattern of out-migration
(Fig. 3.5) broadly corresponds with that of in-migration. The highest rates
are again to be found in the London ring while, despite their high absolute
numbers of out-migrants, the conurbation centres have generally low
rates. Perhaps the major difference between the patterns of in- and out-
migration is that the resort/retirement towns have less out- than in-migration. In general, comparison of Fig. 3.4 and 3.5 shows that areas with low

49

out-migration tend to have low in-migration and, conversely, high out-migration corresponds with high in-migration. This means that some SMLAs have a low turnover of population by migration; most important in this category are the conurbation centres, but also included are a number of centres of heavy industry, like Middlesbrough and Swansea. In these areas of low 'total mobility' (in-migration plus out-migration), comparatively little overall pressure on the local housing market from migration would be expected. However, there might be pressure on particular sectors of the housing market, depending upon the type of migrants and upon the existing natural increase of population and the housing stock in the destination areas. Where there are high rates of total mobility, as in much of south-eastern England outside London, more active labour and housing markets than are suggested by the map of net migration (Fig. 3.3) would be expected. It is these areas that are most likely to experience pressure on local housing directly from migration.

The discussion so far has referred to all migration to and from SMLAs, regardless of origin and destination of flows. For the purposes of the present study it is useful to review the relative importance of migration between SMLAs to migration from other origins and to other destinations. Fig. 3.6 shows the proportion of total in-migrants to each SMLA originating in other SMLAs. On average, just over half of all migration to SMLAs was from other SMLAs but the amount varied considerably. Fifteen SMLAs had more than 70 per cent of their migrants from other SMLAs while, at the other extreme, eight areas had less than 40 per cent from that source. The areas with the highest proportions of inter-SMLA migrants were usually those on the fringes of the large conurbations. It is likely that this is an expression of one of the problems of defining SMLAs in continuous urban zones, since some of these migrants will be commuters to the central city.

The areas receiving fewest migrants from other SMLAs are diverse. Some, such as Norwich, Chester, Carlisle, Shrewsbury and Lincoln, are relatively isolated from other SMLAs, and thus are likely to have few short-distance migrants from adjacent SMLAs. Many of the migrants to these places will be from surrounding rural areas. Other places with a comparatively low proportion of migrants from SMLAs attract people from outside England and Wales. This applies particularly to the conurbation centres, especially London and Birmingham. In fact, although London has the highest absolute number of in-migrants from other SMLAs, at the same time it receives only a low proportion of its total in-migration from that source. Some SMLAs in northern England, like Carlisle, receive a well-above-average proportion of their in-migrants from Scotland, thus

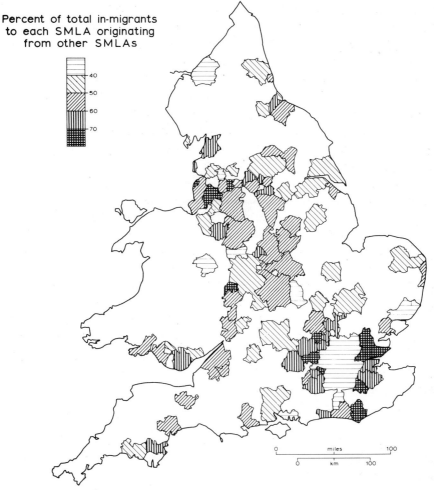

Fig. 3.6   Percentage of total in-migrants to each SMLA originating from other SMLAs, 1965–66.

reducing the proportions from other SMLAs.

Although in total only 51 per cent of all in-migrants to SMLAs came from other SMLAs, 61 per cent of out-migrants from SMLAs went to other SMLAs, perhaps indicating the 'redistributive' function of some places, especially the large cities, in the nation's overall migration pattern. Fig. 3.7 shows the percentage of total out-migrants from each SMLA moving to other SMLAs. Although on the whole the pattern is broadly similar to that in Fig. 3.6, overall the proportions are higher. London, for example, had less than 40 per cent of its in-migrants from other SMLAs, but sent over 50 per cent of its out-migrants to them. Only one SMLA in

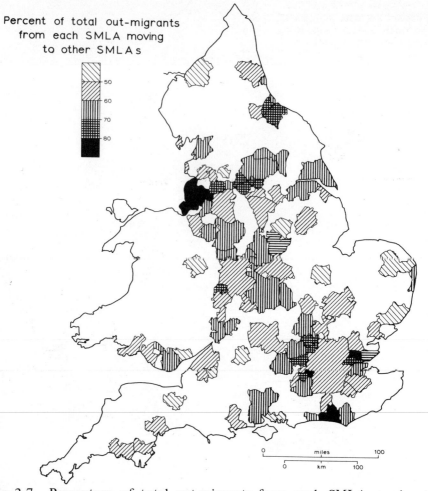

Percent of total out-migrants
from each SMLA moving
to other SMLAs

50
60
70
80

Fig. 3.7 Percentage of total out-migrants from each SMLA moving to other SMLAs, 1965—66.

eight sent less than half of its out-migrants to other SMLAs, while one in three received less than half its migrants from other SMLAs.

The employment characteristics of SMLAs

As already indicated, four employment characteristics were considered: change in the workforce; unemployment; the proportion of the labour force in managerial and professional categories; and the proportion in manual employment. The first two of these indicate the general economic well-being and degree of activity of the labour market areas, the last two

Percent change of workforce

DECREASE

5
10
15
20

INCREASE

miles   100

km   100

Fig. 3.8 Change in the workforce 1961—66, as a percentage of total workforce, 1961.

provide some guide to the type of labour they contain.

Figure 3.8 shows the pattern of overall change in the workforce. The highest increases were concentrated on the London periphery, while in the north only Wigan/St. Helens, Harrogate and Grimsby had increases of over 10 per cent. Conversely decreases were mainly concentrated in the north-west and west Yorkshire; outside these areas only Rhondda and Kidderminster had decreases.

The pattern shown in Fig. 3.8 yields greater insights when compared with change in residential population (Fig. 3.2). The map of workforce change exhibits greater spatial variability. More places experienced a decrease in their workforces than showed a reduction in their residential populations (13 against 11). More SMLAs recorded an increase of above 10 per cent in their workforces than underwent a similar increase in their residential populations. Moreover, the conurbation centres as a whole experienced decreases in their residential populations but increases in their workforces. These comparisons suggest divergent trends in these two phenomena when measured at this scale, with decentralisation of residential population, but at the same time concentration of employment.[3]

A complement to the map of change in total employment is the distribution of unemployment — usually regarded as the key variable in judging the economic health of an area. Some of the principal features of unem-

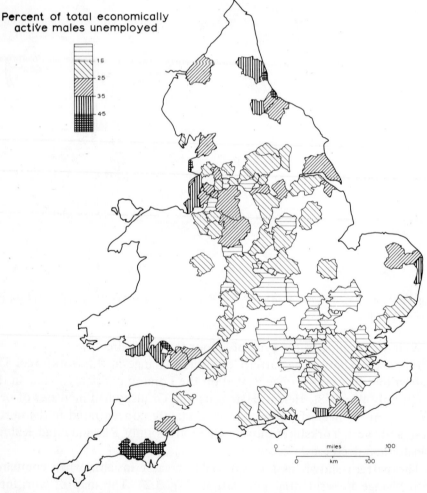

Percent of total economically
active males unemployed

Fig. 3.9   (Note: Figs. 3.9–3.11 and 3.13–3.15 refer to 1966)

ployment in England and Wales have already been discussed in Chapter 1, and Fig. 3.9 attempts to pick out the main variations between SMLAs. The data are derived from the census and pose problems of interpretation. They refer to one month only and hence display no trend; furthermore the month referred to is April and therefore they embody the effect of winter seasonal unemployment, especially in coastal resorts. The difficulties of fitting Employment Exchange data on unemployment to SMLA boundaries precluded the use of Department of Employment statistics. In any case, the more comprehensive nature of census statistics on unemployment provides a better picture of the real unemployment situation at one point in time.

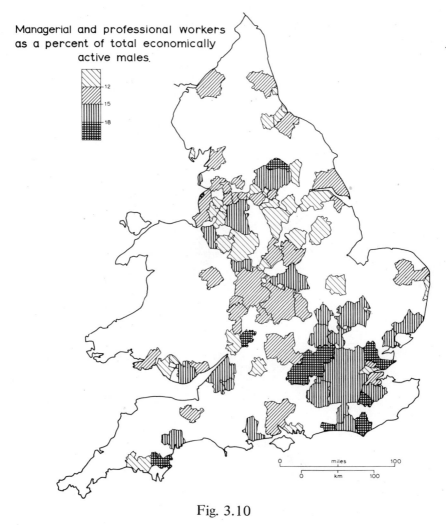

Fig. 3.10

In fact, Fig. 3.9 provides a fair representation of the regional distribution of unemployment in England and Wales in the mid-1960s, which was a time of very low national unemployment. The lowest rates are to be found in the main urban-industrial axis extending from the south-east into Yorkshire and, to a lesser extent, into Lancashire. In most of this area rates were less than 2·5 per cent. Areas of high unemployment were of two types: (1) the older industrial areas in the north-east, parts of Lancashire and south Wales, and including the port areas of the Mersey and the Humber; and (2) coastal areas of seasonal unemployment, including Blackpool, Torquay, Plymouth and the south coast resorts. However, only Blackpool, Torquay and Plymouth (tourist industry) and Sunderland,

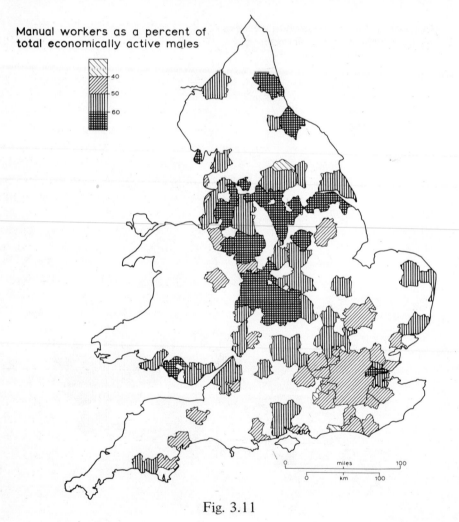

Fig. 3.11

West Hartlepool and Rhondda (shipbuilding and coal) had more than 4·5 per cent unemployment.

In addition to indicating the economic buoyancy of SMLAs, it was thought necessary to consider the importance of those sectors of the labour force regarded as the most mobile and the least mobile. Fig. 3.10 and 3.11 demonstrate the spatial distribution of these two extremes: managerial and professional workers, and manual workers. Only three SMLAs (Harrogate, Aldershot and Worthing) had less than 40 per cent of their workforces in the manual category. Areas with less than 50 per cent were almost entirely concentrated in southern England, including London. In the north and Midlands only Blackpool, Southport, Chester, Shrewsbury, Stafford and Cheltenham had less than 50 per cent manual workers. In contrast, south of the Severn—Wash axis only Thurrock had over 60 per cent. There was thus a marked regional contrast with high concentrations of manual workers in all the main industrial areas associated with coalfields, including the west Midlands, Lancashire, Yorkshire, south Wales and the north-east, and low concentrations in the south-east.

Bearing in mind the mapping interval used, it seems that the percentage of managerial and professional workers varied more between SMLAs within regions than the percentage of manual workers. In many respects the distribution of managerial and professional workers is complementary to that of manual workers. As might be expected, the highest concentrations of these more highly-paid workers were in London and surrounding SMLAs, with outliers at such places as Torquay, Worthing, Eastbourne, Cheltenham and Harrogate almost certainly reflecting the location of their retirement. Fewest managerial and professional workers were found in those areas where manual workers were most concentrated, especially in Lancashire, north Staffordshire, Yorkshire, Lincolnshire and the north-east.

The housing characteristics of SMLAs

The total amount of information available on housing for SMLAs is fairly extensive. Unfortunately, most of the variables that can be derived are of little use for the present study, and some of the most important information, on house prices for example, is unobtainable. Accordingly, four characteristics were considered. The first of these was the rate of house building, measured by additions to stock. Second, in order to get some idea of likely points of pressure on the housing market, differences in rates of overcrowding were mapped. Finally, two variables reflecting housing tenure were introduced into the analysis.

57

Rates of housebuilding at national and regional level have already been referred to in Chapter 1; Fig. 3.12 shows marked variations which existed between SMLAs. Only two areas had decreases, London and Bath. London is particularly interesting in that the nation's largest labour and housing market and focus of attention for migrants experienced a decrease in its housing stock.

However, with this notable exception, additions to stock formed a higher proportion of dwellings in the south-east than in other parts of England and Wales, the highest figures being for Aldershot (19·8 per cent)

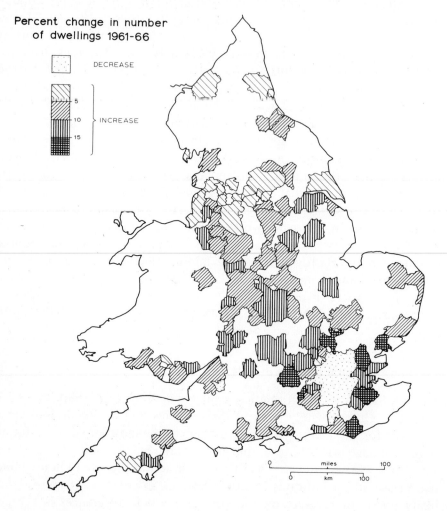

Fig. 3.12   Change in the number of dwellings 1961−66, as a percentage of total dwellings, 1961.

— also the most 'mobile' SMLA with the highest proportion of both in- and out-migrants — Basildon (19·3 per cent) and Maidstone (18·7 per cent). All seven SMLAs with over 15 per cent increase in housing stock were found in a ring around London.

In contrast, the majority of SMLAs with increases of less than 5 per cent lay north of a line from the Dee to the Wash, with Lancashire and the West Riding of Yorkshire being notable as areas with low additions to stock. In general, the Midlands had levels of increase interme-diate between those found in the south-east and the north, although the older industrial areas of both west and east Midlands had lower increases than some of the newer areas, such as Stafford and Coventry.

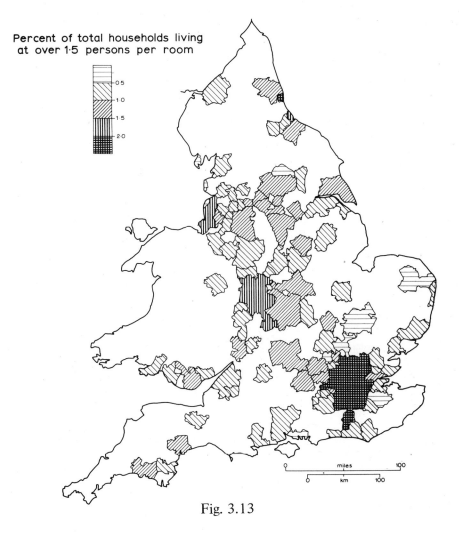

Fig. 3.13

The rate of additions to housing stock cannot itself indicate housing shortage. The presence of overcrowded dwellings does not necessarily indicate pressure on the local housing market, but it does represent a situation where society regards the provision of additional dwellings to be beneficial. To that extent it indicates an unsatisfied demand for houses.

Fig. 3.13 shows the pattern of overcrowding in SMLAs, using information from the 1966 Census on households living at densities of over 1·5 persons per room. No clear regional pattern emerges, except that the conurbations tended to have more overcrowding (and perhaps, therefore, more unsatisfied demand for housing) than other areas, with London, Birmingham and Liverpool being particularly notable. Only Sunderland

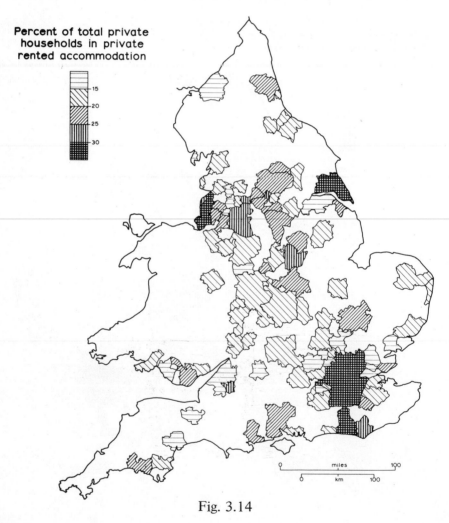

Fig. 3.14

and West Hartlepool, both in the north-east, reached the levels of over-crowding found in the main conurbation centres. It seems, then, that additions to housing stock in the ring of SMLAs around London kept pace with the net migration into this area, with the result that the number of overcrowded dwellings there is below average.

Possible relationships between housing tenure groups and migration have already been discussed in Chapter 1. Fig. 3.14 and 3.15 show the proportions of the housing stock of SMLAs held under the main types of tenure. Fig. 3.14 shows there is no clear regional pattern in the distribution of private-rented accommodation, and SMLAs which were otherwise diverse in characteristics had common high or low levels. The highest

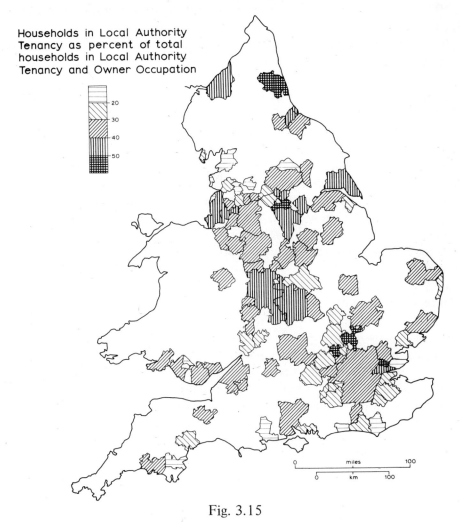

Fig. 3.15

proportions of private-renting were in London and Brighton in the south, and Liverpool and Hull in the north, all of which had over 30 per cent. Next came Dewsbury, Rochdale, Manchester, Nottingham, Southport, Bath and Eastbourne, all with over 25 per cent. These areas were of three basic types: (1) the large cities of London, Manchester, Liverpool and Nottingham (but not including Birmingham); (2) smaller, older industrial areas, including Dewsbury, Rochdale and also Hull; and (3) places associated with retirement — Bath, Southport, Brighton and Eastbourne. The places with the lowest proportions of private renting were mainly in the south-east, outside London and away from the south coast resorts, in the Midlands and in East Anglia.

The distribution of owner-occupied and local authority housing, shown in Fig. 3.15, differed from that of private renting. Again no clear regional distinction emerged and within different parts of the country considerable variation was found between SMLAs. Most places had more dwellings in owner-occupation than in local authority renting. In the south-east only the three new-town SMLAs of Hemel Hempstead, Stevenage and Basildon had more local authority houses than owner-occupied ones, a situation existing elsewhere only at Newcastle and Barnsley. The central parts of conurbation areas usually had more local authority houses than other areas. This is especially true in the south-east where, outside London, local authority housing generally represented less than a third of the combined total of local authority and owner-occupied housing. Comparison of Fig. 3.14 and 3.15 shows that, with few exceptions, there was little relationship between the proportion of private-rented accommodation and the local authority/owner-occupied ratio.

The classification of SMLAs

In this discussion of SMLA conditions, certain places have repeatedly emerged with common characteristics — for example, the conurbation centres, resort/retirement towns, and the ring of centres around London. But because of the large number of variables considered and the range of conditions found, no obvious synthesis has emerged to allow a categorisation of all SMLAs. However, the use of these variables in a statistical classification procedure, details of which are given in Appendix 1, allows the identification of SMLAs with similar migration, housing and employment characteristics. The method uses a form of clustering analysis and Fig. 3.16 indicates in graphical form the manner in which the 100 SMLAs were clustered into groups of similar places, thus producing a hierarchy

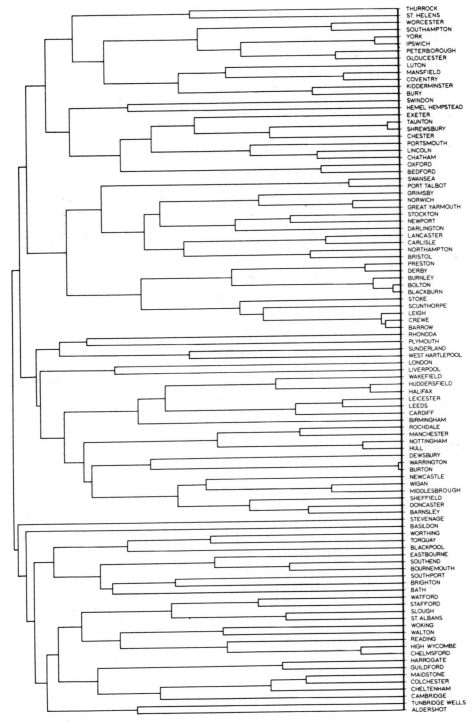

Fig. 3.16 Standard Metropolitan Labour Area classification diagram.

63

from which significantly different groups could be isolated. A cut-off point giving five groups was eventually chosen after testing confirmed the statistical significance of the groups.[4] These five groups embraced all the SMLAs in England and Wales except two, the new towns of Basildon and Stevenage (see Fig. 3.17 and Table 3.1). The characteristics of the SMLAs in each group may be summarised as follows:

Group A. SMLAs with high gross in-migration, together with a large net increase by migration. Dwelling stock is characterised by a high rate of

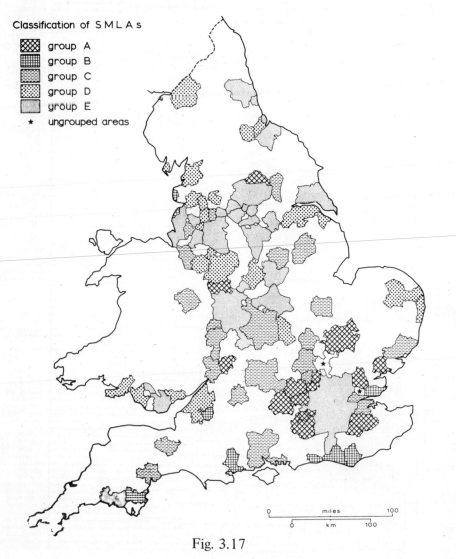

Fig. 3.17

Table 3.1

SMLAs in each group

Group A	Group C	Group D	Group E
Aldershot	Bedford	Barrow	Barnsley
Tunbridge Wells	Oxford	Crewe	Doncaster
Cambridge	Chatham	Leigh	Sheffield
Cheltenham	Lincoln	Scunthorpe	Middlesbrough
Colchester	Portsmouth	Stoke-on-Trent	Wigan
Maidstone	Chester	Blackburn	Newcastle
Guildford	Shrewsbury	Bolton	Burton-on-Trent
Harrogate	Taunton	Burnley	Warrington
Chelmsford	Exeter	Derby	Dewsbury
High Wycombe	Hemel Hempstead	Preston	Hull
Reading	Swindon	Bristol	Nottingham
Walton and Weybridge	Bury	Northampton	Manchester
Woking	Kidderminster	Carlisle	Rochdale
St. Albans	Coventry	Lancaster	Birmingham
Slough	Mansfield	Darlington	Cardiff
Stafford	Luton	Newport	Leeds
Watford	Gloucester	Stockton	Leicester
	Peterborough	Gt. Yarmouth	Halifax
Group B	Ipswich	Norwich	Huddersfield
Bath	York	Grimsby	Wakefield
Brighton	Southampton	Port Talbot	London
Southport	Worcester	Swansea	Liverpool
Bournemouth	St. Helens		West Hartlepool
Southend	Thurrock		Sunderland
Eastbourne			Plymouth
Blackpool			Rhondda
Torquay			
Worthing	Two unclassified: Basildon, Stevenage		

additions to stock, and an average ratio between local authority tenants and owner-occupiers. High employment growth is coupled with low unemployment, and a resident male population consisting of a high proportion of executives and professional workers, and a low proportion of manual workers.

Group B. SMLAs again with high gross migration rates and a large net increase by migration. Dwelling stock is characterised by average additions to stock, a low ratio of local authority tenants to owner-occupiers, and a large private-rented sector. Average employment growth is coupled with very high unemployment and again the resident male population consists of a high proportion of executive and professional workers, and a low proportion of manual workers.

Group C. SMLAs with average migration rates. Dwelling stock is characterised by high additions to stock and an average local authority to owner-occupier ratio. Average employment growth is coupled with average unemployment, and the resident male population consists of a low proportion of executive and professional workers, and an average proportion of manual workers.

Group D. SMLAs with below average gross migration rates, and little net increase by migration. Dwelling stock is characterised by an average local authority to owner-occupier ratio, and a small private-rented sector. A small increase in employment growth is coupled with above average unemployment, and the resident male population consists of a low proportion of executive and professional workers and a high proportion of manual workers.

Group E. SMLAs with low migration rates and no increase by net migration. Dwelling stock is characterised by a very low rate of additions to stock, a high overcrowding rate, a large local authority sector in relation to owner-occupiers, and a large private-rented sector. Low employment growth is coupled with a high rate of unemployment and the resident male population consists of a low proportion of executive and professional workers, and a high proportion of manual workers.

Fig. 3.17 indicates the geographical distribution of these different groups of SMLAs. The SMLAs characterised by high migration rates, employment growth, good housing stock and a high social-status population were almost entirely confined to the south and east of the country. In contrast, the north and Midlands were distinguished by areas of comparatively little movement, poorer employment prospects, poorer quality housing, and a population containing more manual workers. Between these groups are areas representing a range of less extreme conditions. The seaside resorts are isolated as a group by the contrast of high migration rates, and a range of housing conditions, a high-status population, but with poorer economic conditions.

Conclusion

This chapter has demonstrated that there are significant differences in migration, employment and housing characteristics between individual local labour markets in England and Wales, and that on the basis of these characteristics it is possible to identify 'type' areas, groups of labour markets within which similar conditions exist but which are significantly different from other groups. These groups will be used to provide a framework for more detailed study of the labour migration—housing relationship

66

(Chapters 6—9). So far, however, little has been said about the direction and volume of the flows of migrants between individual SMLAs. This interaction will be examined in more detail in the following chapter.

Notes

[1] J.R. Drewett, 'The definition of Standard Metropolitan Labour Areas', Urban Growth Study, Political and Economic Planning, *Working Paper* no. 1, 1968.
More recently, the PEP work has been fully described in, P. Hall, et al., *The Continent of Urban England*, vol. 1, 1973, especially Part Two, pp. 115—444.
[2] For details see N. Hadjifotiou, 'The multivariate classification of local labour markets areas', Housing and Labour Mobility Study, Department of Geography, University College London, *Working Paper* no. 2, 1971.
[3] P. Hall, 'Spatial structure of metropolitan England and Wales', in M. Chisholm amd G. Manners (eds.), *Spatial Policy Problems of the British Economy*, Cambridge 1971, pp. 96—125.
[4] N. Hadjifotiou, op. cit., pp. 13—22.

4 Migration between Labour Market Areas in England and Wales: the Aggregate Pattern

No information is available about the total pattern of labour migration in England and Wales at any date. In spite of the importance of labour migration for social and economic planning, it also seems unlikely that any regular monitoring can be expected in the foreseeable future. In fact, detailed information for small areas about any form of migration within Britain did not become available until the results of the Sample Census of 1966 were published. In our attempts to make some generalisations about the magnitude and pattern of labour migration, therefore, we were faced with the task of applying some form of analysis to the 1966 Census data on total migration. Data on the gross movements of population between local authority areas during both the one-year period from April 1965 to April 1966 and the five-year period from April 1961 to April 1966, are published only for administrative areas which had more than 1,000 one-year and 2,000 five-year migrants (in- and out-migrants). Unpublished statistics on all the flows between local authority areas are therefore necessary for detailed analysis and form the basis of what follows. The one-year migration statistics are more reliable, since respondents possess greater accuracy of recall over a shorter period, and in any case, the Registrar General's Office itself was unable to explain some of the detailed figures for local authorities, where the numbers of migrants over five years appeared to be less than those over one year. Our analysis therefore makes use of the one-year (1965–66) migration flows, based upon a question in the census about the place of residence of respondents in April 1965.

The flows between local authority areas refer to residential mobility. The main limitation of these data for our purpose is that a high proportion of the moves so defined will not have incurred any locational change in the employment of the migrant workers. On the other hand, migration flows between large standard regions can be assumed to include a high proportion of labour migrants, since most of the moves involve changes of residential location over distances which would not allow employed migrants to keep jobs in the origin regions (assuming that short distance moves across the borders between contiguous standard regions are insignificant). Such inter-regional flows, however, exclude labour migration which takes place within the standard regions.

The principal problem in employing the census residential migration data for our purposes was therefore one of selecting those flows which predominantly consisted of labour migrants, eliminating from consideration those which included few people changing jobs. Since, as already discussed, commuting tolerances provide the key to the distances over which people may change their job before moving house, and *vice versa*, the commuter-defined Standard Metropolitan Labour Areas seemed to be most appropriate, both on the grounds of their geographical scale and functional basis. The use of these areas rests on the assumptions that residential change within them should not normally require labour migration, since the distances involved do not generally exceed the commuting tolerance of their inhabitants, and that residential change between them would be expected to require a change in the place of the worker's employment.

It is clear that these are gross assumptions; moves within a labour market area (particularly from one side to another) may well be associated with job changes, while moves to a contiguous SMLA may only be over a short distance and have little effect on the journey to work, especially if the place of employment is on the periphery of the SMLA. Implicit in the use of these areas, therefore, is the assumption that national patterns of employment are dominated by 100 urban nodes, and that labour migration predominantly takes place between their hinterlands. Table 4.1 indicates the imperfection of these assumptions, by showing that only one half of migration into the SMLAs in 1965—66 was from other SMLAs, although, as was shown in Chapter 3, the proportions varied greatly between different areas (Fig. 3.4). Conversely, 61 percent of the 987,120 persons who moved out of a SMLA in 1965—66 moved to another SMLA, although again the proportions varied considerably (Fig. 3.5). The

Table 4.1

Major origins of migrants moving into SMLAs, 1965 — 66

Total no. of persons moving into all SMLAs	Percentage of total from:				
	other SMLAs	Scotland	rest of England and Wales	elsewhere in British Isles	abroad
1,176,310	51·0	3·4	25·1	2·7	18·0

boundaries of the SMLAs must therefore be regarded as no more than indicating the lines across which residential change is also likely to involve a relatively high proportion of labour migration. This likelihood might be expected to be less marked in some areas, such as around large metropolitan centres where the overlapping of commuter flows between labour markets is common, and will also apply less strongly than average to some income and socio-economic groups, especially better-off managerial and professional workers.

In spite of these reservations about the degree to which inter-SMLA residential migration is a surrogate for the most significant flows of labour migration, the same difficulties would arise with any set of areal units which could be used. It is believed that SMLAs represent the best solution to the problem of separating labour migration from movement not involving a change of job. In the absence of better information, the patterns of inter-SMLA migration should provide an *aggregate* picture of the labour migrant flow structure of England and Wales, although its validity for examining local or sub-regional patterns may be more dubious. These technical considerations will be returned to in evaluating the conclusions of the analysis at the end of this chapter. A further complication concerns the relationship between total population movement and the migration of employed persons. In undertaking the examination of inter-SMLA migration, the number of workers in the various migration flows is assumed to be a constant proportion of the total flow involved.

The census information was used to compile a matrix of flows in and out of the 100 SMLAs during 1965—66. This involved examining the groups of local authorities which comprised each labour market area and calculating, from the unpublished data, the flows to all the other 99 SMLAs. The largest individual flow of migrants during the year was of 6,410 people from the London to Brighton SMLAs. On the other hand, a number of possible flows were zero. The total numbers of persons entering and leaving each SMLA with an origin or destination in another SMLA is shown in Table 4.2.

The analysis of inter-SMLA migration flows

The 100x100 matrix of migration flows between labour market areas forms a complex pattern of interlinkage which presents many difficulties for summary analysis. Consideration in Chapter 2 of the likely theoretical relationships between flows and the characteristics of their origin and destination areas suggests that two approaches to the analysis are worth

Table 4.2

Total number of persons entering or leaving each SMLA with an origin or destination in another SMLA (1965 – 66)

SMLA	In-migration from other SMLAs	Out-migration to other SMLAs	SMLA	In-migration from other SMLAs	Out-migration to other SMLAs
1 Aldershot	7,730	6,230	51 Liverpool	13,360	25,880
2 Barnsley	2,070	2,060	52 London	86,660	140,160
3 Barrow-in-Furness	1,080	1,110	53 Luton	7,970	6,870
4 Basildon	6,510	3,990	54 Maidstone	7,050	3,550
5 Bath	2,650	1,850	55 Manchester	21,010	26,420
6 Bedford	3,050	2,440	56 Mansfield	3,040	2,050
7 Birmingham	23,020	27,430	57 Middlesbrough	4,900	4,430
8 Blackburn	1,370	2,220	58 Newcastle-upon-Tyne	9,820	11,200
9 Blackpool	5,400	3,500	59 Newport	2,290	1,980
10 Bolton	3,820	4,470	60 Northampton	1,890	2,200
11 Bournemouth	9,000	4,910	61 Norwich	3,870	3,160
12 Brighton	10,630	7,750	62 Nottingham	10,350	10,960
13 Bristol	11,190	9,180	63 Oxford	8,580	7,150
14 Burnley	1,390	1,200	64 Peterborough	2,140	1,670
15 Burton-on-Trent	2,430	1,780	65 Plymouth	5,120	6,280
16 Bury	5,220	2,790	66 Portsmouth	9,480	7,850
17 Cambridge	5,360	4,210	67 Port Talbot	2,650	2,270
18 Cardiff	6,430	6,830	68 Preston	2,670	3,200
19 Carlisle	850	1,360	69 Reading	11,840	6,670
20 Chatham	8,950	5,560	70 Rhondda	540	1,570
21 Chelmsford	5,870	2,460	71 Rochdale	2,490	2,310
22 Cheltenham	2,830	2,880	72 St. Albans	3,430	3,410
23 Chester	2,230	2,400	73 St. Helens	7,510	4,170
24 Colchester	3,880	2,570	74 Scunthorpe	2,120	1,740
25 Coventry	13,770	11,980	75 Sheffield	8,220	9,560
26 Crewe	1,830	1,670	76 Shrewsbury	1,680	1,310
27 Darlington	2,190	2,220	77 Slough	10,330	9,210
28 Derby	5,430	5,590	78 Southampton	7,510	7,700
29 Dewsbury	2,330	2,840	79 Southend	9,840	6,180
30 Doncaster	2,590	3,030	80 Southport	3,490	1,930
31 Eastbourne	4,600	2,280	81 Stafford	1,470	1,980
32 Exeter	3,940	3,670	82 Stevenage	3,870	2,660
33 Gloucester	3,720	2,740	83 Stockton-on-Tees	3,950	2,880
34 Great Yarmouth	2,790	2,210	84 Stoke-on-Trent	4,960	5,320
35 Grimsby	2,350	1,890	85 Sunderland	2,110	2,900
36 Guildford	7,190	5,950	86 Swansea	2,780	2,150
37 Halifax	2,680	3,080	87 Swindon	3,870	2,910
38 Harrogate	3,800	3,070	88 Taunton	2,070	1,340
39 West Hartlepool	1,120	1,510	89 Thurrock	4,940	3,710
40 Hemel Hempstead	4,090	3,220	90 Torquay	4,360	2,660
41 High Wycombe	10,340	6,510	91 Tunbridge Wells	4,680	2,540
42 Huddersfield	2,740	3,060	92 Wakefield	2,290	3,100
43 Hull	5,170	4,780	93 Walton and Weybridge	5,570	3,800
44 Ipswich	3,330	2,690	94 Warrington	2,940	3,060
45 Kidderminster	2,510	1,690	95 Watford	6,150	5,990
46 Lancaster	2,860	2,450	96 Wigan	3,740	2,830
47 Leeds	15,770	16,760	97 Woking	4,580	3,660
48 Leicester	8,620	6,750	98 Worcester	2,720	2,520
49 Leigh	2,470	2,110	99 Worthing	5,420	3,000
50 Lincoln	3,280	2,740	100 York	3,900	2,840

pursuing. The first of these assumes that labour migration patterns, to some extent at least, are hierarchical in character, with the form of relationships between larger and smaller centres being governed by the range of employment opportunities which they offer and by the relative mobility (in terms both of volume and distance likely to be covered) of different occupation or socio-economic groups. Second, it is also likely that labour migration will be relatively high within regional groups of labour market areas, if the effect of the different sizes of area is allowed for.

Two stages of analysis were therefore pursued, in order to examine the major flows and also the salient structures of the minor flows. First, an inspection of the raw data matrix allowed the patterns of the largest flows of migration between SMLAs to be traced. These patterns tended to be dominated by the larger areas. Second, a more elaborate analysis was needed to allow for the different sizes of the labour market areas, seeking out more subtle relationships based upon regional groupings or upon complementary or similar qualities in the origin and destination areas.

If inter-SMLA migration provides an effective surrogate for labour migration, the structure of flows is significant as an index of important trends in the national space economy. Most migration studies, in analysing all forms of residential mobility, whether accompanied by employment changes or not, have attempted to explain flows with reference to fundamentally heterogeneous types of motivation. Although labour migration is a complex phenomenon in itself, its aggregate pattern should be more coherent and capable of being related to other economic indices than, for example, are patterns of migration between local authority areas.

The magnitude of flows between SMLAs

As an aid to the clarification of the complex pattern of inter-SMLA flows, and to emphasise the most important gross flows of population, the pattern of moves which involved more than 60 sample migrants was examined cartographically (Figure 4.1). If the census sample is assumed to be representative, this threshold reflects a total movement of 600 persons during the year. In the following discussion, all sample figures will be multiplied by 10 on the basis of this assumption. Below this level, the number of inter-SMLA flows increased rapidly, to make generalised analysis more difficult.

Concentrating first on the largest flows, of more than 2,000 migrants during the year, a very large proportion of these (25 out of 38) were of out-migrants from London, mainly to other centres in south-east England.

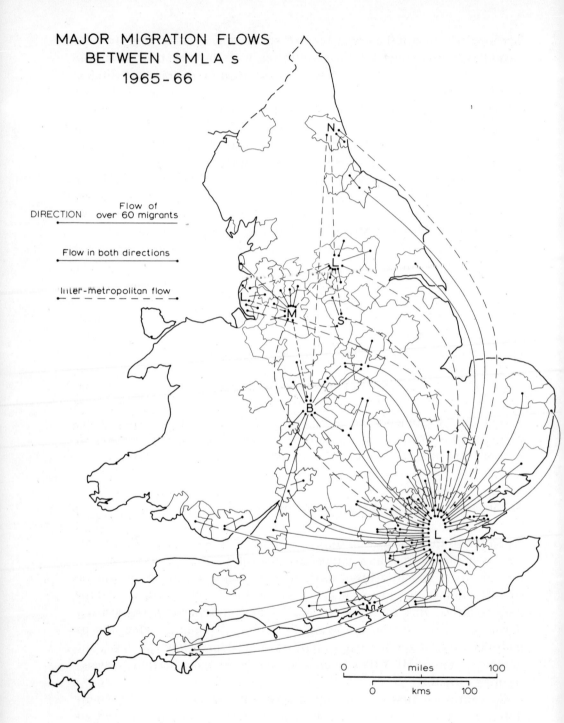

MAJOR MIGRATION FLOWS
BETWEEN SMLAs
1965-66

DIRECTION   Flow of over 60 migrants

Flow in both directions

Inter-metropolitan flow

miles   0   100

kms   0   100

Fig. 4.1

Only six flows of this magnitude linked other SMLAs to London in the opposite direction, including migration from Birmingham, Liverpool and Manchester and from three SMLAs in the south-east. Moves of more that 2,000 persons outside the south-east took place only within Lancashire (from Manchester to Bury and Blackpool and between Liverpool and St. Helens), and the west Midlands (between Birmingham and Coventry and from Birmingham to Kidderminster).

When the threshold level of significant flows is lowered to 600, these patterns of interchange become denser and movements between SMLAs in the Midlands and north become more evident. Inflows into London also take on a greater significance. Three types of flow pattern can be discerned from the total picture of migrant flows of over 600 persons (Fig. 4.1):

1   Inter-metropolitan migration between the seven largest SMLAs (those with the most connections with other large SMLAs). These were London, Birmingham, Manchester, Leeds, Liverpool, Sheffield and Newcastle. 24 of the 173 flows involving more than 600 migrants were in this category, shown by pecked lines in Figure 4.1.
2   Flows between these regional centres and the smaller SMLAs in their surrounding regions. 54 of the flows involved moves into the seven metropolitan areas, and 67 were from these centres to other SMLAs, excluding the other large centres. London contributed by far the largest proportion of these moves: 40 inflows and 44 outflows. The balance of large in- and out-flows for Birmingham was 4:8, for Manchester and Leeds 4:5, for Liverpool 1:3, Newcastle 1:1, and Sheffield possessed one outflow of this size.
3   Flows between SMLAs in the various regions, excluding the seven largest centres. Various sub-systems could be identified, linked by 28 flows of more than 600 persons. The local significance of these movements will be discussed at the end of this chapter, when the relative importance of inter-SMLA moves between different places will be examined. At this stage, the patterns of large absolute flows suggest a 'western Home Counties' group of SMLAs, with links between Slough, High Wycombe, Reading and Oxford, and an Essex group, mirroring this pattern to the east of London between Southend, Basildon and Thurrock. Outside the south-east, Nottingham, Derby, Burton-on-Trent and Mansfield constituted a 'north-east Midlands' group, and a south Wales group included Cardiff, Newport and Port Talbot. Another set of interconnections linked Portsmouth, Southampton and Plymouth on the south coast, the only sub-system to disturb the general predominance of London over

central-southern and south-western England. In addition to these small systems, a number of other exchanges took place between pairs of towns in various parts of the country. Large movements of population took place between the SMLAs of Aldershot in Hampshire and Guildford in Surrey, on Teesside (Middlesbrough and Stockton), between Coventry and Leicester, and between Chatham and Maidstone. Like many of the other

LONDON
IN-MIGRATION
1965-66

UNDER 500 NOT SHOWN

500 - 2000 ————

7000
6000
5000
4000
3000
2000
1000

IN

Fig. 4.2

interregional flows, it is impossible to judge the proportion of these movements which were purely residential in character, following the extension of the commuter hinterlands of the towns, rather than involving labour migration.

The flows centred on the largest SMLAs will now be analysed in more detail, to examine their significance as the principal national nodes of movement. Then, migration flows that define the various regional systems of interconnection (flow patterns 2 and 3) will be examined in more detail by standardising the data to allow for the varying sizes of the SMLAs.

The London-centred flow pattern

Undoubtedly, the main feature of the structure of migration flows between SMLAs in England and Wales was the volume and wide geographical influence of London-oriented flows. Forty-eight SMLAs, in fact, sent their largest outflows of migrants in 1965—66 to London, and these included all SMLAs south of the line from the Wash to the Severn estuary as well as several important provincial centres beyond this line, such as Cardiff, Swansea, Liverpool, Nottingham, Sheffield, Leeds and Newcastle. The two major provincial centres, Birmingham and Manchester, also sent large numbers to London, although these moves were less important when compared with other flows from these cities, especially to their surrounding regions. In addition, a large proportion of migrants to London (over 60 per cent) during the sample year came from non-SMLA areas: from rural areas and small towns in England and Wales, from elsewhere in the British Isles and from overseas.

Perhaps of even greater general significance than the attraction of the London SMLA was migration from the capital, which resulted in a strong net balance of out-migration during the sample year, with 86,660 moving in and 140,160 moving out. If the volume of London-oriented movement was of a different order from that moving to and from other centres, so was the manner in which it spread over relatively long distances. A comparison of the gross flow maps for in-migration and out-migration (Figs. 4.2 and 4.3) indicates a strong movement from the Midlands and north, but many fewer migrants returning to Liverpool and Nottingham. A high proportion of out-migration from the London SMLA went to the south-east region and to such southern and south-western centres as Bristol, Bournemouth, Portsmouth and Southampton.

If these patterns are interpreted as reflecting the principal flows of inter-SMLA labour migration in England and Wales, the significance of the

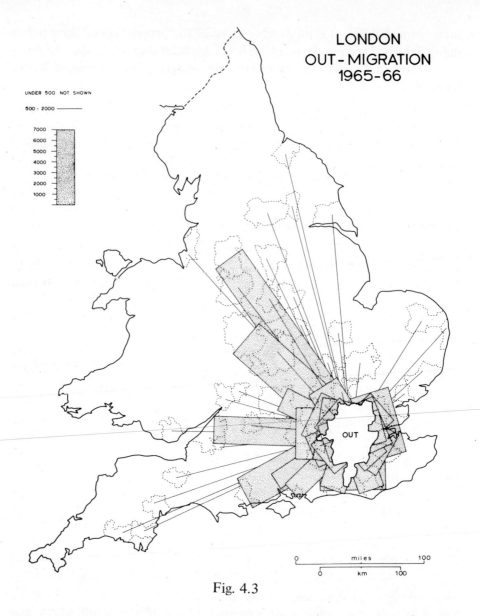

LONDON
OUT- MIGRATION
1965-66

UNDER 500 NOT SHOWN

500 - 2000 ———

7000
6000
5000
4000
3000
2000
1000

OUT

miles

km

Fig. 4.3

London labour market in sustaining national mobility levels is difficult to underestimate. The occupational characteristics of the various flows under discussion cannot be investigated, but it is likely that a high proportion of the mobile, managerial, professional and other non-manual groups would be found in these London-oriented movements, as well as young workers of all categories, moving to the wide range of opportunities provided by the Greater London area. Perhaps some indication of the social character of this movement can be gained from the fact that a high proportion of the towns that principally exchange migrants with London were in the A and B categories in the multivariate classification of SMLAs discussed in Chapter 3. These were places with relatively high levels of in-migration, high owner-occupation of houses, high rates of employment growth and large proportions of managerial and professional workers.

The London-oriented pattern was unique in its national extent, with very wide-ranging implications for the changing geographical balance of national employment opportunities. A net flow southwards was clearly one feature, as can be seen from the maps of absolute flows to and from London (Figs. 4.2 and 4.3). A second feature was a net gain of migrants by many areas in southern and south-eastern England. Part of the latter pattern must have included commuter movements to the London fringe, as well as people retiring to south coastal areas, but the volume of movements to the major cities of the south, such as Bristol, Portsmouth and Southampton, suggests that labour migration was also a most important element of movement within the southern part of the country.

The Birmingham-centred flow pattern

No other centre generated a pattern of inter-SMLA flows which compared with that of London in its volume or geographical extent. None of the remaining networks were national in their extent. The Birmingham SMLA was the centre of the most important network of movements outside London and it maintained a national significance of a more limited type. Fifty thousand people were involved in migrating to or from the area during the sample year. Birmingham's primary area of attraction lay within its own west Midlands region, where the other major urban centres, such as Coventry, Stoke-on-Trent, Kidderminster, Shrewsbury, Stafford and Worcester, all sent their greatest flows to the Birmingham SMLA. Some of this movement between adjacent SMLAs may not have involved changes of employment, but there was also a considerable contribution by longer-distance migration to Birmingham, which must have consisted very largely of labour migration. In-migration from Manchester, Liverpool, Leeds, Newcastle, Derby and Nottingham resulted in a marked gross movement southwards to Birmingham, only partly balanced by moves in the opposite direction, mainly to Manchester and Liverpool. (Figs. 4.4 and 4.5). In the Midlands itself, however, out-migration to Coventry and Nottingham provided a strong counterflow to the attraction of the Birmingham SMLA, in the case of Coventry perhaps affected somewhat by commuter-based residential moves. The southern part of the Birmingham-oriented migration

Fig. 4.4

flow pattern, on the other hand, was fairly balanced between inward and outward components, both in its volume and geographical extent, although London attracted more people from Birmingham than Birmingham from London.

On balance, the Birmingham SMLA received 23,020 in-migrants during 1965–66 and lost 27,430 out-migrants. Much of this discrepancy was probably accounted for by the extending commuter hinterlands of

80

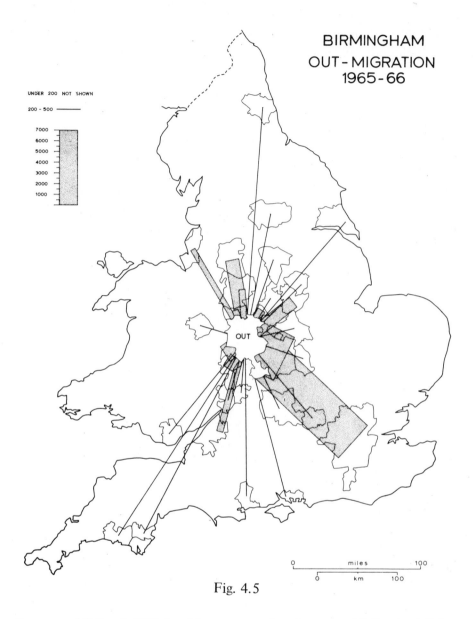

BIRMINGHAM
OUT - MIGRATION
1965 - 66

UNDER 200 NOT SHOWN

200 - 500

7000
6000
5000
4000
3000
2000
1000

OUT

0   miles   100
0   km   100

Fig. 4.5

the west Midland SMLAs. Most towns in the west Midlands fell into
category C in the classification of SMLAs, being industrial centres with
average economic growth. Stoke-on-Trent and Crewe were more static and
heavily industrial, like some of the northern cities that also made a net
contribution of labour migrants to the Birmingham SMLA. The general
role of the Birmingham SMLA in the national system of migration may
therefore be different from that of London, with a greater emphasis on

81

the mobility of manual workers within industrial Britain, than on the mobility of white-collar workers to or from Metropolitan Britain.

The Manchester-centred flow pattern

The inter-SMLA migration generated by Manchester in 1965—66 was very similar in volume to that of Birmingham: 21,010 in-migrants and 26,420

MANCHESTER
IN - MIGRATION
1965 - 66

UNDER 200 NOT SHOWN

200 - 500

7000
6000
5000
4000
3000
2000
1000

Fig. 4.6

out-migrants. The geographical pattern of its migration was much more confined to the local north-west region, however, being dominated by exchanges with centres such as Preston, Blackpool, Bolton, Burnley, Bury, Leigh and Rochdale. It is also significant that, unlike Coventry in the west Midlands (which sent its largest flow of out-migrants to Birmingham), Liverpool, the second largest SMLA in the north-west, was primarily oriented towards London rather than Manchester.

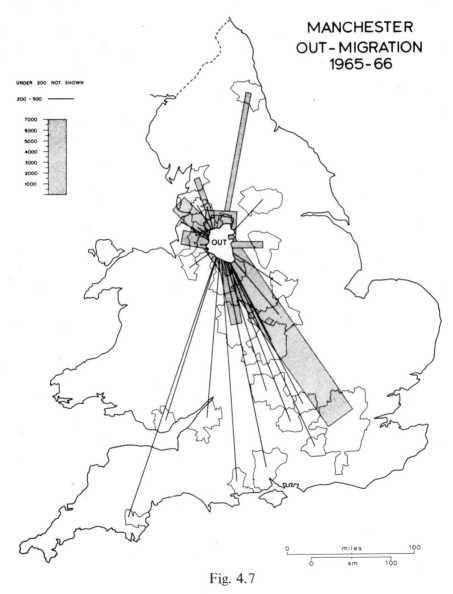

Fig. 4.7

The large flows to Manchester from outside the north-west mainly consisted of contributions from Leeds, London and Birmingham. On the other hand, out-migrants from the Manchester area moved to many areas of England and Wales, to Newcastle, Preston, Blackpool and Sheffield in the north, and to a variety of SMLAs in the Midlands and south (Figs. 4.6 and 4.7). In terms of labour migration, the Manchester SMLA seemed therefore to import migrants mainly from its surrounding areas, but to distribute them over wider areas of the country, especially farther south.

Fig. 4.8

In addition, the Manchester SMLA exchanged workers with the other large cities, such as London, Birmingham and Newcastle. Most of the SMLAs that exchanged their most important flows of migrants with Manchester were placed in category D in the classification of SMLAs: towns with little net in-migration themselves, relatively low rates of employment growth and small proportions of managerial and professional workers. Again, it may be inferred that, compared with London and Birmingham,

Fig. 4.9

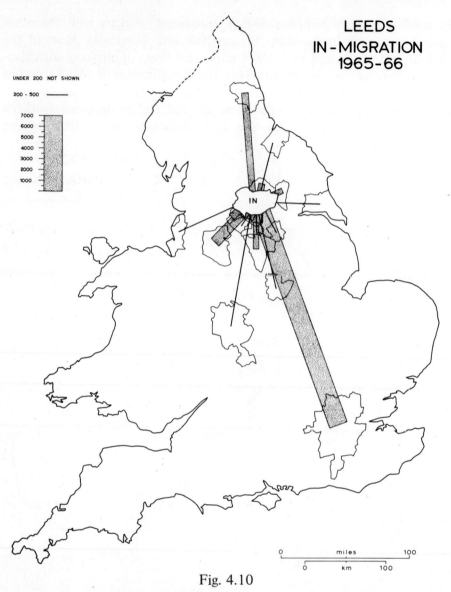

LEEDS
IN-MIGRATION
1965-66

UNDER 200 NOT SHOWN

200 - 500 ⸻

7000
6000
5000
4000
3000
2000
1000

IN

0   miles   100
0   km   100

Fig. 4.10

the role of the Manchester SMLA may be functionally as well as geographically distinctive, although more evidence is needed to substantiate this
inference.

Other Networks: Liverpool and Leeds

The most significant remaining SMLAs, in terms of the total numbers of
migrants moving to and from them in 1965–66, were Liverpool (39,240)

86

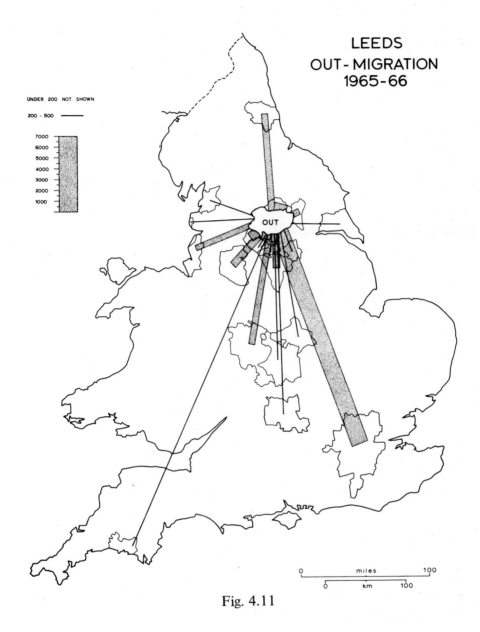

LEEDS
OUT-MIGRATION
1965-66

UNDER 200 NOT SHOWN

200 - 500

7000
6000
5000
4000
3000
2000
1000

OUT

miles

km

Fig. 4.11

and Leeds (32,530). These were followed by Coventry (25,750), Nottingham and Newcastle (both about 21,000 migrants gross). The situation of the last three can be quite adequately deduced from the map of total gross flows of over 600 migrants, (Fig. 4.1) but brief consideration of Liverpool and Leeds provides a useful complement to the three largest centres already discussed.

The most important longer-distance moves to Liverpool (Fig. 4.8) were from London and Leeds, while the pattern of out-migration from Liverpool was particularly dominated by London (Fig. 4.9). Local or intra-regional exchanges were mainly with Manchester and Chester. Apart from this, labour migration around Liverpool consisted of an exchange of population with other SMLAs in Lancashire, Yorkshire and the Midlands. The balance of migration was strongly outwards, with only 13,360 in-migrants replacing 25,880 out-migrants during the pre-census year.

The migration pattern for the Leeds SMLA (Figs. 4.10 and 4.11) was similar in its geographical pattern to that of Manchester, although it included a smaller volume of movement and resulted in a much closer balance of loss and gain during the year: 16,760 out-migrants and 15,770 in-migrants. Like Manchester in Lancashire, Leeds had a marked regional influence in the West Riding and a balanced exchange with another large SMLA nearby, Sheffield (which, like Liverpool, still sent its largest flow to London). Migration inwards to Leeds from outside the West Riding was confined to important flows from Newcastle, Manchester and London, but, again like Manchester, its pattern of out-migration was spread over a relatively wide area of England and Wales, especially the Midlands and coastal areas of northern England.

Regional patterns of inter-SMLA migration

So far the analysis of migration flows between SMLAs has concentrated on the gross pattern of movements, to emphasise their volume and the significance of London and the major provincial SMLAs in a national context. The influence of the large SMLAs, however, is somewhat overwhelming, especially as their size includes the population of their commuting hinterlands. In the initial review of the major flows (Fig. 4.1), three types of flow pattern were identified. Type 1, inter-metropolitan flows, has been examined together with important elements of type 2, migration to and from the major regional centres and smaller SMLAs nearby. However, at an intra-regional scale (especially including smaller type 2 and most type 3 flows) single flows of less than 600 persons in the sample year may be locally significant either for the exporting or importing SMLA. Even the larger flows already described need to be related to other movements taking place within the regions. Standard Metropolitan Labour Areas of different size, character and location within the same region may play different roles in the structure of regional migration. An appropriate procedure was therefore sought to elicit regional and other patterns from amongst the smaller flows. A number of methods of simplifying the data matrix into its most important elements were explored and tried. A discussion of these methods and the results of some of them have been published by N. Hadjifotiou.[1] Q-mode and R-mode factor analyses were carried out on the flow matrix to identify origin SMLAs with similar patterns of destinations, and also destination SMLAs with similar patterns of origins. The standard factor analysis programe BMD X72[2] was used, and those factors with eigenvalues greater than unity were subjected to a biquartimin rotation. The results of this procedure have already been presented in a graphical form in a project working paper.[3]

Several of the factors, however, were not readily interpretable, and others linked together groups of apparently dissimilar SMLAs. Because of the complexity of the technique and its resulting output, and because of interpretation difficulties, it was decided to adopt a simpler technique to pick out regularities in inter-SMLA flows. The method adopted was simply to express the flows from an individual SMLA to every other SMLA as a percentage of the total outflow from that SMLA. Similarly, the flows into each SMLA from the other areas were expressed as proportions of the total in-movement. The largest of these percentages were then isolated and mapped, and the results, in fact, accorded quite closely with those derived from factor analysis.

Figures 4.12 to 4.15 summarise the results of this analysis, the first two demonstrating that the importance of the London SMLA is not simply a result of its large absolute size. Figure 4.12 shows that movement to London attracted a significant share of out-migrants from all SMLAs south of the Wash—Severn Estuary line. The same pattern emerges in Figure 4.13, which reveals the share of in-migrants that came from London, and the number of London-dominated SMLAs in this case is even greater than in Figure 4.12. In effect, these maps confirm the earlier evidence of the special character of London's role in the national pattern of labour migration by demonstrating how most other SMLAs in southern and eastern England are of only local significance in comparison.

Elsewhere in the country, the standardisation of inter-SMLA migration flows according to their local contributions to the total numbers of out-migrants (Fig. 4.14) and in-migrants (Fig. 4.15) allows the significance of other flows to emerge from behind the dominance of the London-oriented patterns, generally highlighting intra-regional patterns of connection. If allowance is made for the size of the largest SMLAs, it appears that these patterns of connection are quite complex and result in extended patterns of migration exchange around the regional capitals. The maps show only the most important flows (including more than 10 per cent of the contri-

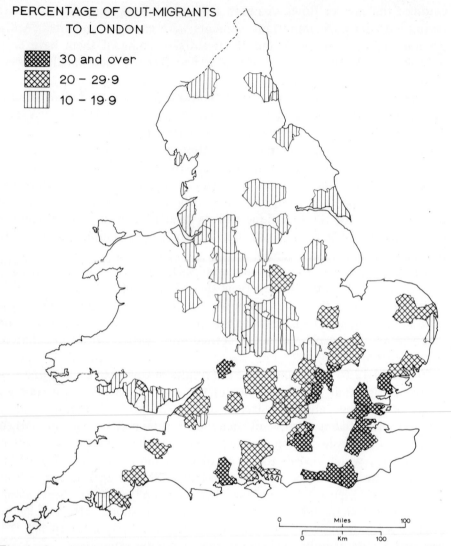

PERCENTAGE OF OUT-MIGRANTS
TO LONDON

30 and over
20 – 29·9
10 – 19·9

Fig. 4.12 (SMLAs sending less than 10 per cent of their out-migrants to London in 1965–66 not shown)

bution from or to each SMLA), excluding those involving London. The analysis of the destination patterns of out-migrants (Fig. 4.14) and that of the origin patterns of the in-migrants (Fig. 4.15) show broadly similar regional groupings. In effect, the two analyses examine the same flows, first from the point of view of their significance for the origin areas (Fig. 4.14) and second, for the destination areas (Fig. 4.15). The similarity of pattern therefore reflects the basic process of migration exchange be-

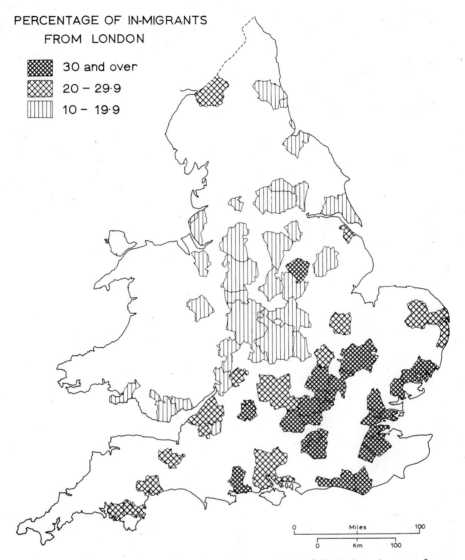

Fig. 4.13 (SMLAs receiving less than 10 per cent of their in-migrants from London in 1965–66 not shown)

tween areas, which forms the most persistent feature of inter-SMLA migration (including, as we have seen, London-oriented moves and those between the large SMLAs in the provinces).

Although some of the short-distance movement between contiguous SMLAs must have consisted of residential moves without change of employment location, the distances moved by many migrants were long

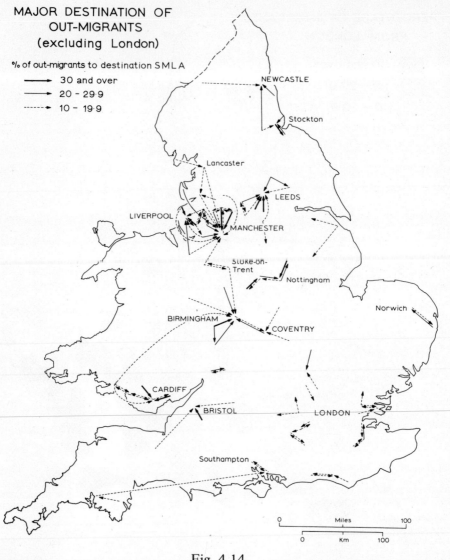

MAJOR DESTINATION OF
OUT-MIGRANTS
(excluding London)

% of out-migrants to destination SMLA

→ 30 and over
→ 20 - 29·9
⤍ 10 - 19·9

Fig. 4.14

enough to suggest that labour migration and retirement were the predominant types of move taking place. Generally speaking, the regional
patterns in Fig. 4.14 (showing the importance for the origin areas of migration to other SMLAs) were more compact and involved less overlap between regions than in Fig. 4.15. This is because out-migrants from an
SMLA are likely to move to many areas, including London and other
large regional centres, so that many single flows did not reach the 10 per

92

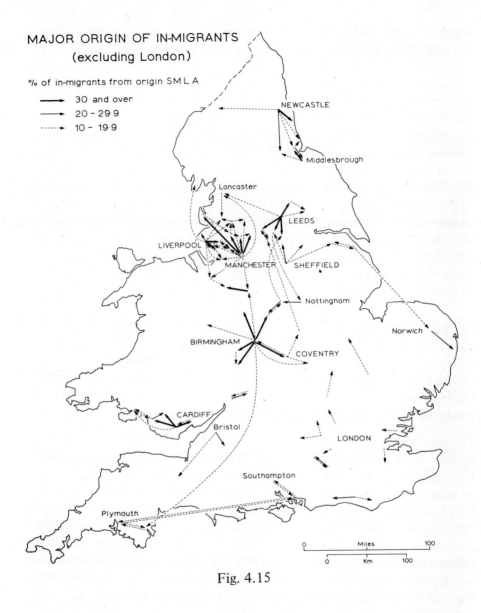

MAJOR ORIGIN OF IN-MIGRANTS
(excluding London)

% of in-migrants from origin SML A

30 and over
20 - 29·9
10 - 19·9

NEWCASTLE
Middlesbrough
Lancaster
LEEDS
LIVERPOOL
MANCHESTER
SHEFFIELD
Nottingham
Norwich
BIRMINGHAM
COVENTRY
CARDIFF
Bristol
LONDON
Southampton
Plymouth

Miles
Km
0
100
0
100

Fig. 4.15

cent 'threshold' share of total out-migration required to be shown on the map. In contrast, the patterns in Fig 4.15 (based on the importance to the destination areas of migration from other SMLAs) are likely to be dominated by a relatively few places (generally speaking, those nearby and with perhaps one or two contacts with places outside the local region), several of which may contribute more than 10 per cent of the total inflow and thus be shown on the map. The two maps should therefore be considered together so that differences between them can be evaluated in relation to the basic similarities between the flow patterns that they display.

A further general observation underlines the importance of the London SMLA in southern and eastern England. With one exception (in the Bristol area) no part of these broader regions apparently escaped the dominating influence of London, even when allowance is made for the relative sizes of the migration flows. Only local exchanges of migrants between pairs of SMLAs around London, on the south coast, in the south-east Midlands and in East Anglia seemed to be of sufficient local importance to challenge the influence of London. The sparcity of sub-regional interlinkages on the maps in these areas is probably affected by the large number of possible origins and destinations for each SMLA, both within the south and east and in other regions of England and Wales. Individual flows are thus again less likely to reach the 10 per cent 'threshold' and appear on the map.

Seven regional systems of interlinkage can be defined once the influence of London is removed.

The north-west. This is a region with much interconnection between the numerous small SMLAs around the major centres of Manchester and Liverpool. Its influence extended in the north to Preston and Lancaster (which also received a high proportion of out-migrants from Barrow-in-Furness) and in the south to Stoke-on-Trent. The boundary with the Yorkshire areas to the east is quite distinct.

The west Midlands. A dual structure was clearer here than in the north-west because there are fewer SMLAs and the pattern was clearly dominated by Birmingham and Coventry. As noted in the discussion of absolute volumes of migration, Kidderminster, Coventry, Shrewsbury, Stafford and Stoke-on-Trent exchanged significant proportions of migrants with the Birmingham SMLA, while Birmingham, Northampton and Leicester were strongly connected with the Coventry SMLA. Stoke-on-Trent sent significant proportions of its migrants to both this region and to the north-west while overlap also occurred between the west Midlands and the north Midlands, through movements from Birmingham to Burton-upon-Trent.

The north Midlands. Here, interchange took place between Burton-upon-Trent, Derby, Nottingham and Mansfield, to form a surprisingly self-contained group of SMLAs (apart, of course, from their ties with London). Only the link from Birmingham to Burton-upon-Trent and some significant exchanges with the West Riding of Yorkshire provided significant overlapping with other regions on Fig. 4.15.

The West Riding of Yorkshire. The Leeds-based system of exchange included Halifax, Huddersfield, Barnsley, Wakefield, Harrogate and York. Movements between this area and the north Midlands also had some significance in both regions, but the only significant connection with the north-west involved moves from Leeds to Lancaster – a flow which must have contained a considerable share of retirement moves. Perhaps more striking in the area south of Leeds was the relative absence of important connections involving Sheffield and Doncaster. Apart from moves from Sheffield to Doncaster, Dewsbury and Barnsley, which were significant to the receiving areas (Fig. 4.15), flows to the south Yorkshire SMLAs were too diffuse for any clear regional pattern to emerge at this level of analysis. Hull is similarly placed, being isolated from all other SMLAs, at least if the criteria used for drawing both these maps are applied as a basis for assessment.

The north-east. Out-migration to many other places outside the region reduced the importance of nearby areas as destinations for people moving out of SMLAs in the north-east (Fig. 4.14) but a larger proportion of in-migrants came from SMLAs in the local region (Fig. 4.15). Newcastle, with Sunderland and Carlisle, were linked with Middlesbrough, Stockton, Darlington and West Hartlepool into a clearly-defined north-eastern region of labour migrant exchange.

South Wales. This region was similar in its general position and pattern of interchange to the north-east. Cardiff, Port Talbot, Rhondda, Newport and Swansea formed a well-defined group, although Swansea seemed to be less regionally-oriented than the other SMLAs, having a significant proportion of migrants going outside the region to Birmingham.

The Bristol region. This region provided the sole possible exception to the diffuseness of the patterns in southern England, once migration to and from London has been allowed for. Here a small network of interchange could be distinguished, including Bath, Swindon and Taunton, each of which sent or received significant numbers of migrants from the Bristol SMLA.

These various groupings indicate that the most significant affinities between areas with respect to migration exchange are regional in character. No doubt, relatively high movement levels occur between SMLAs in different parts of the country outside this regional framework, but the volumes of such flows are evidently not sufficient to overcome the influence of the regional and London-oriented patterns. Nevertheless, the maps provide a few single examples of such 'non-regional', long-distance flows, to give an indication of the type of affinity between SMLAs that might be more in evidence if a lower threshold of interchange were examined. The same types of linkage may, of course, take place within the regionally-defined groupings, but are subsumed within them.

The first type of long-distance affinity is exemplified by the relatively large proportion of in-migrants to Torquay who came from Birmingham; retirement moves are frequently important in linking coastal areas into the patterns of regional inter-connection, although many such moves must also go to non-SMLA areas. A second type of move over long distances is exemplified by those between Portsmouth and Plymouth. Movement of the armed forces and their families (in this case, naval personnel) is significant at this level of analysis, although it is of minor general importance. Third, the movement from Swansea to Birmingham, and also perhaps that between the West Riding and the north Midlands already referred to, provide examples of inter-regional flows between areas with similar types of industry but different levels of prosperity within them. It may appear surprising that these types of connection, suggested in our general discussion in Chapter 2, do not appear more commonly. It should be remembered, however, that the principal manifestation of moves to an area of better opportunity lies in the dominance of London and perhaps also the other major provincial centres.

Conclusion

The geographical patterns of inter-SMLA migration exhibit large gross volumes and complex networks of flows between labour market areas in England and Wales. The total extent of mobility between and around the largest cities in England and Wales should not be forgotten in discussing such concepts as 'the labour market' or 'the housing market' in modern circumstances. The short-term character of these markets is almost certainly determined more by the level of activity taking place within them than by any marginal effect of net growth or decline.

The net balance of migration between SMLAs is also important, especially in creating longer-term alterations in local balances of supply and demand for both labour and housing. The parts played by the London and Birmingham SMLAs in the national pattern of economic change contrasts with more northerly cities, and this contrast is reflected in relative housing prices, wages, levels of unemployment, activity rates and vacancy rates. In examining the balance of inter-SMLA movements, with their implications for fundamental shifts in the economic geography of England and Wales, our analysis has very clearly emphasised the enduring nature of the movement from north to south in the mid 1960s.

The use made in this chapter of inter-SMLA migration patterns to provide a guide to the geographical structure of labour migration in England and Wales has a number of deficiencies which have already been outlined. Nevertheless, the framework that has emerged seems sufficiently robust to reveal the major types of labour migrant flow in England and Wales. Although still at a fairly broad level of generalisation, associated groups of labour market areas have been identified more precisely than previously. It is within these groups that the geographical mobility of labour is likely to exert greatest pressures on resources such as housing. Much more investigation is required into the details of the very large numbers of moves involved (about 600,000), and future inquiry should also investigate the economic and social forces which may change these patterns, since the use of a single year's figures implicitly assumes that they are stable in the short term.

Three types of flow pattern have been recognised, and the distinction between these types is partly concerned with the different opportunities to be found in different areas of the country, partly with the distances over which migrants may be willing to move to new areas, and partly with the occupational groups and aspirations of the migrants themselves. These topics will be taken up again in the second half of this book, but it is clear that little can be done in an aggregated analysis of census data to pursue the relationships which lie beneath the patterns.

The first type of flow is numerically the most dominant, and consists of moves to and from the London SMLA. The quantitative importance of this pattern for long-distance migration has already been commented upon, but there are good reasons for regarding the influence of London as unique in several other respects, compared with other large cities in England and Wales. This is most obviously indicated by the extent of its geographical influence, but probably is also reflected in the distinct economic and social structure of the migrant populations involved, although specific information on this topic is lacking. The importance of the London SMLA in the national pattern of in- and out-migration suggests that forms of tenure within the metropolis should perhaps be more flexible than elsewhere in the country, to allow households of different types and income to move in and out as freely as possible. The pressure consistently placed upon certain sectors of the London housing market, such as private-rented accommodation and certain types of owner-occupied housing, indicates that the capital's association with a sizeable proportion of the country's labour migration is one of the major contributory factors in producing some of its housing difficulties.

Outside London itself, the influence of the metropolis pervades many SMLAs in southern and eastern England when workers are considering moving to new jobs. Similarly, workers moving out of the London SMLA are most likely to move to other areas in the south-east. Thus, employment and housing conditions in the metropolis extend their influences over a wide area and probably make labour migration in the south-east distinct from that in other parts of Britain.

The second type of labour migration has attracted less comment in the literature than the London-based system of movement. This type consists of the migration which takes place between the major provincial centres outside London. In relative terms these flows are much less important than those to London, but the absolute numbers involved are quite large and the distances are substantial. An interesting feature of these flows is the different roles apparently played by the major provincial cities. Thus, the movement pattern around Birmingham contrasts with that around Manchester, which is more comparable with the pattern for Leeds. Cardiff and Newcastle also seem to be similar in the ways in which they connect their regional systems into the national pattern of labour migration. Although there is no direct evidence, these provincial centres may well generate a somewhat different type of movement from that centred on London, with industrial workers forming a higher proportion of the migrants. Certainly the evidence of the characteristics of SMLAs presented in Chapter 3 would support such a contention.

The third type of pattern consists of the exchange of labour migrants within regional groups of SMLAs. It is more difficult to equate these moves solely with labour migration, since over shorter distances (particularly between contiguous SMLAs) they become merged with residential changes involving commuting to an unaltered place of employment. In some cases, too, moves to resorts on retirement may also form part of these more localised patterns of flows. Nevertheless, their outer boundaries probably indicate significant functional boundaries, which combine localised commuting and wider-scale labour migration spheres of influence. They therefore define the main regional labour and housing markets, within which competition for regional resources takes place most intensively.

Thus, the main inter-SMLA migration patterns which have been identified hold clear implications for the study of housing. These migration patterns indicate that the labour market operates on a range of scales, of which three stand out most clearly. Housing markets must also be studied on these different levels, since there is good reason for believing that they are functionally connected to labour markets. It is likely that labour migrants view local housing markets differently if they form part of different patterns of movement; and to understand the housing needs of labour migrants it is necessary to appraise the housing market in terms of who are migrating, what parts of the country they are moving to and from, and why they are doing so.

Notes

[1]   N. Hadjifotiou, 'The Analysis of migration between Standard Metropolitan Labour Areas in England and Wales', Housing and Labour Mobility Study, Department of Geography, University College London., *Working Paper* no.4 1972, pp. 5—11.

[2]   The program BMDX72 is described in W.J. Dixon (ed.) *BMD: Biomedical Computer Programs. X-series Supplement* University of California Publications in Automatic Computation, no.3 1970.

[3]   Hadjifotiou, op. cit., pp. 23—34, 39—48.

5 Previous Studies Relevant to Labour Migration

In a review of previous work on migration and its relation to housing, considerable difficulty is created by differences in the areal units and time periods used by various studies. Most empirical work on migration in Britain has analysed data either on movement between Standard Regions or on movement between local authorities. As discussed in Chapter 2, neither of these scales is fully adequate for the study of labour migration.

The few attempts at explaining regional migration patterns in England and Wales have relied on the gravity model approach, usually in combination with selected variables representing regional differentials, such as unemployment rates,[1] industrial growth[2] or, in one case, the supply of new houses.[3] The highly aggregated approach adopted by these studies has inevitably meant that the actual motives of individual migrants have remained hidden. It is clear that any attempt to explain the patterns of labour migration described in Chapter 4 must be through an examination of the characteristics and motivations of individual migrant households. But first it is necessary to review other studies that have attempted to explain why families move in order to isolate those characteristics that seem to be associated with migration.

Unfortunately, surveys of housing in Britain have been concerned with mobility of all types, including movement within local authority areas. Investigations of migration over varying time periods are also difficult to compare. An additional problem for the analysis of labour migration is that most studies of long-distance movement include migrants who are not economically active, such as retired people moving to coastal resorts or elsewhere.

Characteristics of migrants

Previous work on residential migration has suggested a number of generalisations about the process of moving and about those who are likely to migrate.[4] Of particular relevance to this chapter is work on the differential propensities to migrate of groups within the population.[5] Attributes which have been associated with migration propensity include life-cycle stage, education, employment status, income, socio-economic group, previous migration experience, and type of housing, some of which are likely to be closely correlated with each other. It is relevant, where possible, to examine the interaction of these factors on migration propensity; and it is also important to examine studies of the effects of migration.

Life cycle and career pattern

Age is perhaps the best-established variable affecting migration. The reasons for the relationship between age and propensity to move include both the effects of life-cycle stage and of career pattern. The age of the household head is likely to be closely related to his stage in the family life-cycle, but the correlation is not perfect, as age at marriage and the length of the period of child-bearing may vary.

Cullingworth presents a 'family housing cycle' which generalises the experience of many British households.[6] The first stage of this cycle starts with the creation of a new household when the parental home is left on marriage or when a job is taken in a new area. In this stage, households often live in small 'rooms' or 'converted flats', usually in privately rented accommodation. When the first child is born, the household requires more space for storage and privacy; a separate bathroom and a garden become more desirable. Mobility is greatest at this stage, and more householders become owner-occupiers and council tenants. As the family grows, overcrowding remains the major problem and further movement may be necessary to adjust to changes in space requirements. The importance of crowding diminishes, however, when the older children marry and split off to start their own independent housing history. The final stages of the cycle may vary for different types of household. Comfort, convenience and warmth become increasingly important to older people, but the inclinations of households to move to more suitable accommodation may be restrained by falling income and by a wish to retain the stability and familiarity afforded by their old house and district.

Life-cycle theories, however, do not explain labour migration as such, for there is no reason, unless it be housing availability, why movement to adjust to changing family needs should be accompanied by job changes. Hunter and Reid discuss the effects of career pattern on mobility:

> In his twenties, the worker is likely to be in a favourable position to make regional job shifts, as both money and psychological costs will be low. The older worker will be more likely to have found work

102

which he regards as permanent, but there are other reasons linked with age which can as readily explain the lower mobility of the age groups 30–40 and above. Some of these are associated with *continued employment* in a single firm, such as seniority, job security and the effect of pension and welfare plans linked with age ... and insofar as these affect mobility within a local labour market area, they apply *a fortiori* to inter-regional movement of labour.[7]

Older men may also find inter-regional job changes difficult because of discrimination against them by employers. Hunter and Reid also point out that age is related to other characteristics of a potential migrant, such as family circumstances and the quantity of his moveable possessions. Thus both the money and the psychological costs of movement will increase with age.[8] Becker makes the additional point that very specific training may only be useful for a particular job. He argues that, if people receive general training from their formal education and specific training on their jobs, their mobility should be greatest before they have received much specific training.[9]

Both life-cycle and career-pattern variables indicate that the probability of residential movement will be greatest for young people in their twenties, and will steadily decline with increasing age. Life-cycle factors do not require that such residential movement should also involve a change of job, but it may be argued that the desirability of a change of accommodation may make a prospective migrant more willing to undertake a long-distance move, if this is being considered in any case. An insight into this can be obtained by examining the number of labour migrants who gave housing factors as their main reasons for moving (see Chapter 8).

Life-cycle stage is related to a number of distinct attributes of a migrant household, including marital status, family type and family size as well as the age of the household head. Similarly, career pattern has implications for the socio-economic group of the labour migrant as well as his age. Both life-cycle stage and career-pattern factors lead us to expect a diminution in propensity to move with age, a result borne out by almost all empirical studies. Harris and Clausen[10] found that movement rates in Great-Britain (the proportion of their sample that moved house at least once in the previous ten years) were highest for the 25–30 age group (86·1 per cent moved), followed by the 31–44 age group (69·4 per cent) and 20–24 age group (66·2 per cent). In the United States in 1963–64, the percentage of employed males moving between states declined from 6·7 per cent for those aged 18–24 to 0·9 per cent for those aged 45–64.[11] Lansing and Mueller found that the percentage of their sample of household heads who had moved across the boundaries of labour market areas in the USA in the last five years declined from 35 per cent (for those aged 18–24), to 28 per cent (25–34), 14 per cent (35–44), 11 per cent (45–54), 8 per cent (55–64) and 5 per cent (65 and over). [12] Hunter and Reid cite a number of other studies confirming the same trend. [13]

Marital status

Although life-cycle theories of residential mobility stress the frequency of moves in the early stages of marriage, it should be remembered that single people are also prone to labour migration. One might expect one-person households to be more mobile than families headed by people of equivalent age, for they are without such ties as the spouse's employment and the children's schools, and are likely to find it easier to obtain suitable housing due to their low space requirements. On the other hand, changes in marital staus often involve moves for one or both parties. This may explain Bogue's finding that, for moves crossing county boundaries in the United States, single people under 45 were less migratory than married people, while over 45 the single were more migratory; at all ages the widowed, divorced and separated were more migratory than either. [14]

Harris and Clausen found that 57·9 per cent of people in their sample who were married at the time of the survey had moved house within the preceding ten years, compared with 42·3 per cent of single people and 38·7 per cent of the widowed. However, the proportion of single people moving for work reasons (21 per cent) was considerably higher than that of married people (16 per cent). [15] This may indicate that single people are better represented among labour migrants than among short-distance movers.

Household size and type

Conflicting arguments have been advanced about the effects of household size on the propensity to move. As stated earlier, life-cycle theories of migration suggest that mobility is likely to be fostered by the need to adjust to changes in family size; in this respect, larger households are more likely to have to make such an adjustment. On the other hand, costs of movement may be greater for larger households and ties to the origin area stronger.

Cullingworth found that the average number of people in a migrant household was 3·29, somewhat higher than the average for non-moving households (3·04). He also reported that one-person households were less mobile than average, and three-person and four-person households rather more mobile. [16] This study, however, concerned residential mobility of all types and its findings may not be applicable to labour migration. Friedlander and Roshier found that, among households headed by manual workers, large families were less likely to move from one local authority area to another than small families, but the reverse was true for non-manual workers, large families being more likely to move. [17]

Household type is also closely related to mobility. The studies by both Cullingworth [18] and Woolf [19] showed that households classified as 'individuals under 60 years of age', 'small adult households', 'small families' and 'large families' were overrepresented among moving households, as compared with 'large adult families' and 'older small households'. It is surprising that 'individuals under 60 years of age' should have been mobile, although one-person households were not; a partial explanation may be that a large number of one-person households consisted of old people. [20]

Education

The level of education of the family head appears to be related to geographical mobility. It might be expected that better-educated persons would be more aware of the existence of opportunities elsewhere and hence would be more likely to migrate. Indeed, Friedlander and Roshier found that those in England and Wales with grammar school education were twice as mobile as those not educated in grammar schools, and that this difference was greatest for long-distance movers. [21] Again, Harris and Clausen showed that, although 70·8 per cent of those with university education had moved in the preceding ten years, under 50 per cent of those from comprehensive or secondary modern schools with no higher education had done so. [22] Lansing and Mueller, however, have pointed out that education levels are strongly related to age group, as the quality and availability of education have increased greatly over the last few decades.[23] Bogue, however, found that the relationship between education and mobility persisted when he controlled for the effect of age. [24]

Employment and income

Traditional theories of labour migration have stressed the importance of employment level, and many economic models have included unemployment as a predictor of inter-regional migration. [25] Clearly, the unemployed have more to gain from a move, but in the real world they may have more difficulty raising the money required for movement. There is little firm information on this matter for England and Wales, but in the United States the migration rate during 1963—64 for unemployed males was 6·3 per cent compared with 2·9 per cent for employed males.[26] Lansing and Mueller reported that over a quarter of the migrants in the five years before their survey had been unemployed before the move.[27] Daniel, however, found that movement was least when unemployment was greatest, and that the unemployed moved only after considerable delay.[28] According to Lansing and Mueller, people who had been unemployed for more than three months were distinctly more likely to have moving plans than those who had only recently been put out of work.[29]

The income of a household head is likely to be correlated both with his socio-economic group and with his age. Willis has suggested that higher-income groups should be more mobile because the cost of movement forms a smaller proportion of their total wealth or income.[30] In contrast, Lansing and Morgan found, from United States data, an inverse relationship between income and labour migration, with the incomes of migrants tending to be lower than those of non-migrants.[31] Bogue explored this relationship in more detail:

> At each age, the least migratory segments of the population were those with large (above-average) incomes and those with almost no income. This would seem to indicate that a person might be 'too poor to migrate' as well as 'so rich that he has no need to migrate' ... The same situation that is responsible for an adult person's poverty might prevent him from migrating, even if he wanted to.

Bogue also suggested that very wealthy groups may be somewhat more migratory than those in the upper-middle income brackets.[32]

The preponderance of British data, however, has suggested a rather different pattern. Woolf tabulated the weekly income of heads of migrant households (excluding those formed in the last four years) and heads of non-migrant households, and found an apparent increase in propensity to move with income.[33] Cullingworth's results were in accordance with this conclusion.[34] It is open to question whether this difference is a result of divergence between British and American experience or of the inclusion of short-distance movers in the British figures.

Socio-economic groups

After life-cycle stage, socio-economic group is perhaps the attribute with the best-authenticated relationship to migration selectivity. The tendency for professional and managerial people to be more mobile, especially over long distances, has been explained in Chapter 2 in terms of the scale at which the labour market operates for them. [35] Members of these groups are likely, in Merton's terms, to be 'cosmopolitans' rather than 'locals'. [36] They exemplify Watson's image of 'spiralism':

> The progressive ascent of the specialists of different skills through a series of higher positions in one or more hierarchical structures, and the concomitant residential mobility through a number of communities at one or more steps during the ascent, forms a characteristic combination of social and spatial mobility. [37]

As Burn states, 'this does not mean that unskilled persons are not found among migrants, but rather that those in career type jobs view migration as an integral part of the job and are, therefore, more willing to move'. [38]

Most studies of longer-distance migration show marked differences between socio-economic groups. Tarver has reported that professional, technical and kindred workers are the most mobile groups in the United States population. [39] Ladinsky pointed out that mobility among professional people may be very variable, depending on their investment in non-transportable 'capital' (such as equipment, clientele and fringe benefits). [40] In England and Wales, Friedlander and Roshier found that only 18·5 per cent of the top professional and executive group had lived in the same local authority area all their lives, compared with 47·8 per cent of the unskilled manual group; of those moving over 50 miles, 30 per cent were professionals and only 13 per cent were unskilled manual workers. [41] In Jansen's Bristol study, where migrants and non-migrants were matched by age, sex, marital status and employment status, 69·3 per cent of migrants compared with 44·1 per cent of residents were in career-type occupations, while 27·7 per cent more residents than migrants held manual jobs. [42] Donnison found that skilled manual workers and foremen were more strongly represented among those trying to move than among actual movers;[43] this perhaps indicates some degree of frustration among this group. However, a comparison using 1966 data of migrant household heads and heads of all households showed relatively little difference between their socio-economic groups. [44] Moore suggests that such findings reflect the superimposition of two types of migration. One consists of intra-urban migration, in which working-class movement predominates, and the other of longer-distance moves, in which, as suggested above, the higher socio-economic groups are best represented. [45]

Past migration experience

Those households and individuals which have moved frequently in the past appear to be more likely to move again than do those who have stayed for long periods in the same area. Blumen, Kogan and McCarthy observed that their stochastic model of mobility was more successful if the population was divided into two groups — movers and stayers. [46] McGinnis explained the same phenomenon by his 'Axiom of Cumulative Inertia', which states that an individual's propensity to move declines as his length of stay in the same area increases. [47] This decline might be caused by a gradual increase in social and personal ties to an area, so that greater perceived benefits elsewhere will be required to induce the individual to move. Alternatively, this duration-of-stay effect may be produced by the more frequent movement of people who are intrinsically prone to move anyway. A division of the population into movers and stayers could explain this phenomenon without recourse to ideas of cumulative inertia.

The operation of the migration differentials already discussed would lead one to expect that past migration behaviour would be repeated in the future. If the young and the high-status are more prone to move, they are still young and high-status after the move, and thus possess a high propensity to move again. A number of other factors are also relevant. Besides the lower intensity of personal and psychological ties to an area of relatively short residence, it can be suggested that a learning process may blunt inertia, making it easier to move again. [48]

Taylor, concerned with the role of personality traits in explaining the selectivity of migration, found that out-migrants from Durham mining villages had greater prior mobility than those left behind. [49] He also reported that migrants were more likely than non-migrants to have travelled extensively, usually the result of service in the forces or extended periods of work away from home. [50] He described migrants as characterised by a sense of 'dislocation', compared with the non-migrants' sense of 'belonging'; while migrants 'aspire', non-migrants are 'satisfied'. [51]

Housing

It is clear that housing is a dominant consideration in most changes of residence. It was given as the main reason for moving by 56 per cent of Harris and Clausen's sample. [52] Housing itself is not often the main reason for labour migration, but it may act as a stimulus or as a contributory factor to a decision to undertake a long-distance move. In some cases, particularly movement away from a central city to outer suburbs or over-spill estates, it may still be the prime reason; McDonald, for example, found that more workers moving into Scottish new towns gave housing as their primary reason for movement, than gave work.[53]

Housing requirements are complementary to life-cycle stage as factors impelling migration: movement takes place in response to a disparity between the household's requirements and the existing dwelling, particularly with respect to space. It has also been argued that movement takes place in order to reconcile housing aspirations with the household's ability to pay for housing of various types. [54]

One might assume from both these lines of reasoning that migrants motivated by housing needs are more likely to originate in small dwellings, in flats or lodgings and in privately rented accommodation, and less likely to originate in large owner-occupied, detached or semi-detached houses. However, the higher long-distance mobility rates of the high-income and high-status groups run counter to this assumption.

Tenure

The likely effects of tenure on labour mobility are discussed in Chapter 1. Cullingworth found that mobility rates were highest for those who had been renting private furnished accommodation, 58 per cent of this group having moved in a 15-month period. The rates for previous owner-occupiers, local authority tenants and private tenants of unfurnished accommodation were roughly equal at about 14 per cent. [55] Of those who had moved recently, 41 per cent were now owner-occupiers, 26 per cent were private tenants of unfurnished accommodation, 20 per cent were local authority tenants, and 9 per cent were renting private furnished accommodation. [56]

It has also been demonstrated, however, that the mobility of house-holds within the tenure groups is rather different if only long-distance moves are considered. Although, according to Cullingworth's survey, the largest tenure groups had approximately equal rates of movement, only 13 per cent of local authority tenants moved over an hour's journey away, compared with 27 per cent of owner-occupiers and 29 per cent of tenants of private unfurnished accommodation. Tenants of furnished accommodation had a far higher rate of mobility and also were more likely to move long distances (37 per cent moved over an hour's journey away).[57] Further evidence of this is presented by Pennance and Gray, who computed an index of geographical mobility based on 'household miles moved per year'. Differences between the tenure groups emerged clearly; the mobility of local authority tenants was 4·9 miles per year against 14·3 for private tenants, 11·1 for owners without a mortgage and 10·1 for owners with a mortgage. [58]

Flows between tenure groups

The number of households within each of the main tenure groups is not static and it seems there is substantial movement within and between them. Unfortunately, the available evidence for distinguishing the direction and magnitude of these movements is limited. However, information based on three studies carried out at intervals during the 1960s and early 1970s does allow some analysis to be made. [59] Results should be treated with caution because the studies are not directly comparable.

Table 5.1 ranks the size of flows within the three main tenure groups. Two of the sources show that owner-occupation was associated with most movement and private-renting least, while the third shows the private-renting sector as having the most internal movement. In each case, the local authority sector had less internal movement than the owner-occupied sector.

Table 5.2 is concerned with movements between sectors; movements

Table 5.1
Ranked volume of movement within tenure groups

Tenure group	Ranking		
	1960 – 62	1967	1971
Owner-occupation	2	1	1
Local authority	3	2	2
Private renting	1	3	3

Table 5.2
Ranked volume of movement between tenure groups

Rank	1960 – 62	1967	1971
1	PR – OO	PR – LA	PR – OO
2	PR – LA	PR – OO	PR – LA
3	OO – PR	LA – OO	LA – OO
4	LA – OO	⎰LA – PR⎱	OO – PR
5	LA – PR	⎱OO – LA⎰	OO – LA
6	OO – LA	OO – PR	LA – PR

110

Table 5.3

Summary ranking of movement between tenure groups

Flow	Ranking			
	1960 – 62	1967	1971	Summary ranking
PR – OO	1	2	1	4
PR – LA	2	1	2	5
LA – OO	4	3	3	10
OO – PR	3	6	4	13
LA – PR	5	4	6	15
OO – LA	6	4	5	15

In the above tables: OO = Owner-occupation
                      LA = Local authority
                      PR = Private renting

are ranked according to size of flow. Quite clearly the predominant flows are out of the private-renting sector into owner-occupation and local authority housing. There are, however, discrepancies between the sources in the rankings of flows out of the owner-occupied and local authority sectors. On balance, it seems that flows out of the local authority sector, especially to owner-occupation, exceed those out of owner-occupation.

Table 5.3 attempts to summarise the pattern of flows by summing the individual rankings. It suggests that outflows from the private-renting sector are much larger than other flows, and that movement out of local authority housing to owner-occupation is third in importance. Movements from local authority to private renting; and from owner-occupation to local authority renting, represent, on balance, the smallest flows.

Further detail on movement between housing of different tenures is supplied by Woolf. [60] Over half the households in her sample remained in the same tenure after their move. Almost all owner-occupiers and local authority tenants did so, but tenants of private landlords were much more likely to change tenure. Those in unfurnished accommodation were split into three groups, moving into owner-occupied housing, local authority housing, and privately-rented unfurnished housing. Those in furnished accommodation were most likely to stay in the same tenure group, although some moved to unfurnished privately-rented dwellings and some became owner-occupiers.

Housing costs

Pennance and Gray supply data on British households' weekly expenditure on housing. [61] Their results showed that owner-occupiers with mortgages paid substantially more than people in other tenures. They averaged £4·3 per week, compared with £2·4 for local authority tenants, £2·5 for private tenants and £2·8 for owner-occupiers. In general, those who had moved recently had higher housing costs than other households, although this was not true of local authority tenants. Migrants to private-rented accommodation averaged £3·6 per week, and owner-occupiers who had recently moved in paid an average of £4·9 per week (with a mortgage) or £3·9 (without).

Housing costs averaged 10 to 15 per cent of household income, varying according to tenure group from 11·4 per cent for owners without a mortgage, to 15·4 per cent for private tenants. The averages for recent movers were somewhat higher, being 19·1 per cent for private tenants, 18 per cent for owners with a mortgage, 15 per cent for owners without a mortgage and 13·8 per cent for local authority tenants. [62] If these proportions are compared with household income, it is clear that poor households spend a much higher proportion of their income on housing than do richer households.

Reasons for moving

An obvious strategy for studying the process of migration is to ask people why they moved. Unfortunately, this does not always provide the information needed for a full understanding of the process. This is partly because most moves are the product of many factors, partly because many movers cannot or are reluctant to recall their state of mind at the time of decision, and partly because it is a question allowing answers of different, and incompatible, types. The last point is discussed by Rossi, who points out that such a question may be answered at several different levels of generalisation. [63] Nevertheless, the answers given do at least provide some indication of the factors uppermost in the mind of the respondents. It should also be remembered that such terms as 'job reasons' and 'housing reasons' may cover a multitude of diverse situations.

A number of British surveys of housing and residential mobility have investigated reasons for movement. The studies by Cullingworth, [64] Donnison [65] and Harris and Clausen [66] all found that 17—18 per cent of mobile households gave job reasons as the primary ones for movement. These figures refer to all households, not just those engaged in labour migration. The North Regional Planning Committee study of movement into the urbanised sectors of the Northern Region found that 'employment factors

Table 5.4

Distance moved, analysed by reason for moving (all last moves)

Main reason for last move	Distance moved				
	Up to 10 miles %	11 – 30 miles %	31 – 100 miles %	Over 100 miles %	All distances %
Marriage (including prospective marriage)	11·9	9·7	5·3	3·0	10·7
Slum clearance/redevelopment	8·2	1·0	0·3	0·1	6·5
Given notice	4·1	1·0	0·3	1·0	3·3
Wanted better/modern accommodation	28·0	17·3	8·1	1·7	24·0
Wanted different size dwelling	18·4	6·8	2·2	0·3	15·1
Wanted home of own	9·3	6·2	2·8	1·6	8·1
Work reasons	8·5	34·7	46·0	56·7	16·5
To be near friends/relatives	3·7	9·0	11·8	19·3	5·7
Wanted better surroundings	5·0	10·7	20·6	11·0	6·9
All other reasons	2·9	3·6	2·6	5·3	3·2
No. of persons on which percentage based	7,947	927	648	695	10,217

Source: Harris and Clausen, Table 21, p. 18

formed the major influences behind in-migration to the survey area'. [67]

The study by Harris and Clausen showed that moves over long distances were ascribed to work reasons much more frequently than shorter moves (Table 5.4). Work reasons were given for 8·5 per cent of moves of up to 10 miles, but for 56·7 per cent of moves of over 100 miles. The other reasons occurring most often for long-distance moves were the wish to be near to friends or relatives and the desire for better surroundings; housing reasons were also given by a few households which had moved long distances. [68]

The reasons given for moving may be compared with various attributes of the population, including age, marital status, household type, education, income, socio-economic group and tenure. Harris and Clausen found that age bore little relation to reasons for moving, except that marriage was mentioned far more often by people in the 20–30 age group, and that older people were more likely to move to better surroundings or to be near relatives. [69] Single people were most likely to move for work reasons, and widowed or divorced people least likely. The latter group, however, moved to be near relatives or friends at a much higher rate than married people, with single people being in an intermediate position. [70]

Lansing and Mueller found that the proportion of movers giving eco-

nomic reasons for moving increased with family income. They also reported a similar relationship with socio-economic status, professional and technical workers giving economic reasons for moving more frequently than
did other workers. [71] Donnison found that 42 per cent of households
whose heads were in administrative, professional, managerial or proprieta-
ry jobs mentioned a change of job as a reason for moving, compared with
11 per cent of those whose heads were in other occupations. [72] In
Simmie's study of migrants to Southampton, the importance of housing
and social reasons for moving tended to increase with successively lower
social classes, as employment reasons decreased. [73] Job reasons for movement were more likely to be given by those moving to private-rented
furnished accommodation, and far less likely to be given by local authority tenants. [74]

Consequences of moving

The consequences of changing both home and job must be of major
importance in the life of a labour migrant. In many cases, the migrant can
have only a vague idea of the changes the moves will bring; even if his new
house and new job are exactly as he intended, they may prove to have
unanticipated disadvantages. To some extent, the migrant's evaluation of
his move is a matter of personality; but it is also true that an objective
evaluation can be made of some aspects of his situation.

When Lansing and Mueller asked the 690 people in their sample who
had moved within the last five years whether their move had been a good
idea or not, 89 per cent evaluated it favourably, and only 6 per cent indicated that it had been a mistake. [75] Economic reasons were cited as the
basis for the evaluation by 63 per cent of respondents. After the move,
65 per cent of heads of families were earning more than before, and
24 per cent were earning less. Of those moving to get a better job, 73 per
cent were earning more than before. Similarly, 61 per cent liked their new
job better.

Woolf provides information specifically about movers' evaluations of
their new accommodation. Overwhelmingly (74 per cent), they thought
their new housing was better, only 9 per cent claiming it to be worse. [76]
Simmie collected evaluations from migrants to Southampton about their
satisfaction with their housing, the new district, their social life and their
job. A majority felt that their present situation was better than the previous
situation on each of these criteria. [77] Working in the different housing
context provided by the United States, Butler and his associates found a
higher rate of dissatisfaction with the new neighbourhood than with the
new home. [78]

Simmie also presents findings on the social adjustment of the migrants after the move. [79] No problems were reported by 56 per cent of his sample, and 24 per cent found settling-in 'fairly easy'. Those with problems settling-in were likely to have negative evaluations of their new housing and other circumstances. They gave loneliness, home-centred reasons and unfamiliar environment as their main reasons for experiencing problems. He also examined the effect of the degree of contact with relatives after the move, and the ability to make new friendships, discussing social class variations in these factors.

Lansing and Mueller found that seven out of ten of the moves they studied were made to places where the migrant household had either friends or relatives. [80] However, they point out that moves may not have been made because of these contacts; people from the same area may make similar moves independently of each other, for example from a rural area to the nearest large city.

The process of moving home

A move involving changes of both home and job is a complex process for most migrants, and there must be many different ways of going about it. A labour migrant, who may find himself in difficulties if he cannot complete both changes at about the same time, is particularly liable to encounter problems in finding a satisfactory home and job within an acceptable distance of each other.

Evidence has already been presented to indicate that most migrants succeeded in obtaining the kind of housing they had in mind. Cullingworth found that 85 per cent of migrants accomplished a move to their preferred tenure. [81] This figure may overstate, however, the success of potential migrants in making a satisfactory move. For one thing, those who fail completely to find the accommodation they hoped for may be deterred from moving altogether. Secondly, those who move to something other than what they had in mind may adjust to their new situation and express satisfaction with it, in the knowledge that it is fruitless to hanker after the unattainable.

The choice of residence

Cullingworth asked his respondents for their reasons for choosing their present dwelling. [82] The most common response was that it was the only one, or the best one, available (23 per cent). Others made the choice to be

E

near to their job or to friends or relatives (17 per cent), because they liked the area (17 per cent), or the house (17 per cent), or because the price was right (13 per cent). There were considerable differences in the responses of different groups. Thus 38 per cent in private-rented unfurnished accommodation chose their present home because it was the best or the only one available, compared with only 13 per cent of owner-occupiers. The most common reason given by local authority tenants was simply that they had been allocated the house. Owner-occupiers were more likely to respond that they liked the house or the area, or that the price was right. Herbert asked his sample of local movers within Swansea to evaluate a number of factors according to their importance for their choice of residence. [83] Dwelling-unit space was the most highly-rated characteristic, and dwelling design and type of neighbourhood were also highly valued by respondents in a high-cost area. Those in a low-cost area, however, tended to give more importance to access to shops and to work.

The range of alternatives

Investigating the range of choice available to households, Herbert found that 43 per cent in the high-cost area and 57 per cent in the low-cost area claimed not to have considered any other alternatives seriously. [84] Butler and his associates also reported the number of dwellings seriously considered by movers before making their final choice. [85] Many movers (68 per cent of inter-metropolitan migrants moving to the city, and 45 per cent of those moving to the suburbs) seriously considered no other dwellings apart from the one eventually chosen; only 12 per cent and 20 per cent, respectively, gave serious consideration to more than one other alternative. However, a high proportion (39 per cent of those moving to the city) believed that they did not have an opportunity to look at a suitable number of housing alternatives that might have been appropriate.[86]

Information about housing

The first and possibly still the most detailed study of the process of moving is Rossi's monograph concerning intra-urban residential mobility in Philadelphia.[87] Among other contributions to the study of mobility, he provided information on the use of various channels of search. He found that the most commonly employed information sources were newspapers, followed by personal contact, 'walking or riding around', and real estate agents, all employed by more than half his sample. House

116

buyers tended to make more use of estate agents and newspapers, and prospective renters to use personal contacts and direct search. Herbert asked his respondents to evaluate six information channels according to their importance in the search process. [88] 'Looking around' was judged to be the single most important source of information; friends and family were highly rated as sources of information, but work contacts were regarded as unimportant. Well below half of the respondents considered that agents or newspaper advertisements were important, although those in the high-cost area made rather more use of these sources.

Rossi found that personal contact was the most effective medium of search, in that a higher proportion found their eventual home through this source than through others. [89] Herbert found that family and friends were most important in the low-cost area, 58 per cent of vacancies being discovered with their help, compared to 21 per cent through 'looking around', 13 per cent through newspapers and 8 per cent through estate agents. In the high cost area, 'looking around' (39 per cent) was most effective, followed by family and friends (25 per cent), estate agents (17 per cent) and newspapers (11 per cent). [90]

Summary

This account of previous work must leave the reader impressed by the amount of research carried out on various aspects of household mobility. Throughout the chapter, examples have, of necessity, been drawn from studies of residential mobility in general where the majority of movers were not labour migrants. A migrant moving into a new area, changing his job as well as his house, is faced with additional problems to those of the man who knows the area well and can call on many local friends to help. Many of the findings cited have often been from the United States, where housing conditions are not directly comparable with those in Britain, and several of the British studies that have been referred to were concerned with conditions a decade ago. Nevertheless, this literature gives useful insights into labour migration, as there are many topics where there is no *a priori* reason to suppose that labour migrants have experiences greatly different from those of intra-urban movers, or that American experience is any different from British.

The first part of this chapter was concerned with relationships between migration and various personal and economic characteristics of the population. The findings of many previous students of migration lead us to expect that the sample of labour migrants interviewed in the course of our study will differ from the total population in certain ways. It can be anticipated that the migrants will tend to be young, relatively well-educated, in the higher socio-economic groups, and, for their age, in high-income groups; a high proportion are likely to be in new housing, and others will be tenants of furnished accommodation; they will tend to pay more for their housing than average. In Chapter 7, the characteristics of the migrant sample are outlined, generally confirming the findings of others, but occasionally modifying and often extending them.

The section on 'reason for moving' in the second part of this chapter is intended to provide a background for the discussion of the motivations of our sample of labour migrants in Chapter 8, where attention is also given to their evaluations of the move. In Chapter 9, an examination of the problems encountered by some individual migrant households is followed by a description of the labour migration process and results are presented concerning the method and the success of the search for accommodation. In these chapters, much information is reported on topics which have not been investigated in previous studies. Before the description of the survey findings, however, it will be helpful to describe the rationale and methods of the survey itself. Chapter 6 gives an account of the selection of the sample and the questions they were asked.

Notes

[1] F.R. Oliver, 'Inter-regional migration and unemployment 1951–61' *Journal of the Royal Statistical Society (A)* 127, 1964, pp. 42–75.

[2] R.A. Hart, 'A model of inter-regional migration in England and Wales' *Regional Studies 4*, 1970, pp. 279–96.

[3] K.G. Pickett, 'Aspects of migration in N.W. England 1960–61' *Town Planning Review* 38, 1967, pp. 233–44.

[4] Bibliographic reviews of much of this literature are provided by J.J. Mangalam, *Human Migration,* Lexington, Ky., 1968; and R.L. Welch, *Migration Research and Migration in Britain: A Selected Bibliography,* Occasional Paper no. 14, Centre for Urban and Regional Studies, University of Birmingham, 1971.

[5] An early review of this topic is D.S. Thomas, *Research Memorandum on Migration Differentials,* Social Science Research Council Bulletin 43, New York 1938.

[6] J.B. Cullingworth, *English Housing Trends,* Occasional Papers on Social Administration, no 13, London 1965, pp.101–2.

[7] L.C. Hunter and G.L. Reid, *Urban Worker Mobility,* OECD, Paris 1968, pp. 49–50.

[8] Ibid., p. 50.
[9] G. Becker, *Human Capital*, New York 1964, pp. 29 and 50.
[10] A.I. Harris and R. Clausen, *Labour Mobility in Great Britain: 1953–63*, HMSO, London 1967, p. 9.
[11] US Dept. of Commerce: Bureau of the Census, 'Mobility of the population of the United States March 1963 to March 1964' *Current Population Reports: Population Characteristics* P-20, 1965, p. 141; quoted by Hunter and Reid, op. cit., p. 48.
[12] J.B. Lansing and E. Mueller, *The Geographic Mobility of Labor* Ann Arbor, Mich., 1967, p. 40.
[13] Hunter and Reid, op. cit., p. 68.
[14] D.J. Bogue, *The Population of the United States*, Glencoe, Ill., 1959, p. 414.
[15] Harris and Clausen, op. cit., p. 9.
[16] Cullingworth, op. cit., p. 67.
[17] D. Friedlander and R.J. Roshier, 'A study of internal migration in England and Wales. Part II: Recent internal migrants – their movements and characteristics' *Population Studies* 20, 1966, pp. 54–5.
[18] Cullingworth, op. cit., p. 67.
[19] M. Woolf, *The Housing Survey in England and Wales: 1964*, HMSO, London 1967, p. 104.
[20] Cullingworth, op. cit., p. 41.
[21] Friedlander and Roshier, op. cit., p. 51.
[22] Harris and Clausen, op. cit., p. 9.
[23] Lansing and Mueller, op. cit., p. 43.
[24] Bogue, op. cit., p. 414.
[25] For example, Oliver, op. cit.
[26] US Dept. of Commerce: Bureau of the Census, op. cit., quoted by Hunter and Reid, op. cit., p. 51.
[27] Lansing and Mueller, op. cit., p. 68.
[28] G.H. Daniel, 'Some factors affecting the movement of labour' *Oxford Economic Papers* 3, 1940, pp. 144–79.
[29] Lansing and Mueller, op. cit., p. 75.
[30] J. Willis, 'Population growth and movement', Centre for Environmental Studies *Working Paper* 12, 1968, p. 35.
[31] J.B. Lansing and J.N. Morgan, 'The effect of geographical mobility on income' *Journal of Human Resources* 2, 1967, p. 449.
[32] Bogue, op. cit., p. 416.
[33] Woolf, op. cit., p. 104.
[34] Cullingworth, op. cit., p. 67.
[35] See also A.M. Rose, 'Distance of migration and socio-economic status

R.K. Merton, *Social Theory and Social Structure*, Glencoe, Ill., 1957.

W. Watson, 'Social mobility and social class in industrial communities' in M. Gluckman (ed.) *Closed Systems and Open Minds: The Limits of Naïvety in Social Anthropology*, Edinburgh 1964, p. 147.

S.M. Burn, 'Local Authority Housing: Implications for Labour Mobility' M. Phil. thesis, Department of Town Planning, University College London, 1972, p. 49.

J.D. Tarver, 'Occupational migration differentials' *Social Forces* 43, 1964, pp. 231–41.

J. Ladinsky, 'Occupational determinants of geographic mobility among professional workers' *American Sociological Review* 32, 1967, pp. 253–64.

Friedlander and Roshier, op. cit., p. 50.

C.J. Jansen, 'Some sociological aspect of migration' in J.A. Jackson (ed.) *Migration*, Cambridge 1969, p. 70.

D.V. Donnison, 'The movement of households in England' in D.V. Donnison, C. Cockburn, J.B. Cullingworth and A.A. Nevitt, *Essays on Housing*, Occasional Papers on Social Administration, no. 9, London 1964, p. 59.

See Burn, op. cit., p. 49.

E.G. Moore, 'Residential Mobility in the City' *Resource Paper* 13, Commission on College Geography, Association of American Geographers, 1972, p. 11.

I. Blumen, M. Kogan and P.J. McCarthy, *The Industrial Mobility of Labor as a Probability Process*, Ithaca, N.Y., 1955.

R. McGinnis, 'A stochastic model of social mobility' *American Sociological Review* 33, 1968, pp. 712–22.

A further discussion of this issue can be found in P.A. Morrison, 'Theoretical issues in the design of population mobility models', *Environment and Planning* 5, 1973, pp. 125–34. Another relevant study is that of M.D. Van Arsdol, Jr., G. Sabagh and E.W. Butler, 'Retrospective and subsequent metropolitan residential mobility' *Demography* 5, 1968, pp. 249–67.

R.C. Taylor, 'Migration and motivation: a study in determinants and types' in J.A. Jackson (ed.) *Migration*, Cambridge 1969, p. 110.

Ibid., p. 111.

Ibid., p. 116.

Harris and Clausen, op. cit., p. 14.

G.C. McDonald, *Social and geographical mobility: studies in the New*

Towns, Department of Geography, University College London, Occasional Paper no. 12, 1970.

[54] B.S. Morgan, 'Why Families Move: a re-examination' *Professional Geographer* 25, 1973, pp. 124–9.

[55] Cullingworth, op. cit., p. 60.

[56] Ibid., p. 66.

[57] Ibid., p. 60.

[58] F.G. Pennance and H. Gray, *Choice in Housing*, The Institute of Economic Affairs, London 1968, p. 63.

[59] The data are from the following sources: D.V. Donnison, *The Government of Housing*, Harmondsworth, Middx., 1967, p. 205; A.E. Holmans, 'A forecast of effective demand for housing in Great Britain in the 1970's' *Social Trends* 1, 1970, p. 37; and Department of the Environment, 'Survey of Movers 1972' (not yet published).

[60] Woolf, op. cit., p. 106.

[61] Pennance and Gray, op. cit., pp. 45–6.

[62] Ibid., p. 51.

[63] P.H. Rossi, *Why Families Move: a Study in the Social Psychology of Urban Residential Mobility*, Glencoe, Ill., 1955; see Chapter VII, especially pp. 124–7.

[64] J.B. Cullingworth, *Scottish Housing in 1965*, HMSO, Edinburgh 1967, p. 34.

[65] Donnison, 'The movement of households in England', p. 52.

[66] Harris and Clausen, op. cit., p. 14.

[67] North Regional Planning Committee, *Mobility and the North*, 1967, vol. 2, p. 63.

[68] Harris and Clausen, op cit., p. 18.

[69] Ibid., p. 15.

[70] Ibid.

[71] Lansing and Mueller, op. cit., p. 60.

[72] Donnison, 'The movement of households in England', p. 53.

[73] J.M. Simmie, 'The sociology of internal migration', Centre for Environmental Studies *University Working Paper* 15, 1972, p. 36.

[74] Cullingworth, *English Housing Trends*, p. 62.

[75] Lansing and Mueller, op. cit., pp. 246–58.

[76] Woolf, op. cit., p. 107.

[77] Simmie, op. cit., pp. 42–6.

[78] E.W. Butler, F.S. Chapin. Jr., G.C. Hemmens, E.J. Kaiser, M.A. Stegman and S.F. Weiss, 'Moving Behavior and Residential Choice: National Survey' *National Cooperative Highway Research Program Report* 81, Highway Research Board, 1969, p. 42.

[79]   Simmie, op. cit., pp. 46–60.
[80]   Lansing and Mueller, op. cit., p. 132.
[81]   Cullingworth, *Scottish Housing in 1965*, p. 38.
[82]   Cullingworth, *English Housing Trends*, p. 63.
[83]   D.T. Herbert, 'The residential mobility process: some empirical observations' *Area* 5, 1973, p. 46.
[84]   Ibid., pp. 45–6.
[85]   Butler *et al.*, op. cit., p. 41.
[86]   Ibid., p. 40.
[87]   Rossi, op. cit.
[88]   Herbert, op. cit., p. 45.
[89]   Rossi, op. cit., p. 161.
[90]   Herbert, op. cit., p. 45.

122

6 Questionnaire Survey Strategy

The migration between SMLAs in England and Wales described in Chapter 4 probably serves as a useful surrogate for the general pattern of labour migration because of the scale of analysis adopted. However, as Chapter 5 has indicated, it cannot be assumed that all these migrants moved for job reasons. Information on the social and economic characteristics of the migrants between SMLAs is not revealed by the available census information, thus restricting any discussion of migration patterns to the analysis already presented of the volume and direction of flows. In any case, census information gives no real insight into the complex web of motives surrounding an individual labour migrant household, nor does the census give any specific indication of the role of housing in influencing migration. As a result, it was thought necessary to contact labour migrant households directly by means of a questionnaire survey in order to uncover more information about the characteristics of labour migrants, the results of migration and the factors influencing the decision to migrate. In particular, a survey approach was thought to offer the best means of assessing the influence of housing availability as a factor in the migration decision.

The choice of SMLAs for household survey

It was decided to use four of the groups of SMLAs that emerged from multivariate classification as a framework for the selection of individual SMLAs for more detailed study. One group was excluded – that which was largely dominated by seaside resorts, where in-migration was heavily weighted with people who were leaving the workforce on retirement. The SMLAs within each of the four remaining groups were ranked in order of their proximity to the group averages for migration, housing and economic characteristics and the population size for each area was also inspected. It was then decided to choose areas of similar population size for ease of sampling and later comparison. Census information suggested that a minimum population of 150,000 would provide an adequate number of labour migrants from which the sample could be drawn. In selecting individual SMLAs from within each group a further criterion of geographical location within the major urban axis of England and Wales was applied.

Table 6.1

Some attributes of the chosen SMLAs

	In-migration 1965 – 66	Out-migration 1965 – 66	Net migration 1965 – 66	Additions to stock 1961 – 66	Over crowding 1966	LA/OO ratio 1966	Private rented sector 1966	Employment growth 1961 – 66	Unemployment 1966	SEG 1, 2, 3, 4, 1966	SEG 9, 10, 11, 1966	Total population
	A	B	C	D	E	F	G	H	I	J	K	
Chatham	6·20	3·74	2·46	11·99	0·62	28·48	16·60	7·10	1·80	13·02	52·92	220,870
High Wycombe	7·03	4·45	2·58	14·19	1·00	25·58	13·90	13·37	1·37	24·27	45·29	215,340
Huddersfield	2·34	2·08	0·26	1·81	1·43	29·29	21·02	-1·85	1·31	13·70	62·33	195,080
Northampton	3·21	2·20	1·01	7·27	0·53	30·20	15·83	9·28	1·30	14·10	58·19	160,390

A In-migration Percentage of total residential population (1966) which moved into each SMLA, 1965 – 66.

B Out-migration Percentage of total residential population (1966) which moved out of each SMLA, 1965 – 66.

C Net migration Migration balance 1965 – 66 as a percentage of total residential population in 1966.

D Additions to stock Change in the number of dwellings 1961 – 66 as a percentage of total dwellings in 1961.

E Overcrowding Percentage of total households living at over 1·5 persons per room in 1966.

F Local authority/ owner-occupier ratio Local authority tenants as a percentage of total of local authority tenants and owner-occupiers (1966).

G	Private rented sector	Percentage of total households in private rented accommodation (1966).
H	Employment growth	Change in the workforce 1961 – 66 as a percentage of total workforce 1961.
I	Unemployment	Percentage of economically active males 'out of employment' in 1966.
J	Executive and professional workers	Percentage of economically active males in socio-economic groups 1, 2, 3 and 4 (1966).
K	Manual workers	Percentage of economically active males in socio-economic groups 9, 10 and 11 (1966).

Table 6.2

Percentage of total migrants moving into each selected SMLA 1965 – 66, by area of origin

	Source of migrants					
	Other SMLAs (urban sources)	Elsewhere in England and Wales (rural sources)	Abroad	Scotland	Elsewhere in British Isles	Total in-migrants
Chatham	65·33	20·12	13·08	2·14	0·99	13,700
High Wycombe	68·25	13·33	15·12	1·78	1·52	15,150
Huddersfield	59·83	18·78	15·72	3·28	2·40	4,580
Northampton	36·70	46·02	13·01	0·78	3·50	5,150

The final selection consisted of four areas: Chatham, High Wycombe, Huddersfield and Northampton, each drawn from a different classification group.[1]

Information in the 1966 Census showed important differences between these four SMLAs in terms of their housing stock, employment prospects and area of origin of their in-migrants (Tables 6.1 and 6.2). Most in-migrants were from other parts of England and Wales, but whereas Chatham and High Wycombe both had about two-thirds of their in-migration from other SMLAs, the proportion going to Huddersfield from other SMLAs was somewhat less and that to Northampton was only a third. Conversely almost half of Northampton's in-migration was from more 'rural' parts of England and Wales. In all areas the proportion of migration from abroad was fairly constant and relatively unimportant in relation to the total in-migration.

To supplement this census information and to provide a necessary background for the questionnaire survey a study was made of the physical stock of housing and the nature of employment opportunities in each of the chosen SMLAs during 1971.[2] At the same time, some assessment was made of the attitudes and policies adopted by local authorities, building societies and estate agents in the different areas. This study confirmed that a wide range of housing and labour market conditions existed in the four selected labour areas during 1970 and 1971. In particular, several points emerged that would have been important to a labour migrant household contemplating a move to any of these areas.

Conditions in the selected SMLAs: a summary

The four labour markets suffered a relative decline in levels of economic activity from 1970 onwards, indicated both by an increase in their rates of unemployment and by a decrease in their numbers of unfilled vacancies. This decline in economic activity had noticeably affected the expansion programme for Northampton, which depended heavily on increasing the employment opportunities in the area. A further limitation on the range of opportunities in this area may have been imposed by the concentration of employment in the boot and shoe industry, although quite a wide range of types of employment was being advertised here in 1971. The dependence of the Huddersfield area on the textile industry has similarly restricted the range of jobs available in that area. High Wycombe, on the other hand, provided a very wide range of opportunities for all grades of employment. In the Chatham area, white-collar employment was more restricted than in the other three labour markets. This area also experienced the highest rate of unemployment for the 1970—71 period. Opportunities for the employment of women were restricted in the Chatham area, whereas the other areas maintained a high level of demand for female labour. It may be suggested that the difficulties experienced by migrants seeking employment in any of these areas would relate as much to the nature of their occupational skills and experience as to the strengths or weaknesses of the local economy.

Housing market conditions also varied between the four areas. For the country as a whole there was ·a phenomenal rise in house prices during 1970 and 1971, and each of the four areas experienced this trend. Some differences occurred, however, between the areas in the prices of similar properties. Migrants to Northampton, particularly, were encouraged to buy dwellings both by their availability and by their relative cheapness, and a further inducement was the ready availability of mortgages. Huddersfield was characterised by a stable housing market, and although house prices had risen, there was still a large number of very cheap properties available. Although more expensive than both Northampton and Huddersfield, house prices in the Chatham area appeared relatively cheap compared to many parts of south-east England. The availability of cheap accommodation in High Wycombe was extremely limited and the area was characterised by large properties.

The availability of mortgages for buying properties varied both between and within the four areas because of the different policies adopted by building societies. Both the potential security of income of the applicant and the age and type of property involved affected the amount of mortgage advanced by the building societies, but the relative weight given to these factors differed between societies. As a result, it would have been to the advantage of many labour migrants to contact several societies in any of the areas studied. For example, a branch of one particular society was prepared to accept a borrower even though he was not in employment at the time of application; few other societies would have considered such an applicant.

In all four areas there was a high level of demand for all types of private-rented accommodation. In some instances this demand was unsatisfied through scarcity of supply. The difficulties of obtaining private-rented accommodation are liable to increase as the number of dwellings in this sector of the market continues to decline.

As in the private housing sector, access to local authority housing for migrants varied between the four areas. The designation of Northampton as a new town had resulted in very easy access to local authority and, more particularly, Development Corporation housing for specific groups, although at the time of the survey the amount of new town house construction was relatively restricted. In the Huddersfield area access to local authority housing was also relatively easy, especially in the outlying areas where there was less demand for accommodation from the local population. Access to local authority housing in the two labour markets located in south-east England was more difficult, but housing was available for those in real housing need in the Chatham area within two to three years of application. In contrast to the other areas, local authority housing was difficult to obtain in High Wycombe, with a waiting period varying between three and seven years. Housing might be easier for the labour migrant household to obtain in one or two local authorities in this area, since considerable variations occurred between the authorities in the qualifications required of the applicant and the allocation policies adopted.

It is possible to indicate the relative ease or difficulty likely to be experienced by the labour migrant household in moving to any of the four areas. The Chatham and High Wycombe areas were characterised by an imbalance between their housing and job opportunities. In Chatham, housing was relatively accessible to all groups, but employment opportunities within the area had been declining. The opposite situation occurred in High Wycombe, where job opportunities were plentiful but access to housing restricted to those in the higher income groups. Some opportunities for both housing and employment existed in the Huddersfield area, but potential migrants have shown a marked reluctance to move to this area. Possibly this reluctance is related to some sort of psychological barrier

128

towards moving to the north of England. Northampton would appear to be the easiest of the four areas to which a labour migrant household could have moved during 1970 and 1971, since formal channels existed to assist migrant households to the area. Whereas professional groups may have found little difficulty in moving to any of the four areas, the expansion programme for Northampton offered unique opportunities for housing for the non-professional groups. Most highly favoured for assistance were the skilled manual groups from London boroughs, but migrants from other areas have not been excluded.

These findings suggest that a labour migrant household moving to any one of these areas would have experienced some difficulties in obtaining either housing or employment, or perhaps both. The degree of difficulty would, however, be affected by the characteristics of each individual household (for example its size and type, and the income and educational level of its members). As already suggested, the ability of a labour migrant household to negotiate its position in the housing and labour markets would depend both on its occupation skills and its awareness of the opportunities available.

The identification of labour migrant households

Fairly straightforward procedures for sampling households in general already exist, but migrant households pose more difficult problems. Not only are they a small proportion of the population (the 1966 Census shows that 9·9 per cent of the population was migrant during the previous year), but they are more difficult to contact because they are changing address. An even smaller proportion of the population (probably about 2 per cent) is likely to be involved in labour migration.

Because of these difficulties, several methods of obtaining a sample of migrant households for the questionnaire survey were examined. Of the four methods described briefly below, the first two were discarded and the others tested.

1. *Survey of new houses*

One possible method involved choosing an area of new housing and identifying those households which had moved from another labour market area within the last year. Of these, the labour migrant households would be those in which the principal wage earner changed job in association with moving to the new labour market area. The danger of bias, however, is very great with this method, since areas of new housing are very likely to be developments for owner-occupation or for the local authority, households in the privately-rented sector being automatically excluded. In addition, households in areas of new housing may be atypical in a number of ways; for instance, there may be conditions specific to the housing development which have prevented other people from moving there. As a result this method was discarded.

2. *Market research firms' general surveys*

It was thought that one of the larger market research agencies might be willing to include questions in its regular survey which could be used to identify labour migrant households. There are some rather obvious dangers in using this method, for these agencies often use a quota sample which would be inappropiate to this study. Much would also depend on the willingness of these people, who had already undergone a market research inquiry, to submit themselves to the further extensive interview necessary to investigate their housing and job conditions. A further drawback was the wide variation in the nationwide coverage of these agencies. This method was not, therefore, considered a viable one.

3. *Use of local employment exchanges*

A more promising method involved contacting local employment exchange managers in areas which appeared to have been experiencing economic growth in the last two years. These managers were asked to suggest employers in the labour market area whose workforces had recently expanded, and where some employees might, therefore, be members of migrant households. Firms known to have employees on Department of Employment allowances were considered good prospects and much depended on the employment exchange manager's intuition as to the likelihood of the personnel staff of those firms having both the time and the inclination to co-operate in the project. The managers of six employment exchanges within fairly easy reach of London showed considerable interest in the project. Following discussion, a group hospital management committee and three firms engaged in engineering and electronics were successfully approached. Two personnel officers supplied names and addresses very promptly; for another, responses to a letter circulated among his staff drifted in too slowly to be of use; and the fourth, faced with unexpected redundancies, was in the end unable to help. From the names and addresses supplied, nine successful interviews were carried out at the labour migrants' homes using a preliminary draft of the question-naire.

The households were very co-operative and provided valuable informa-tion about their experiences in moving house and job, but reservations were held about the way in which the households had been chosen, and on the applicability of this method on a large scale. Selection tends to be biased in favour of expanding firms and there is a danger of neglecting whole areas of static or declining employment. It is difficult to find a reasonable basis for the final choice of employers, and a great deal de-pends on a whole series of personal contacts between the research team and employment exchange managers, between employment exchange managers and the personnel staffs of firms, between the research team and the personnel staffs, between the personnel staffs and their employees, and eventually between the research team and actual employees. It seem-ed only too easy for this elaborate chain to be broken.

4. *Additions lists of the electoral register*

Bearing these doubts in mind, a fourth method was also explored and, after testing in Chelmsford, was finally adopted. This method involved the use of the 'Additions' or 'B' lists of the Electoral Registers covering the selected Labour Market Areas. The 'Additions List' is published each year at the end of November and comprises people newly eligible to vote since the register was drawn up in the October of the previous year. Some of these are young people who have reached voting age and, as the trial run showed, the remainder is made up of people who have changed address for various reasons. From this latter group a sample can be drawn from the households that moved into the area from another SMLA. It is possible to eliminate several categories of people from the list of those newly eligible to vote. The first group are those who will reach voting age in the coming year, and, as their birth date is given, they are easily identified. Other groups which may be eliminated are merchant seamen and service voters. Large residential institutions, long-term mental hospitals, old peoples' homes, teacher training colleges, and so on, are unlikely to contain labour migrants except among the staff, whose quarters are usually listed sepa-rately. Where several people of the same name are living at the same address, the person who appears to be head of that household can be selected and the rest of the household excluded. A sampling proportion is then applied to the usable names and addresses that have been obtained, in order to produce a sample list. To each person selected a letter is sent briefly outlining the purposes of the study and asking for a short questionnaire to be completed and returned. Pre-paid replies are received only from those persons who have changed their addresses. They are also asked to name the area in which they lived prior to the move, to indicate the nature of their employment and to state whether a change of job took place in association with the change of address. This procedure allows the identification of labour migrant households (that is, those who have moved from outside the SMLA and have been involved in a change of job). On the basis of this preliminary postal survey a list of labour migrant households can then be prepared for further investigation by means of a detailed questionnaire, administered by personal interview.

Some comments on the survey strategy

There are well-known hazards in using electoral registers as a sampling frame. Some households do not bother to register themselves. Others, such as aliens, do not appear. Immigrants from the Commonwealth and the Republic of Ireland may be under-represented. The additions list may in fact contain people who changed address eighteen month ago, although the majority will have moved within the last year. Another hazard is that the electoral register gives no indication of marital status; hence it is difficult in some cases to establish the identity of the head of the household. Such features produce certain systematic biases in the registers. For example, middle-class households are perhaps more likely to ensure that their names have been added to the list of electors. Immigrants from overseas may be less sure of their rights to appear on the register. Young

Table 6.3

Details of questionnaire survey

	Chatham	High Wycombe	Huddersfield	Northampton	Total
Initial letters sent	1,982	1,989	1,988	1,992	7,951
Reminders	703	698	740	724	2,865
Additional letters sent	479	–	501	–	980
Replies received	1,014	927	959	844	3,744
Labour migrants identified from replies	199	246	118	221	784
Labour migrants as a percentage of all respondents	19·6	26·5	12·3	26·2	20·9
Final response to interview and accepted as labour migrants	126	178	76	171	551
Percentage of labour migrants from each SMLA	22·9	31·9	13·8	31·0	100·0

heads of households under eighteen will be omitted, and people in rented furnished accommodation are also more likely to be missed.

On the other hand, the revisions list of the electoral register gives a very convenient list of people who have changed their address. It is a source that can be used to cover the whole of a SMLA, both outside as well as within the legal limits of a town. It should also be recalled that the electoral registers were merely being used as part of a preliminary screening process in order to find labour migrants for further study. The resources available for survey work placed a restriction on the number of interviews that it was possible to undertake. The survey examined the migration experience of over 500 households, living in the contrasted economic and housing contexts provided by four different SMLAs. Some statistical details of the household survey are provided in Tables 6.3 and 6.4. These households were drawn from a wide range of social backgrounds and from random locations within the SMLAs being studied; but it was never considered possible to interview a large enough sample of labour migrants to make statistically-valid statements about the total population of migrants in England and Wales or even in the four areas being studied.

The aim of the questionnaire used in the survey was to elicit from the different groups of households sampled the relative importance of housing, job, attachment to area and other components of the household's net advantage calculation and their eventual combination in the migration decision. The questionnaire, which is reproduced in Appendix 2, began by confirming that a labour migrant household was in fact being interviewed and then established the household's size and composition, its stage in the life cycle, and the occupations and formal qualifications of the head and other employed members of the household. Details of housing accommodation were also recorded, including the type of tenure.

Following this basic information, other data which appeared relevant were gathered. To begin with, the costs of obtaining housing services were ascertained as accurately as possible and some attempt was made to find out the income of the household. Information on the journey to work was also sought, including distance involved, time taken, mode of transport used and financial cost. Then details about the actual move of home were collected, including information about members of the former household left behind, the nature of accommodation previously occupied, including its cost and tenure. Details about the former occupation and journey to work were also recorded to complete the picture of the previous job and home environment.

A third section of the questionnaire asked how the migrant household went about looking for a job and house in the new area and tried in

133

Table 6.4

Numbers of labour migrants actually interviewed during field survey

SMLA	Addresses from postal survey	Not in fact labour migrants	Refused interview	Empty house and moved away	Unsatisfactory forms	Others	Productive interviews
Chatham	199	19	9	29	–	16	126
High Wycombe	246	12	20	24	6	6	178
Huddersfield	118	10	7	21	3	–	77
Northampton	221	9	7	15	6	14	170

various ways to assess the problems associated with moving home and job at the same time. Some attempt was made to record if the spouse of the labour migrant had different assessments from the head of the household. This section of the questionnaire also attempted to note the effect of moving home on social and family life. In this context informants were not only asked to record if there had been an effect, but they were also invited to comment at greater length on the changes that had taken place and to say whether these changes were expected or not. A series of questions towards the end of this section then attempted to summarise the results of the move of home for a particular household by asking whether the change of home had produced a loss or gain for various aspects of life. In effect, these questions were designed to record the evaluation of the householders themselves of their present situations compared with their former ones.

The last part of the questionnaire was intended to record the full migration experience of the various members of the household, and it was thought that such experience might have played a vital part in the decision of the household to move again. An attempt was also made to relate these various past moves to life-cycle changes. Finally, the informants were asked to list the three most important reasons for moving in order of importance, a task which they were asked to undertake in the light of the detailed information they had already given to the interviewer, but without any other prompting. Apart from its own intrinsic interest, this information gave a cross-check on some of the other details given earlier in the questionnaire.

The approach that was adopted allows attention to be focused on different types of migrant households, classified in various ways, and gives insights into their contrasting evaluations of housing and labour markets on becoming labour migrants. It has, of course, various limitations. In particular, it cannot examine those potential migrants who found themselves completely prevented from moving for various reasons — an important, but most difficult group to investigate. On the other hand, the questionnaire made it possible to collect information about some of the problems which labour migrants encounter in moving between homes, to record some of the tangible results of such moves, and to place the migration experience of households in specific social and economic contexts.

Notes

[1] H. Robinson, 'Survey method and questionnaire design', Housing and Labour Mobility Study, Department of Geography, University College London, *Working Paper* no. 3, 1971.

[2] N. Hadjifotiou and H. Robinson, 'Employment and housing conditions in four selected labour market areas in England and Wales', Housing and Labour Mobility Study, Department of Geography, University College London, *Working Paper* no. 5, 1972.

7 Characteristics of the Labour Migrants

In this chapter the sample of labour migrants and their characteristics in relation to the population in general are described. The way in which the sample was selected was discussed in Chapter 6. Although some bias was unavoidably introduced in the course of identifying and locating labour migrants, data on the structure of the sample are of interest for two reasons. First, accurate and up-to-date information is provided for a sample of labour migrants; although one must be cautious in drawing inferences from the sample about the behaviour of the total population, it seems reasonable to suppose that many of the major differences found between migrants and the population as a whole are valid beyond the limitations of the sample. Second, much of the survey is directed towards elucidating the process of moving both house and job as it affects labour migrants of different types. In this context, the information presented in this chapter should be regarded as a backcloth against which to view the findings of subsequent chapters.

The sample consisted of 551 labour migrant households which had recently moved into one of the four sample Standard Metropolitan Labour Areas (SMLAs). It was thus composed entirely of successful movers, and hence is impossible to compare with a control group of non-movers. However, where data are available, it is possible to compare the characteristics of movers with the total population and sometimes with the population in the migrants' destination areas. It is also possible to compare the status of the migrants with respect to these and other variables before and after the moves. In this way, we can gauge the extent to which residential mobility has been accompanied by social and occupational mobility; in particular, changes in employment status or in housing tenure may throw light on the structure and the efficacy of the labour migration process.

The sample was drawn from four contrasted areas, and it is to be expected that the four areas should differ markedly in the characteristics of the migrants attracted to them. Many of these differences appear to mirror variations in the attributes of the resident populations of these areas. Although the size of the sample within each area is too small for complete confidence in the significance of some of these differences, attention will be drawn to variables for which the migrants to one or more of the areas show a major discrepancy from the sample as a whole.

The chapter will be composed of a series of sections, each devoted to the examination of a variable or group of variables relevant to labour migration. It is based on tabulations of responses to questions in the first part of the questionnaire (see Appendix 2). The variables are examined in the order in which they are discussed in Chapter 5: life-cycle factors, including age, sex, marital status, household size and composition; educa-

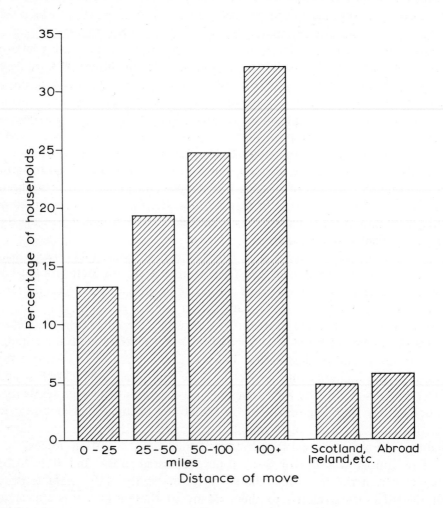

Fig. 7.1   Distance moved by labour migrants.

tion; employment; income; socio-economic group; migration experience; housing factors, including tenure, housing costs, and house type. Findings concerned with the distance of the move are also presented.

Personal characteristics of the labour migrants

A labour migrant is a person who has changed both place of employment and address. If two members of the household had made these changes, the head of the household was taken to be the labour migrant, and the other considered as a member of his or her household. Of the 551 households, 126 were in Chatham SMLA, 178 in High Wycombe SMLA, 76 in Huddersfield SMLA and 171 in Northampton SMLA. Most of the households (57·4 per cent) had been at their current address between six months and one year, but 12·3 per cent had been there less than six months and 30·3 per cent had been there for more than one year. Thus, most moves had taken place during 1971.

The distances moved by labour migrants to their new areas are shown in Fig. 7.1 (see also Table 7.1); 13·4 per cent moved less than 25 miles (40 km) and 32·1 per cent moved over 100 miles (160 km). Just over 10 per cent came from Scotland, Ireland, the Channel Islands, and from abroad. It should be remembered in interpreting these figures that the areas and the populations within each distance band are not of equal size. If potential labour migrants were distributed uniformly within 100 miles (160 km) of the labour market area, one would expect three times as many to come from the 25–50 mile (40–80 km) zone as from the 0–25 mile (0–40 km) zone, and twelve times as many to come from the

Table 7.1

Distance moved by labour migrants

Distance moved	Chatham		High Wycombe		Huddersfield		Northampton		Total	
	No.	%	No.	%	No.	%	No.	%	No.	%
Under 25 miles	13	10·3	31	17·4	15	19·7	15	8·8	74	13·4
25 – 50 miles	34	27·0	26	14·6	10	13·2	37	21·6	107	19·4
50 – 100 miles	12	9·6	39	21·9	19	25·0	66	38·2	136	24·7
Over 100 miles	52	41·3	65	36·5	22	29·0	38	22·2	177	32·1
Scotland, Ireland, the Channel Islands	6	4·8	10	5·6	4	5·3	6	3·5	26	4·7
Abroad	9	7·1	7	3·9	6	7·9	9	5·3	31	5·6
Total	126		178		76		171		551	

50–100 mile (80–160 km) zone. The survey data are thus consistent with the distance-decay effect found in most studies of migration.

The patterns of distances moved to the individual labour market areas show considerable divergence from each other, probably due in part to the different locations of the labour markets in relation to the main population centres of the country. The low proportion of migrants to Northampton from under 25 miles (40 km) is probably a reflection of the

SOURCES OF SAMPLE LABOUR MIGRANTS TO CHATHAM

Fig. 7.2 (Note: in Figs. 7.2–7.5 each dot is the former place of residence of one of the survey respondents)

relatively low population in the area, and the high proportion in the 50–100 mile (80–160 km) zone may be due to the fact that London falls within this zone. Similarly, the high proportion of Chatham migrants in the 25–50 mile (40–80 km) zone may be connected with the location of London.

The places from which individual members of the sample have moved are plotted on Figures 7.2 to 7.5.

Fig. 7.3

- GLENROTHES
- LANGHOLM
- GLASGOW

- SOUTH AFRICA
- H.M. FORCES
- W. GERMANY
- ARGENTINA
- CANADA

Fig. 7.4

Age, sex and marital status

As shown in Table 7.2, 483 (87·7 per cent) of the labour migrants in the sample were male and 68 (12·3 per cent) female. The proportion of female labour migrants is conspicuously lower in Huddersfield (7 per cent) than in the other areas.

Fig. 7.6 shows the age distribution of the labour migrants. They were mostly in the age ranges 20– 24 (25·1 per cent), 25–34 (35·6 per cent) and

SOURCES OF SAMPLE
LABOUR MIGRANTS TO
NORTHAMPTON

• DUMBARTON
• ABERDEEN
• • GLASGOW
• • DUNDEE

• CO. FERMANAGH

• SWITZERLAND
• W. GERMANY
• AUSTRALIA
• BAHAMAS
• • CANADA

Fig. 7.5

35—44 (22·1 per cent). If it is assumed that the ages of labour migrants are evenly distributed within each age group, the mean age of labour migrants is 33·3 years; the SMLA means range from 31·9 at Northampton to 35·5 at High Wycombe.[1] However, the age group best represented among the labour migrants is the 20—24 group (because the population at risk is bigger in the 25—34 group). Chatham and Northampton appear to have a rather greater number of 20—24 year olds, High Wycombe more

Table 7.2
The labour migrants: sex, age, marital status and working status

	Chatham		High Wycombe		Hudders-field		North-ampton		Total	
	No.	%	No.	%	No.	%	No.	%	No.	%
Sex										
Male	108	85·7	154	86·5	71	93·4	150	87·7	483	87·7
Female	18	14·3	24	13·5	5	6·6	21	12·3	68	12·3
Age										
0 – 4	–		–		–		–		–	
5 – 14	–		–		–		–		–	
15 – 19	2	1·6	5	2·8	–		2	1·2	9	1·6
20 – 24	40	31·8	30	16·9	14	18·4	54	31·6	138	25·1
25 – 34	41	32·5	65	36·5	30	39·5	60	35·1	196	35·6
35 – 44	24	19·1	40	22·5	25	32·9	33	19·3	122	22·1
45 – 59	16	12·7	34	19·1	6	7·9	21	12·3	77	14·0
60 – 64	2	1·6	3	1·7	1	1·3	1	0·6	7	1·3
65 and over	1	0·8	1	0·6	–		–		2	0·4
Marital status										
Married	92	73·0	136	76·4	63	82·9	129	75·4	420	76·2
Single	28	22·2	32	18·0	11	14·5	36	21·1	107	19·4
Widowed	3	2·4	5	2·8	1	1·3	–		9	1·6
Divorced or separated	3	2·4	5	2·8	1	1·3	6	3·5	15	2·7
Working status										
Full-time	122	96·8	175	98·3	71	93·4	167	97·7	535	97·1
Part-time	2	1·6	1	0·6	–		1	0·6	4	0·7
Unemployed	1	0·8	1	0·6	4	5·3	3	1·8	9	1·6
Sick	–		1	0·6	–		–		1	0·2
No information	1	0·8	–		1	1·3	–		2	0·4
Total	126		178		76		171		551	

people in the 35–44 (23 per cent) and 45–59 (19 per cent) groups, and Huddersfield a concentration in the middle age brackets (25–44) with few young or older labour migrants.

These data accord well with other findings on age differentials (see Chapter 5). The scarcity of migrants under 20 may be a result of the use of electoral registers in sample selection. The higher average age of migrants to High Wycombe is in accordance with what is known about property values and employment opportunity in the area.

Married labour migrants made up 76·2 per cent of the sample; 19·4 per cent were single, 1·6 per cent widowed and 2·7 per cent divorced. The proportion of married migrants rose to 83 per cent at Huddersfield.

AGE OF LABOUR MIGRANTS

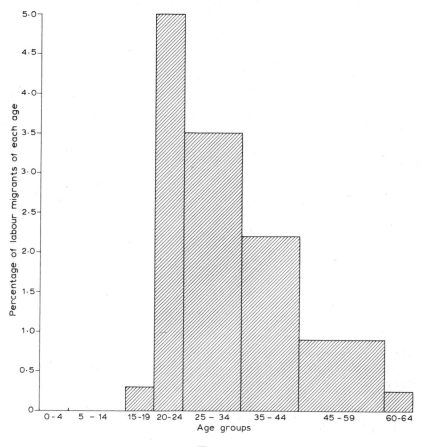

Fig. 7.6

Labour migration, therefore, predominantly involves families, with the additional housing demands that this implies.

The spouse of the labour migrant

Of the 416 spouses of labour migrants, all but one were female; in this one case, a female labour migrant had married following the move. 42·3 per cent were in the age group 25–34, 24·0 per cent between 20 and 24, and 20·9 per cent between 35 and 44.

In accordance with the life-cycle theory of migration propensities, we might expect moves to be associated with increases in family size, and

Table 7.3
Age of members of the labour migrant's present household

Age	Chatham		High Wycombe		Hudders-field		North-ampton		Total	
	No.	%	No.	%	No.	%	No.	%	No.	%
0 – 4	49	12·2	68	11·9	46	17·1	61	12·4	223	12·9
5 – 14	54	13·5	92	16·1	51	19·0	67	13·6	264	15·2
15 – 19	25	6·2	37	6·5	9	3·3	17	3·4	89	5·1
20 – 24	84	20·9	77	13·5	30	11·2	101	20·5	292	16·8
25 – 34	84	20·9	128	22·5	68	25·3	134	27·2	414	23·9
35 – 44	52	13·0	84	14·7	42	15·6	55	11·2	233	13·4
45 – 59	35	8·7	62	10·9	18	6·7	49	9·9	164	9·5
60 – 64	9	2·2	10	1·8	3	1·1	2	0·4	24	1·4
65 and over	9	2·2	12	2·1	2	0·7	7	1·4	30	1·7
Total	401		570		269		493		1,733	

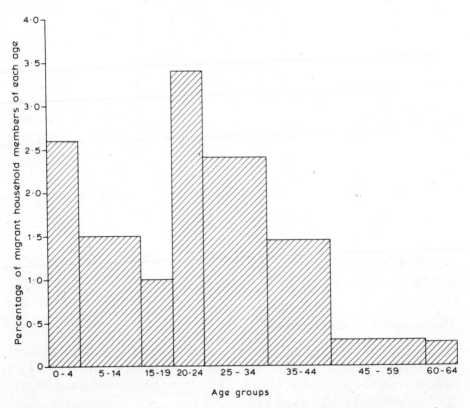

Fig. 7.7   Age of members of labour migrant households. (The area of the column represents the proportion of labour migrants in each age group)

hence that a large proportion of migrants' spouses would be occupied in looking after young children, and thus not in the labour force. On the other hand, the migrant population might include a high proportion of spouses who are engaged in full-time employment, having not yet started a family. Finally, the high socio-economic status and high income of many of the migrants suggest that the spouses might show a relatively low rate of labour force participation, because a second income is less necessary. In fact, 28·8 per cent of the spouses of labour migrants were working full-time, 13·2 per cent part-time, 4·3 per cent were unemployed, and 52·6 per cent not working. The economic activity of spouses will be discussed further in a later section.

The labour migrant's household

There were 1,733 members of the households of the 551 labour migrants, almost equally divided between males and females. In accordance with the greater mobility of young adult household heads, a high proportion of these household members were in the age groups 20–24 and 25–34 (see Table 7.3 and Fig. 7.7). The children of these people produce a further concentration of population in the age groups 0–4 and 5–14. Perhaps the relatively low proportion of the total in the higher age groups (3·1 per cent over 60) indicates the predominance of the nuclear family among migrant households. Table 7.4 shows the relationships of household members to the labour migrant. Only 3·5 per cent of all household members

Table 7.4

Composition of the labour migrant's present household

Relationship to labour migrant	Chatham		High Wycombe		Hudders-field		North-ampton		Total	
	No.	%	No.	%	No.	%	No.	%	No.	%
Labour migrant	126	31·4	178	31·2	76	28·3	171	34·7	551	31·8
Spouse	91	22·7	135	23·7	62	23·0	128	26·0	416	24·0
Parent	15	3·7	22	3·9	11	4·1	11	2·2	60	3·5
Child	111	27·7	178	31·2	101	37·5	132	26·8	521	30·1
Grandparent	1	0·2	–		–		–		1	0·1
Grandchild	1	0·2	2	0·4	–		–		3	0·2
Brother or sister	7	1·7	9	1·6	4	1·5	9	1·8	29	1·7
Other adult relation	12	3·0	13	2·3	5	1·9	4	0·8	34	2·0
Other child relation	6	1·5	7	1·2	3	1·1	1	0·2	17	1·0
Other adult not relation	27	6·7	25	4·4	7	2·6	34	6·9	93	5·4
Other child not relation	4	1·0	1	0·2	–				3	0·6	8	0·5
Total	401		570		269		493		1,733	

F

were classed as parents of the labour migrant, and a further 5·4 per cent were other unrelated adults.

Household size

The number of people in the households of the labour migrants interviewed ranged from one to twelve (see Table 7.5 and Fig. 7.8). The most common household sizes were two (31·0 per cent), three (22·1 per cent) and four (25·4 per cent), with only 8·2 per cent one-person households. If these figures are compared with those presented by Woolf[2] (Fig. 7.9) from the Housing Survey in England and Wales, showing the size distribution for all households, it can be seen that labour migrant households are less likely to contain one person only, and more likely to contain four persons. The mean number of people per household was 3·15, rather more than the 3·00 reported by Woolf.[3] Of the sample SMLAs, Huddersfield had far fewer one-person households and more four-person households than average, while Northampton had more two-person households and fewer larger ones. Additional light is shed on migrant household composition by an examination of the size distribution of the moving households (omitting those who joined the labour migrant in his new residence). This shows a far higher proportion of one-person households (31·4 per cent); in Huddersfield 24 per cent of moving households contained one person, but only 1 per cent of labour migrants' present households were of this size. This may indicate a tendency for single migrants to form households with other single people, perhaps the 'other adults not related' of the previous section.

Table 7.5

Size of the labour migrant's present household

Number of people	Chatham		High Wycombe		Huddersfield		Northampton		Total	
	No.	%	No.	%	No.	%	No.	%	No.	%
1	14	11·1	14	7·9	1	1·3	16	9·4	45	8·2
2	32	25·4	54	30·3	20	26·3	65	38·0	171	31·0
3	31	24·6	40	22·5	17	22·4	34	19·9	122	22·1
4	30	23·8	43	24·2	26	34·2	41	24·0	140	25·4
5	10	7·9	17	9·6	7	9·2	12	7·0	46	8·4
6	6	4·8	4	2·3	2	2·6	1	0·6	13	2·4
7	–		2	1·1	1	1·3	1	0·6	4	0·7
8	3	2·4	3	1·7	–		1	0·6	7	1·3
9	–		1	0·6	1	1·3	–		2	0·4
12	–		–		1	1·3	–		1	0·2
Total	126		178		76		171		551	

HOUSEHOLD SIZE

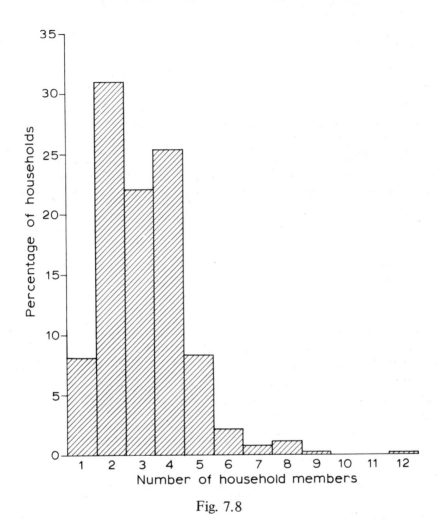

Fig. 7.8

It is noteworthy that households where the labour migrant was female were likely to be considerably smaller than average. Of the 68 female labour migrants, 23 were in single-person households (slightly greater than the number of male single-person households), 22 in two-person households and 13 in three-person households. The age of the labour migrant was also related to household size. The distribution of one-person households was bimodal, with concentrations in the 20–24 and 45–59 age groups; the largest proportion of two-person households was in the 20–24 and 25−34 groups, the 25−34 group becoming predominant for three-person households and the 35−44 group for households with five persons or more. The mean household size increased from 2·5 for labour migrants in the 20−24 age group to 3·1 for the 25−34 group, and 4·1 for the 35−44 group, and decreased to 2·9 for the 45−59 age group. These figures illustrate the effects of life-cycle changes on the migrant population.

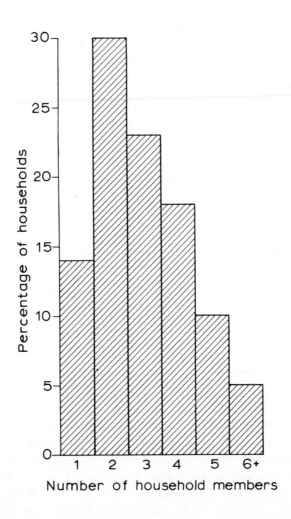

Fig. 7.9   Household size, England and Wales 1964, based on Woolf's survey. *Source*: Woolf, 1967, Table 2.31, p. 150.

It is difficult to detect any systematic relation between household size and the distance moved. There was, perhaps, a tendency for large households to move longer distances than average. Of those moving households containing five or more people, 45 per cent moved over 100 miles (160 km), compared with 32·1 per cent of the whole sample moving this distance.

Household type

Life-cycle theories of mobility suggest that the type of household is likely to be related to the propensity to move; and that movement rates will be high among young families (husband and wife or single parent with all children under 15 years), couples without children and unmarried adults. The survey results indeed showed a great concentration of households in these categories. The concentration of young families in Huddersfield (53 per cent) was noteworthy. However, household type did not appear to have a close relationship to the distance of the move. These findings seem to be in accordance with the expectations generated by both life-cycle and career pattern approaches to migration.

75·8 per cent of households had not changed in household type since moving; the labour migrant had married in 8·7 per cent of cases, a first child had been born in 4·9 per cent and other types of change had occurred in 11·9 per cent of cases. Of those people joining labour migrant households after the move, the most common were other unrelated adults, and parents of the labour migrant or his spouse. In many cases, it may be more accurate to talk of the labour migrants moving to rejoin their parents.

Education

In our sample, 22·7 per cent of labour migrants left school at fifteen; another 20·5 per cent left at sixteen, 13·8 per cent at seventeen and 21·1 per cent at eighteen. The median age was sixteen, but the distribution is bimodal (see Table 7.6 and Fig. 7.10), reflecting a high proportion of subsequent movers staying at school. The proportion who had stayed at school until eighteen ranged from 37 per cent of labour migrants at High Wycombe to 25 per cent at Chatham, suggesting that workers with different levels of education are attracted to different labour market areas.

151

Table 7.6

School-leaving age and other educational qualifications of labour migrants

School-leaving age	Chatham		High Wycombe		Hudders-field		North-ampton		Total	
	No.	%	No.	%	No.	%	No.	%	No.	%
13	2	1·6	2	1·1	0	—	0	—	4	0·7
14	17	13·5	14	7·9	7	9·2	17	9·9	55	10·0
15	32	25·4	31	17·4	18	23·7	44	25·7	125	22·7
16	28	22·2	33	18·5	18	23·7	34	19·9	113	20·5
17	16	12·7	29	16·3	8	10·5	23	13·5	76	13·8
18	25	19·8	38	21·4	14	18·4	39	22·8	116	21·1
19 and over	6	4·8	27	15·2	8	10·5	13	7·6	54	9·8
No information	0	—	4	2·2	3	4·0	1	0·6	7	1·3
Total	126		178		76		171		551	

Qualification	No.	%	No.	%	No.	%	No.	%	No.	%
CSE	2	1·6	2	1·1	0	—	0	—	4	0·8
'O' level	20	15·9	27	15·2	17	22·4	29	17·0	93	17·0
'A' level	18	14·3	39	21·9	12	15·8	27	15·8	96	17·4
HNC	3	2·4	7	3·9	1	1·3	1	0·6	12	2·2
Diploma	8	6·4	10	5·6	4	5·3	15	10·5	37	6·7
Degree	9	7·1	28	15·7	9	11·8	18	10·5	64	11·6
Others	12	9·5	18	10·1	11	14·5	13	7·6	54	9·8
No others	54	42·9	45	25·3	22	29·0	62	36·3	183	33·2
Total	126		178		76		171		551	

Labour migrants were asked about the qualifications required for their job. They were then asked which other educational qualifications (if any) were held; the above table records the responses to the latter question.

Besides those educational qualifications required for their jobs, labour migrants possessed the qualifications indicated in Table 7.6. Again it is clear that a high proportion of labour migrants had a high level of education. The survey results may be compared with Harris and Clausen's data concerning the educational qualifications of the population as a whole.[4] Their figures referred to the highest qualification obtained by men. There are some problems in comparability; for example, the Harris and Clausen data referred to 1963, and may thus provide low estimates for comparison with 1972 figures. Nevertheless, it is clear that the labour migrants were far better qualified than the static population; the differences for degrees (11·6 per cent for labour migrants as against 1·9 per cent for the whole

SCHOOL-LEAVING AGE

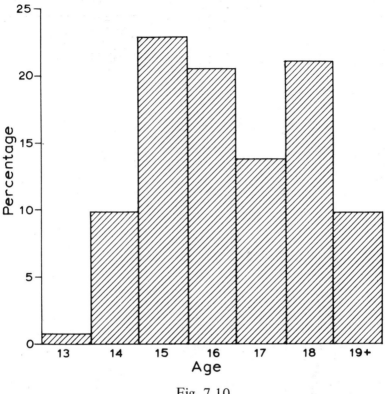

Fig. 7.10

population) and for General Certificate of Education (Advanced Level) qualifications (17·4 per cent as against 1·3 per cent) were particularly great.

Employment

The survey found that virtually all labour migrants had succeeded in obtaining full-time employment following the move (Table 7.2). Only 0·7 per cent were employed part-time and 1·6 per cent were unemployed, whereas 97·1 per cent were employed full-time. Of the total sample, 12·0 per cent had not previously been employed, but only 3·1 per cent of these had been unemployed, most of the remainder (8·4 per cent) being

153

Table 7.7

Present net monthly income of labour migrant

Income (£s)	Chatham		High Wycombe		Hudders- field		North- ampton		Total	
	No.	%	No.	%	No.	%	No.	%	No.	%
Less than £40	5	4·0	3	1·7	3	4·0	3	1·8	14	2·5
£40 – £60	7	5·6	11	6·2	2	2·6	15	8·8	35	6·4
£60 – £80	19	15·1	22	12·4	9	11·8	23	13·5	73	13·3
£80 – £120	42	33·3	34	19·1	19	25·0	48	28·1	143	26·0
£120 – £240	41	32·5	59	33·2	30	39·5	59	34·5	189	34·3
£240 – £400	7	5·6	30	16·9	4	5·3	14	8·2	55	10·0
Over £400	–		10	5·6	2	2·6	3	1·8	15	2·7
Student	–		–		1	1·3	–		1	0·2
Unemployed	1	0·8	1	0·6	4	5·3	3	1·8	9	1·6
No information	4	3·2	8	4·5	2	2·6	3	1·8	17	3·1
Total	126		178		76		171		551	

Table 7.8

Total net income – tax units, England and Wales

Income per month	Number of tax units (thousands)	Percentage
Less than £41·67	1,691	8·8
£41·67 – £58·33	2,347	12·1
£58·33 – £83·33	3,498	18·1
£83·33 – £125·00	5,587	28·9
£125·00 – £250·00	5,472	28·3
£250·00 – £416·67	497	2·6
Over £416·67	233	1·2
Total	19,325	100·0

Source: Adapted from Table 66, p. 116, of *The Survey of Personal Incomes 1969–70*, HMSO, London 1972.

The class intervals are selected to make the data as comparable as possible with the survey data.

students taking up their first job. Only 0·5 per cent were unemployed both before and after the move. More labour migrants to Huddersfield than to the other SMLAs were unemployed before the move, and more became or remained unemployed after moving there.

The unemployed are such a small proportion of the sample that it is difficult to attach much weight to these findings. Five-sixths of unemployed labour migrants succeeded in obtaining employment after moving; this accords with the role frequently ascribed to migration in adjusting regional employment differences. It also indicates the low proportion of moves which are of this type (although the sample method may have led to under-representation of those migrants previously unemployed). Other moves may have been made in response to the threat of unemployment. Despite the frequent use of unemployment rates as a means of predicting migration, our findings suggest that the proportion of labour migrants who were unemployed is very low, and that this factor is not a major determinant of labour migration.

Of the 416 spouses of labour migrants in the survey, 28·8 per cent were employed full-time, 13·3 per cent were in part-time employment and 4·3 per cent were unemployed. Among the remainder, 1·0 per cent were undergoing full-time education, whereas the rest (52·6 per cent of all spouses) were not working. In 12·6 per cent of households with spouses, the migrants had not been married prior to the move. On balance, it seems that labour migration led to a reduction in the number of spouses at work: 41·0 per cent of spouses were not working after the move, while 7·1 per cent were working after the move, although they had not been employed previously.

Changes in the spouse's working status may not always be a direct consequence of the labour market situation in the origin and destination areas. The number of spouses no longer in employment may be related to life-cycle stage; many of them may have stopped work for family reasons. Similarly, some of those beginning work for the first time may have done so on completion of education or training courses. The spouse's working status may have been less central to the household's living standard than the labour migrant's, and many of the spouses not employed in their new area may have searched for work with little urgency, perhaps deferring it until the household was 'settled' in its new home, or until a suitable opportunity presented itself.

Income

Contrary to expectations, only 3·1 per cent of labour migrants refused to give information about their incomes. Table 7.7 shows that, after moving, most labour migrants earned a net monthly income in the range £60 — £80 (13·3 per cent), £80 - £120 (26·0 per cent) or £120 — £240 (34·3 per cent). Only 2·5 per cent earned less than £40 per month, and 2·7 per cent earned over £400. The mean net monthly income (calculated on the basis of an even distribution within the income classes, and excluding unemployed migrants) was £155·4. The means for the SMLAs were £177·5 at High Wycombe, £152·0 at Huddersfield, £145·4 at Northampton and £128·9 at Chatham. Most of the variation in the means is attributable to the frequency of high income migrants − 22 per cent of in-migrants to High Wycombe earned over £240 per month, as against only 6 per cent in Chatham.

There are some difficulties in obtaining comparable data on incomes for the population as a whole, so we cannot be certain of the effect of income as a migration differential. The data presented (Table 7.8) are from the 1969−70 Survey of Personal Incomes,[5] and represent total net income by 'tax unit', either a single person or a married couple, with or without children. This information is presented by size categories incompatible with those used in the survey, and covers the whole of England and Wales. Although the differentials in income between the migrant sample and the total population are exaggerated by the effects of income increases between 1970 and 1972, it is clear that the migrants, on average, earned more than the population as a whole. There seems to be a regular increase in propensity to migrate with income; the £80 − £120 income range was represented roughly equally among the migrants and among the total population, with increasing disparities towards both extremes of the income distribution. Labour migrants may thus be assumed to be earning considerably more on average than the population as a whole. This finding appears in accord with those of Woolf and of Cullingworth (see Chapter 5), and in conflict with those of American students of inter-urban migration.

The incomes of labour migrants prior to moving were less likely to be in the highest ranges (33·9 per cent earned over £120 per month before the move; 47·0 per cent earned this much afterwards). The proportion earning under £40 per month likewise declined from 5·3 per cent before to 2·5 per cent after the move. Although 32·8 per cent of labour migrants (43·1 per cent if those who had been students or unempoyed are included) rose to a higher income level after the move, only 6·7 per cent rose by more than one income group; similarly, 8·8 per cent (excluding currently unemployed labour migrants) had dropped to a lower income group, but only 1·8 per cent had dropped more than one income group. In most income groups, labour migrants appeared most likely to move to the next highest category, with a strong propensity to remain in the same category, and little likelihood of moving to any other group. In the highest income groups, however, labour migrants were more likely to remain in the same category; this last result may be due to the width of the income classes at the upper end of the spectrum.

A comparison of present income with the age of the labour migrant shows a tendency for income to increase with age. If we assume a uniform distribution within each income group, we find that mean monthly net income increased from £95·1 for employed labour migrants in the 20—24 age range to £150·9 for those aged 25—34, £181·8 for those aged 35—44 and £201·2 for those aged 45—59.

If the present income of migrant households is compared to the distance of their move, it is clear that the wealthier households were more likely to have covered long distances than poorer households. Among those with net monthly incomes of under £70 per month, approximately equal proportions came from each of the four distance bands; among those with monthly incomes of over £150 per month, however, only 12 per cent had moved under 25 miles (40 km), compared to 20 per cent between 25 and 50 miles (40—80 km), 28 per cent between 50 and 100 miles (80—160 km) and 39 per cent over 100 miles (160 km). It may also be noted, in contrast to the apparent relationship between present income and length of move, that households with no income prior to the move tended to move long distances (49 per cent moved over 100 miles); this may have been because many were headed by students, whose education enables them to compete for jobs advertised on the national market. Otherwise, previous household incomes showed the same relationship to distance moved as did present incomes. These findings are in accord with the framework advanced in Chapter 2. High-status, high-paying occupations are more likely to be located in large employment nodes at some distance from one another. Hence, people in high income groups are more likely to move longer distances. This also helps to explain the patterns of migration dominated by London and the provincial centres, as described in Chapter 4.

The incomes of the spouses of labour migrants showed less consistent behaviour (Table 7.9). Most spouses were in one of the lowest four income groups, with the highest proportion (28·6 per cent of those in employment) earning between £40 and £60 per month. Comparison with their previous incomes showed that more had suffered a decrease in income following the move than had received an increase, indicating the greater importance attached to the level of the husband's income in the decision to migrate.

Table 7.9

Present net monthly income of labour migrant's spouse

Income (£s)	Chatham No.	%	High Wycombe No.	%	Huddersfield No.	%	Northampton No.	%	Total No.	%
Less than £40	7	18·4	11	22·4	9	37·5	10	15·6	37	21·1
£40 – £60	11	28·9	14	28·6	4	16·7	21	32·8	50	28·6
£60 – £80	7	18·4	12	24·5	4	16·7	19	29·7	42	24·0
£80 – £120	9	23·7	9	18·4	5	20·8	10	15·6	33	18·9
£120 – £240	1	2·6	–		–		2	3·1	3	1·7
Over £240	–		–		–		–		–	
No information	3	7·9	3	6·1	2	8·3	2	3·1	10	5·7
Total	38		49		24		64		175	

The percentages refer to those spouses working full- or part-time.

Table 7.10

Present socio-economic group of labour migrant

Socio-economic group	Chatham No.	%	High Wycombe No.	%	Huddersfield No.	%	Northampton No.	%	Total No.	%
1	7	5·6	31	17·4	4	5·3	10	5·9	52	9·4
2	11	8·7	25	14·0	14	18·4	30	17·5	80	14·5
3	–		–		1	1·3	–		1	0·2
4	16	12·7	40	22·5	13	17·1	26	15·2	95	17·2
5	25	19·8	33	18·5	14	18·4	27	15·8	99	18·0
6	23	18·3	19	10·7	8	10·5	32	18·7	82	14·9
7	1	0·8	4	2·3	1	1·3	5	2·9	11	2·0
8	1	0·8	1	0·6	–		–		2	0·4
9	18	14·3	11	6·2	9	11·8	21	12·3	59	10·7
10	13	10·3	8	4·5	4	5·3	8	4·7	33	6·0
11	3	2·4	3	1·7	3	4·0	2	1·2	11	2·0
12	1	0·8	1	0·6	–		2	1·2	4	0·7
13	1	0·8	–		–		1	0·6	2	0·4
14	–		–		–		–		–	
15	2	1·6	1	0·6	–		4	2·3	7	1·3
16	–		–		–		–		–	
17	2	1·6	–		–		–		2	0·4
18	–		–		–		–		–	
19	–		–		1	1·3	1	0·6	2	0·4
20	2	1·6	1	0·6	4	5·3	2	1·2	9	1·6

The system for numbering the groups is described in Table 7.11.

Socio-economic group

Table 7.10 shows the proportions of labour migrants within each socio-economic group (see also Fig 7.11 and 7.12). It can be seen that groups 2, 4, 5 and 6 were the best represented, followed by groups 1, 9 and 10 (Table 7.11 provides a key to the classification used). These groups are employers and managers (1, 2), professional workers (4), intermediate (5) and junior (6) non-manual workers, and skilled (9) and semi-skilled (10) manual workers. Managerial and professional groups (1—4) constituted 41 per cent of the total sample, a proportion which rose to 54 per cent at High Wycombe and fell to 27 per cent at Chatham. The intermediate and junior non-manual categories (5, 6) accounted for 32·9 per cent of labour migrants. Manual workers accounted for only 18·7 per cent, of which only 2·0 per cent were unskilled workers. High Wycombe had only 12 per cent manual workers, compared to 27 per cent at Chatham, again highlighting the different types of labour migrant attracted to these two places.

A comparison with data for the whole population of the SMLA enables us to determine whether in-migrants differ in socio-economic composition from the existing population. Table 7.12, compiled from the 1966 Sample Census Economic Activity Tables, can be compared with Table 7.10, referring to the migrant sample (see Fig. 7.11). The total population figures are weighted by labour market area to make them directly comparable with the survey data.

Professional, managerial and non-manual workers, including personal service workers, were more strongly represented among the migrants than among the population as a whole. An exception was group 3, self-employed professional workers, who were poorly represented in the sample, probably because they had a greater investment in non-transportable 'capital' (see Chapter 5). In fact, all self-employed workers, as well as manual workers, were less frequently found among the migrants. The differences between migrants and the total population were particularly striking in groups 4 (employed professional workers) and 5 (intermediate non-manual workers), both of which had about four times more labour migrants than would be expected from the frequency of these groups in the total population. These findings appear in accordance with those discussed in Chapter 5, one surprise being the small proportion of skilled manual workers among labour migrants. This is in conflict with Cullingworth's findings,[6] but the discrepancy may be due to his inclusion of short-distance movers, who are not labour migrants as defined in this study.

Sex and marital status were strongly related to socio-economic group.

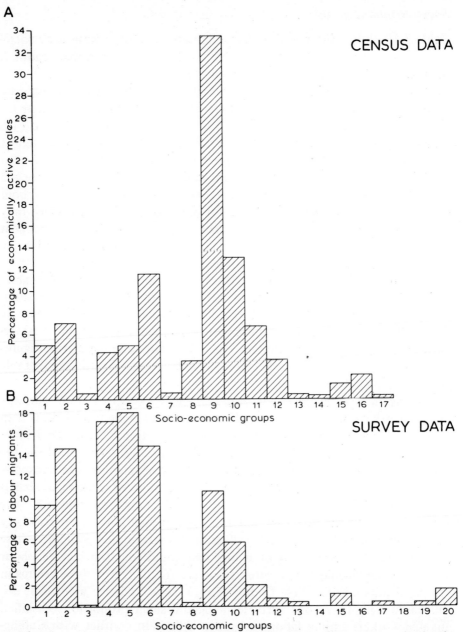

Fig. 7.11 A. Socio-economic groups of economically active males in the four sample SMLAs, 1966. (The percentages are derived from a combination of the figures for the four SMLAs weighted according to their representation in the sample survey.)

B. Present socio-economic groups of labour migrants.

SOCIO-ECONOMIC GROUPS
(Sample SMLAs)

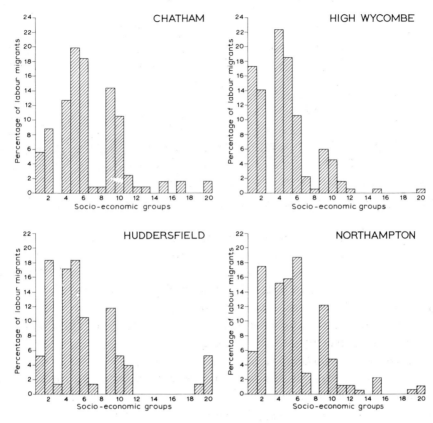

Fig. 7.12

Female labour migrants were concentrated in the intermediate and junior non-manual groups, and in personal service (82 per cent of female migrants were in these categories). Single labour migrants were most concentrated in the intermediate non-manual group, followed by personal service, semi-skilled and unskilled manual workers. Very few employers and managers were single.

The socio-economic groups of the labour migrants prior to the move showed a similar pattern to that already described, the biggest difference being that 8·4 per cent had been students beforehand. Only 5 per cent of in-migrants to High Wycombe had been students before the move, compared with 9 per cent at Huddersfield and 13 per cent at Chathem. Another major

161

Table 7.11
Key to the socio-economic groups
(Groups 1–17 are those used by the census; groups 18–20 have been
added to complete the coverage of labour migrants)

(1) *Employers and managers in central and local government, industry,
commerce, etc. – large establishments.*
   1.1 Employers in industry, commerce, etc.
      Persons who employ others in non-agricultural enterprises em-
ploying 25 or more persons.
   1.2 Managers in central and local government, industry, commerce,
etc. Persons who generally plan and supervise in non-agricultural
enterprises employing 25 or more persons.

(2) *Employers and managers in industry, commerce, etc. – small establishments*
   2.1 Employers in industry, commerce, etc. – small establishments.
      As 1.1 but in establishments employing fewer than 25 persons.
   2.2 Managers in industry, commerce, etc. – small establishments.
      As 1.2 but in establishments employing fewer than 25 persons.

(3) *Professional workers – self-employed*
Self-employed persons engaged in work normally requiring qualifications of university degree standard.

(4) *Professional workers – employees*
Employees engaged in work normally requiring qualifications of university degree standard.

(5) *Intermediate non-manual workers*
   5.1 Ancillary workers and artists.
      Employees engaged in non-manual occupations ancillary to the
professions, not normally requiring qualifications of university
degree standard; persons engaged in artistic work and not employing others thereat. Self-employed nurses, medical auxilia-
ries, teachers, work study engineers and technicians are included.
   5.2 Foremen and supervisors non-manual.
      Employees (other than managers) engaged in occupations in-
cluded in group 6, who formally and immediately supervise
others engaged in such occupations.

(6) *Junior non-manual workers*
Employees, not exercising general planning or supervisory powers,
engaged in clerical, sales and non-manual communications and securi-

ty occupations, excluding those who have additional and formal supervisory functions (these are included in group 5.2).

(7) *Personal service workers*
Employees engaged in service occupations caring for food, drink, clothing and other personal needs.

(8) *Foremen and supervisors — manual*
Employees (other than managers) who formally and immediately supervise others engaged in manual occupations, whether or not themselves engaged in such occupations.

(9) *Skilled manual workers*
Employees engaged in manual occupations which require considerable and specific skills.

(10) *Semi-skilled manual workers*
Employees engaged in manual occupations which require slight but specific skills.

(11) *Unskilled manual workers*
Other employees engaged in manual occupations.

(12) *Own account workers (other than professional)*
Self-employed persons engaged in any trade, personal service or manual occupation not normally requiring training of university degree standard and having no employees other than family workers.

(13) *Farmers — employers and managers*
Persons who own, rent or manage farms, market gardens or forests, employing people other than family workers in the work of the enterprise.

(14) *Farmers — own account*
Persons who own or rent farms, market gardens or forests and having no employees other than family workers.

(15) *Agricultural workers*
Employees engaged in tending crops, animals, game or forests, or operating agricultural or forestry machinery.

(16) *Members of armed forces*

(17) *Occupation inadequately described*

The following were added for the survey:
(18) *Prolonged illness prevented working*
(19) *Never worked; student*
(20) *Unemployed*

Table 7.12

Socio-economic group for the population as a whole: SMLA areas

Socio-economic group	Chatham %	High Wycombe %	Hudders-field %	North-ampton %	Total %
1	3·7	6·9	3·8	4·4	4·9
2	4·7	9·9	5·7	6·5	7·0
3	0·3	1·2	0·5	0·7	0·7
4	3·9	6·5	3·7	2·5	4·3
5	5·3	5·4	4·6	4·4	4·9
6	12·9	11·3	9·9	11·7	11·6
7	0·7	0·8	0·6	0·9	0·7
8	4·2	3·1	4·3	3·4	3·6
9	32·3	29·9	36·5	37·0	33·5
10	12·6	10·5	19·1	13·6	13·1
11	8·0	4·9	6·7	7·6	6·7
12	3·6	4·4	3·0	3·3	3·7
13	0·4	0·5	0·4	0·6	0·5
14	0·1	0·3	0·4	0·5	0·4
15	0·9	1·1	0·6	2·3	1·4
16	6·0	2·7	0·0	0·3	2·3
17	0·4	0·3	0·2	0·3	0·3
Totals on which figures are based	7,047	6,770	6,083	4,922	24,822

Source: Table 4, Economic Activity County Leaflets, Sample Census 1966. The figures refer to economically active males.

The total percentages (final column) are derived from a combination of the figures for the four SMLAs weighted according to their representation in the survey. They are thus directly comparable to the totals in Table 7.10. See Table 7.11 for an explanation of the system for numbering the groups.

change was an increase in the proportion of intermediate non-manual workers following the move, from 11·6 per cent to 18·0 per cent of the sample. This increase was particularly great in Huddersfield and Chatham.

There were several differences between socio-economic groups in the distance of move (see Table 7.13). Those labour migrants in the professional and intermediate non-manual categories were particularly likely to have moved over 100 miles (160 km). Employers and managers seemed more likely to have travelled between 50 and 100 miles (80–160 km) than a longer distance, especially in Huddersfield and Northampton. Migrants

Table 7.13

Distance of move by present socio-economic group of labour migrant

Percentages of entire sample

Socio-economic group	0 – 25 miles	25 – 50 miles	50 – 100 miles	100+ miles	Scotland etc.	Abroad	Total
1	1·6	1·5	3·1	2.4	0·4	0·5	9·4
2	0·9	2·2	5·3	4·4	0·4	1·5	14·5
3	0·2	–	–	–	–	–	0·2
4	1·3	3·1	2·9	8·2	0·9	0·9	17·2
5	2·9	2·2	3·6	8·2	0·4	0·7	18·0
6	2·2	4·0	4·2	3·8	0·5	0·2	14·9
7	0·2	0·7	0·7	0·4	–	–	2·0
8	0·2	–	0·2	–	–	–	0·4
9	1·5	3·8	2·4	1·1	0·7	1·3	10·7
10	1·3	0·9	1·3	1·6	0·7	0·2	6·0
11	0·4	–	0·2	0·9	0·2	0·4	2·0
12	–	0·2	0·2	–	0·4	–	0·7
13	–	–	0·2	–	0·2	–	0·4
14	–	–	–	–	–	–	–
15	–	0·5	0·4	0·4	–	–	1·3
16	–	–	–	–	–	–	–
17	–	–	–	0·4	–	–	0·4
18	–	–	–	–	–	–	–
19	0·2	0·2	–	–	–	–	0·4
20	0·7	0·2	0·2	0·5	–	–	1·6
Total	13·4	19·4	24·7	32·1	4·7	5·6	100·0

For a key to the system for numbering the groups, see Table 7.11.

in other socio-economic groups were less likely to have moved a long distance; this was especially true of skilled manual workers, less than half of whom moved more than 50 miles (80 km). A similar pattern emerged from the comparison of the distance moved with the labour migrant's socio-economic group prior to the move. It is notable here that over half (51 per cent) of those not employed moved over 100 miles (160 km).

The socio-economic status of labour migrants' spouses bore little relation to that of the migrants themselves. Most (57·9 per cent) of the spouses were not in the labour force, but 21·2 per cent were junior non-manual or personal service workers (groups 6 and 7) and 14·2 per cent were intermediate non-manual workers (group 5). Only small proportions were in the professional and managerial groups (3·4 per cent) or the manual worker groups (2·6 per cent). Little change could be observed between present and previous socio-economic groups.

The results of the survey show that labour migration was strongly selective of certain groups in the population, notably the professional, managerial and non-manual workers. A large proportion of migrants were professional and managerial men, almost certainly married, moving within the same socio-economic group. Another group consisted of intermediate and junior non-manual workers of both sexes, many of them single and perhaps in their first job after obtaining qualifications. Manual workers were numerically less important in labour migration than these other groups, constituting only 20 per cent of our sample.

Migration experience

A measure of migration experience was devised to summarise the residential histories of the labour migrants. The labour migrant and his spouse were asked to list the places in which they had lived since birth. Points were allotted for each move, according to the distance involved. A move of under 25 miles (40 km) scored one point, one between 25 and 50 miles (40-80 km) scored two points, between 50 and 100 miles (80-160 km) three points, and over 100 miles (160 km) four points. A move to or from Scotland, Ireland or the Channel Islands was allotted five points, and a move to a foreign country was allotted six points. Four points were given for moves between foreign countries, two for moves within a foreign country, and three for a return from abroad. Service moves within the UK scored one point but those involving foreign travel scored two. Scores were halved for moves back to an area of previous residence. Household migration scores were computed by averaging the scores of labour migrants and their spouses.

Table 7.14 shows the distribution of migration scores for the total

Table 7.14

Migration experience of labour migrant and his spouse

Points score for previous moves	Chatham		High Wycombe		Hudders-field		North-ampton		Total	
	No.	%	No.	%	No.	%	No.	%	No.	%
0 – 2½	16	12·7	10	5·6	9	11·8	16	9·4	51	9·3
3 – 7½	37	29·4	57	32·0	19	25·0	52	30·4	165	30·0
8 – 12½	36	28·6	44	24·7	22	29·0	57	33·3	159	28·9
13 – 20	25	19·8	48	27·0	20	26·3	36	21·1	129	23·4
20½ and over	12	9·5	19	10·7	6	7·9	10	5·9	47	8·5
Total	126		178		76		171		551	

The calculation of points scores is explained in the text.

166

Table 7.15

Distance of move by migration experience of the labour migrant
and his spouse

Points score for previous moves	0 – 25 miles	25 – 50 miles	50 – 100 miles	100+ miles	Scotland etc.	Abroad	Total
0 – 2½	37·3	51·0	9·8	2·0	–	–	51
3 – 7½	15·2	24·2	33·3	23·6	3·6	–	165
8 – 12½	9·4	16·4	25·8	38·4	4·4	5·7	159
13 – 20	10·9	8·5	22·5	38·8	7·8	11·6	129
20½ and over	2·1	8·5	12·8	55·3	6·4	14·9	47

The calculation of points scores is explained in the text. The percentages add to 100 along the rows. Thus the figures are the percentages in each 'migration experience' category moving within each distance band.

sample and for the four SMLAs. The households were approximately equally divided between the three middle categories (3–7 ½, 8–12 ½, 13–20) with smaller proportions in the most and least mobile groups. High Wycombe had relatively few of the least mobile households, and Chatham and Huddersfield had high proportions.

A cross-tabulation of the distance moved by households against their migration scores (Table 7.15) indicates a clear-cut pattern. The least mobile households were most likely to have moved the shortest distances. The more mobile the household had been in the past, the more likely it was to have moved a long distance. In particular, 55 per cent of those with more than 20 points had moved over 100 miles (160 km).

The unavailability of comparable data for the population as a whole makes it impossible to evaluate migration experience as a predictor of movement. Nevertheless, the arguments for the importance of this variable are supported by the relationship found between migration score and distance of move. It is those who have most experience of migration who make the longest moves, in which they are able to keep up few of those links and activities which a shorter-distance migrant finds it easier to preserve.

Journey to work

Because labour market areas were defined in terms of commuting, migrants were asked about the transport mode or modes used in their journey to work, the length of time taken and the cost per week of the journey. The results (Table 7.16) bring out substantial differences between labour market areas in all of these variables. Bus transport was far

Table 7.16

Labour migrant's present journey to work: transport mode, travel time and cost per week

Mode of transport	Chatham		High Wycombe		Hudders-field		North-ampton		Total	
	No.	%	No.	%	No.	%	No.	%	No.	%
Any use of car	74	58·7	116	65·2	36	47·4	109	63·7	335	60·8
bus	11	8·7	8	4·5	18	23·7	18	10·5	55	10·0
train	13	10·3	31	17·4	–		2	1·2	46	8·3
walking	31	24·6	48	27·0	17	22·4	29	17·0	125	22·7
cycling	5	4·0	2	1·1	2	2·6	4	2·3	13	2·4
Other modes	5	4·0	4	2·2	4	5·3	3	1·8	16	2·9
Total	139		209		77		165		590	

Total travel time	No.	%	No.	%	No.	%	No.	%	No.	%
0 – 15 minutes	48	38·1	67	37·6	33	43·4	75	43·9	223	40·5
15 – 30 minutes	38	30·2	27	15·2	23	30·3	54	31·6	142	25·8
30 – 60 minutes	13	10·3	38	21·4	6	7·9	15	8·8	72	13·1
Over 60 minutes	18	14·4	32	18·0	3	4·0	6	3·5	59	10·7
No information/does not travel	9	7·2	14	7·9	11	14·5	21	12·3	55	10·0
Total	126		178		76		171		551	

Travel cost per week	No.	%	No.	%	No.	%	No.	%	No.	%
Less than 50p.	15	11·9	11	6·2	14	18·4	16	9·4	56	10·2
50p. – £1	22	17·5	20	11·2	17	22·4	35	20·5	94	17·1
£1 – £2	22	17·5	21	11·8	13	17·1	35	20·5	91	16·5
£2 – £4	17	13·5	43	24·2	5	6·6	16	9·4	81	14·7
Over £4	14	11·1	29	16·3	1	1·3	4	2·3	48	8·7
Nothing	28	22·2	36	20·2	21	27·6	42	24·6	127	23·1
Company car	7	5·6	15	8·4	5	6·6	20	11·7	47	8·5
No information	1	0·8	3	1·7	–		3	1·8	7	1·3
Total	126		178		76		171		551	

The transport mode figures include multiple use of modes, and do not add up to the total number of labour migrants; the percentages are calculated with respect to the number of labour migrants, and do not add up to 100; they can be thought of as referring to the proportion of labour migrants using the mode of transport in question.

more important in Huddersfield than in the other areas, and train transport more important in High Wycombe. Time and costs were far higher for Chatham and High Wycombe than for the other areas, presumably because some commuters travelled to destinations elsewhere in the south-east.

The mean journey time was 27 minutes (assuming those travelling over 60 minutes had an average journey time of 90 minutes, and excluding those not travelling to work). The SMLA figures ranged from 20 minutes at Northampton and Huddersfield to 35 minutes at High Wycombe. The mean cost of the journey to work per week (assuming those paying less than 50p. averaged 25p., and those paying more than £4 averaged £6 was £1·51; this figure varied from 80p. at Huddersfield, £1·05 at Northampton and £1·60 at Chatham to £2·24 at High Wycombe.

Although the 1966 Sample Census returns on journey-to-work mode[7] are not strictly comparable with our survey results (there is a six-year time lag; census statistics relate to all members of the workforce and to the principal mode of transport, whereas our survey data are concerned with the household head, and with any use of each mode), certain conclusions are clear from Table 7.17. Labour migrants appeared far more likely to use automobile transport in their journey to work (although this was likely to be exaggerated by all three of the factors mentioned above), and far less likely to use bus or cycle. Journeys to work by train and on foot also appeared to be more common among migrants. The latter may be

Table 7.17

Means of transport to work for the working population

Principal transport mode	Chatham		High Wycombe		Huddersfield		Northampton		Total
	No.	%	No.	%	No.	%	No.	%	%
Car	3001	32·6	3813	41·0	2041	22·4	2123	29·2	33·3
Bus	2305	25·0	1752	18·8	4356	47·9	2161	29·8	27·1
Train	929	10·1	782	8·4	61	0·7	30	0·4	5·5
Walking	1627	17·7	1776	19·1	2179	24·0	1544	21·3	20·0
Cycling	543	5·9	629	6·8	85	0·9	747	10·3	6·8
Other	808	8·8	548	5·9	376	4·1	659	9·1	7·2

Source: Table 7, Workplace and Transport Tables, Sample Census 1966. The figures supplied for each area are derived from a 10 per cent sample, and can be multiplied by ten for an estimate for the total SMLA population. The total (final column) is a proportion of the SMLA totals, weighted according to the representation of the SMLAs in our survey.

explained by the success of some migrants in finding housing very close to their place of work, but is more likely to be due to the inclusion of people who walk only to train or bus stops. The basic picture, however, emphasises the selectivity of labour migration in favour of those whose income and aspirations are sufficient for them to use a car, rather than bus or cycle, to travel to work.

The journey-to-work times of the migrants, in relation to those of the population as a whole (Tables 7.16 and 7.18), were likely to fall into the two extreme categories, those of less than 15 minutes and those of over one hour. It will be noticed, however, that those in the latter group were resident mainly in Chatham and High Wycombe labour market areas, and perhaps represented commuters travelling to other centres in south-east England. If these are excluded, it is clear that the labour migrant sample was concentrated mainly in the short journey-to work categories.

The data on cost of travel provided by Harris and Clausen[8] (Table 7.18) are not directly comparable, because of the decrease in the value of money since 1963, and because their data referred to all workers, and not just to heads of households. If one assumes a 60 per cent rise in costs over the period (an estimate based on the movement of the Retail Price Index), it is clear that the labour migrants were spending substantially more on their journey to work. Even among those who had to pay for their travel, 45·6 per cent of Harris and Clausen's sample paid less than £1, whereas only 43·8 per cent of the migrants paid less than £2. On top of this, more than twice as many of the earlier sample paid nothing.

Table 7.18

A.	%	B.	%
Less than 15 minutes	36·7	5p. − 50 p.	30·2
15 − 30 minutes	29·2	50p. − £1	15·4
30 − 60 minutes	21·4	£1 − £2	6·5
Over 60 minutes	6·7	Over £2	1·3
No journey	5·9	Nil	46·6

A. Time taken on journey between work and home (fixed journey; men), 1963.
B. Cost per week of travelling to and from work: all workers, 1963.
Source: Harris and Clausen, Table 98, p. 116 and Table 106, p. 121 (both slightly adapted).

An examination of transport modes used in the journey to work by labour migrants at their previous address shows comparatively little difference from present journey-to-work figures. More differences were apparent in the figures for individual labour markets. In High Wycombe, train and foot transport increased in importance at the expense of the car. In Huddersfield, the bus replaced the car and the train for some labour migrants. The reverse was the case for Northampton, where use of cars increased following the move, largely at the expense of walking.

The times taken by migrants in travelling to work after moving did not show great divergence from their experience beforehand. The major exception was a 50 per cent increase in the number travelling for over an hour, entirely accounted for by Chatham and High Wycombe. In contrast to Chatham, however, a high proportion of in-migrants to High Wycombe (9 per cent) had previously had over an hour's travelling. Among those moving to Huddersfield, the number with a journey to work of over 30 minutes was halved by the move. In Northampton also, the number of in-migrants with journeys under 15 minutes increased substantially at the expense of longer journeys. It can be concluded that labour migration to Huddersfield and Northampton was likely to lead to a shorter journey to work, but moves to High Wycombe and Chatham were frequently associated with a longer journey.

Journey-to-work costs tended to be rather higher after the move than before. The proportion paying nothing decreased from 29 per cent to 23 per cent, and the proportion paying over £2 per week increased from 17 per cent to 23 per cent. In both Chatham and High Wycombe, there was an increase in numbers spending large sums on journeys to work; in Chatham, this was reciprocated by a reduction in the numbers paying nothing, a reduction also observed at Northampton.

The information on journey-to-work perhaps tells us more about differences between labour market areas than about the role of the journey to work in the moving decision. There were certain clear differences between the SMLAs in transport modes used, but it was also the case that many migrants to Chatham and High Wycombe experienced longer and more costly journeys to work than the population as a whole, and than they had previously experienced themselves. Labour migrants to Huddersfield and Northampton, however, were likely to experience shorter and sometimes cheaper travel.

Housing

The availability of suitable housing is a necessity for labour migration to

171

Table 7.19

Age and type of present accommodation of labour migrant households

Age of dwelling	Chatham		High Wycombe		Hudders-field		North-ampton		Total	
	No.	%	No.	%	No.	%	No.	%	No.	%
Pre-1919	24	19·1	29	16·3	18	23·7	29	17·0	100	18·2
1919 – 1938	16	12·7	38	21·4	13	17·1	28	16·4	95	17·2
Post-World War II	84	66·7	111	62·4	45	59·2	113	66·1	353	64·1
No information	2	1·6	–		–		1	0·6	3	0·5
Total	126		178		76		171		551	

Type of accommodation	No.	%	No.	%	No.	%	No.	%	No.	%
Detached house	11	8·7	74	41·6	29	38·2	51	29·8	165	30·0
Semi-detached house	36	28·6	27	15·2	14	18·4	34	19·9	111	20·2
Terraced/town house	32	25·4	15	8·4	16	21·1	19	11·1	82	14·9
Detached bungalow	4	3·2	13	7·3	4	5·3	7	4·1	28	5·1
Semi-detached bungalow	2	1·6	1	0·6	3	4·0	9	5·3	15	2·7
Self-contained flat	11	8·7	16	9·0	3	4·0	27	15·8	57	10·3
Flat with shared facilities	3	2·4	4	2·3	1	1·3	6	3·5	14	2·5
Hostel, bedsitter, living with parents, in-laws, etc.	24	19·1	24	13·5	4	5·3	16	9·4	68	12·3
Caravan	1	0·8	1	0·6	–		–		2	0·4
Other	2	1·6	3	1·7	2	2·6	1	0·6	8	1·5
No information	–		1	0·6	–		–		1	0·2
Total	126		178		76		171		551	

take place, and it is relevant, therefore, to examine the housing of those who have successfully moved. Their housing situation will be a product of their accommodation needs, their financial resources and the housing stock available in the destination area.

Age of housing

Hadjifotiou and Robinson[9] provide information on the housing stock in the labour market areas which may be contrasted with the survey data in Table 7.19. In Chatham, for example, almost half the present number of dwellings in the area existed by 1911; recent development has also been extensive, dwelling stock rising by 10 per cent between 1961 and 1966. In Huddersfield also, 49 per cent of the stock was constructed before 1911. In High Wycombe, one-quarter of the housing stock was built before 1911, and many new houses have been constructed since 1945; the total stock increased by 14 per cent between 1961 and 1966. More complete information is available for Northampton County Borough (which contains 80 per cent of the dwellings in the labour market area). Here 35·6 per cent of dwellings were built before 1914, compared with 27.1 per cent in the period 1914–45, and 37·1 per cent since 1945. In comparison, Woolf's data for England and Wales in 1964 showed that 39 per cent of accommodation units were built before 1919, 29 per cent between 1919 and 1944, and 31 per cent since 1944 (see also Table 1.2). [10]

Comparison of Woolf's findings with those in Table 7.19 shows that the age of housing occupied by labour migrants was substantially less than that occupied by the population as a whole. In particular, the proportion of migrants living in housing built since the Second World War was very much higher, especially in Northampton. Migrants were under-represented in housing dating from earlier periods, although High Wycombe appeared to have a larger proportion of migrants in pre-1914 houses.

House type

The type of house in which a labour migrant was living (Table 7.19; Figs. 7.13 and 7.14) might be expected to reflect the composition of his household and his income level. The larger-than-average size of migrant households would suggest that larger housing units are likely to be in demand among migrants; on the other hand, the early life-cycle stage of many migrants suggests that flats would be well represented. The high average income of migrants indicates that they may be more likely to be found in detached houses than semi-detached or terraced houses.

Table 7.19 may be compared with the findings of Woolf,[11] who collected data on the type of accommodation of all households in her survey. It is clear from this comparison that labour migrants were more likely than average to be living in detached housing (30 per cent of labour migrants did so, compared with 15 per cent of all households). To a lesser extent, they were likely to be found in flats, and to be staying with relatives, or in hostels and bedsitters. They were comparatively unlikely to inhabit semi-detached houses (20 per cent of labour migrants, but 35 per cent of all households) and terraced houses (15 per cent of labour migrants, and 31 per cent of all households).

Changes in housing stock since 1964 (the time of Woolf's survey) may be partially responsible for this difference. In addition, the nature of the housing stock in the four labour market areas may be sufficiently different from that of the nation as a whole to affect the comparison. Data are available on the latter point from Hadjifotiou and Robinson. [12] In 1966, about 90 per cent of all dwellings were houses in both Chatham and High

PRESENT HOUSING TYPE

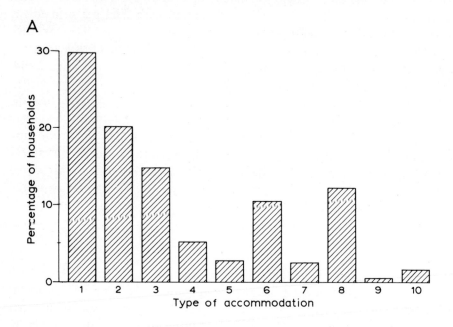

PREVIOUS HOUSING TYPE

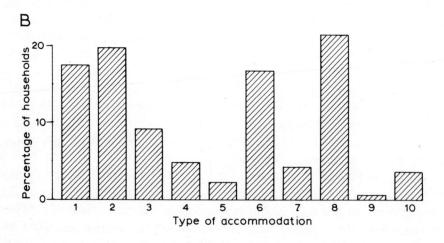

Fig. 7.13

PRESENT HOUSING TYPE (Sample SMLA s)

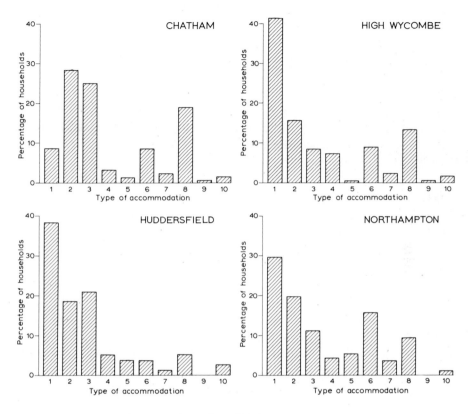

Fig. 7.14

Housing types:
1 detached house
2 semi-detached house
3 terraced/town house
4 detached bungalow
5 semi-detached bungalow
6 self-contained flat
7 flat with shared facilities
8 hostel, bedsitter, living with parents, in-laws, etc.
9 caravan
10 other

Wycombe. This compares with 81 per cent in Woolf's figures for England and Wales, and 67·5 per cent (Chatham) and 73·6 per cent (High Wycombe) for the proportions of labour migrants living in houses or bungalows. In Chatham Municipal Borough, 55 per cent of dwellings in 1971 were terraced houses, 28 per cent semi-detached, 14 per cent detached, and 3 per cent flats (although semi-detached dwellings were more important in other parts of the SMLA); in High Wycombe, the housing stock contained a high proportion of large detached housing. In the light of this information, it seems that houses in general were less likely to be occupied by labour migrants than were dwellings of other types; the apparent exception of detached housing may be due in part to the inclusion of High Wycombe in the sample.

There was considerable variation between SMLAs in the proportion of migrants in each house type. Even granted the scarcity of detached houses in Chatham, the low proportion of migrants moving into them is still surprising. In contrast, Huddersfield had a very high proportion of migrants in houses and bungalows (86 per cent), with only 5 per cent in flats. Northampton had the highest proportion in flats (19 per cent).

The type of house previously occupied by the labour migrant is tabulated in Table 7.20. The proportion of labour migrants living with parents or relatives, or in hostels or bedsitters, was far higher than it was after the move. Many of these labour migrants may have been leaving home to set up an independent household for the first time. There was also a high

Table 7.20

Type of previous accommodation of labour migrant households

Type of accommodation	Chatham No.	%	High Wycombe No.	%	Huddersfield No.	%	Northampton No.	%	Total No.	%
Detached house	9	7·1	51	28·7	16	21·1	20	11·7	96	17·4
Semi-detached house	24	19·1	31	17·4	25	32·9	29	17·0	109	19·8
Terraced/town house	11	8·7	7	3·9	10	13·2	22	12·9	50	9·1
Detached bungalow	5	4·0	7	3·9	1	1·3	13	7·6	26	4·7
Semi-detached bungalow	2	1·6	6	3·4	–		4	2·3	12	2·2
Self-contained flat	27	21·4	28	15·7	10	13·2	27	15·8	92	16·7
Flat with shared facilities	5	4·0	5	2·8	2	2·6	11	6·4	23	4·2
Hostel, bedsitter, living with parents, in-laws, etc.	38	30·2	33	18·5	7	9·2	40	23·4	118	21·4
Caravan	–		–		–		3	1·8	3	0·5
Other	4	3·2	9	5·1	4	5·3	1	0·6	18	3·3
No information	1	0·8	–		1	1·3	2	1·2	4	0·7
Total	126		178		76		171		551	

proportion in flats, and a much lower proportion in detached houses. Differences between the four SMLAs were similar to those noted with reference to present house type.

The majority (51·7 per cent) of labour migrant households were in the same type of accommodation before and after the move. The largest proportion of those who changed (13·2 per cent of all migrant households) moved from a flat to a house, while 7·1 per cent moved from a hostel or from living with parents or relatives to a house, and 5·1 per cent from a bungalow to a house. Only 2·7 per cent moved from a house to a flat, and 5·4 per cent from a hostel, or from living with parents or relatives, to a flat. These figures are in accordance with life-cycle theories of migration, demonstrating a tendency for migrants to take the opportunity of a change in job to adjust their housing to fit the changing needs and resources of their households.

Size of accommodation

Information was collected on the number of living rooms and bedrooms in labour migrants' accommodation (Table 7.21). Most households possessed

Table 7.21

Size of present accommodation of labour migrant households

	Chatham		High Wycombe		Hudders-field		North-ampton		Total	
	No.	%	No.	%	No.	%	No.	%	No.	%
Number of living rooms										
One	45	35·7	68	38·2	23	30·3	70	40·9	206	37·4
Two	61	48·4	67	37·6	32	42·1	77	45·0	237	43·0
Three	10	7·9	25	14·0	15	19·7	12	7·0	62	11·3
Four	1	0·8	7	3·9	5	6·6	3	1·8	16	2·9
Five or more	–		2	1·1	–		–		2	0·4
No information	–		2	1·1	–		–		2	0·4
Number of bedrooms										
One	8	6·4	5	2·8	4	5·3	18	10·5	35	6·4
Two	28	22·2	27	15·2	16	21·1	35	20·5	106	19·2
Three	71	56·4	92	51·7	31	40·8	84	49·1	278	50·5
Four	9	7·1	36	20·2	23	30·3	21	12·3	89	16·2
Five or more	1	0·8	9	5·1	1	1·3	4	2·3	15	2·7
No information	–		2	1·1	–		–		2	0·4
Room used as both living room and bedroom	5	4·0	6	3·4	4	5·3	5	2·9	20	3·6
Bedsitter	9	7·1	7	3·9	1	1·3	9	5·3	26	4·7

Table 7.22

The number of bedrooms and living rooms available to households, 1964

Percentage of all households

Number of living rooms	%	Number of bedrooms	%
None	3·6	None	0·1
One	18·3	One	15·5
Two	56·0	Two	30·1
Three	20·0	Three	46·6
Four or more	2·0	Four	6·0
		Five or more	1·6
Total sample	5,674	Total sample	5,674

Source: Woolf, Table 3.2, p. 51.

one (37·4 per cent) or two (43·0 per cent) living rooms, and three (50·5 per cent) bedrooms. Those moving to Huddersfield and High Wycombe were likely to be in houses larger than average with respect to both living rooms and bedrooms.

A comparison with Woolf's figures[13] (Table 7.22) shows that labour migrants tended to live in accommodation with a larger number of bedrooms than the national average. Whereas only 7·6 per cent of Woolf's sample lived in accommodation with four or more bedrooms, 18·9 per cent of labour migrants in the sample did so; 30·1 per cent of Woolf's sample lived in two-bedroom houses but only 19·2 per cent of migrants did so. These results accord with expectations derived from the family life-cycle approach to migration and from the income differential. If moves are being made by a growing family, regardless of whether space shortage is a motivation for the move, it is reasonable that they should prefer a larger than average dwelling and labour migrants may be better able than others to pay for such accommodation. It was also found that labour migrants, on average, tended to move to houses with fewer living rooms, compared with the households in Woolf's study. Little significance should be attached to this finding, however, as the difference might well be explained by architectural trends towards a combined lounge-dining room in the newer property favoured by labour migrants.

Little difference was found between the distribution of house size of labour migrant households before and after moving. Fewer labour migrants were living in one-bedroom dwellings after the move, and more were living in housing with more bedrooms. The proportion living in bed-sitters declined from 8·4 per cent to 4·5 per cent following the move. These figures mask a considerable amount of change in dwelling size for individual households. Thus 20·0 per cent of households had fewer living rooms and 22·5 per cent more than previously. Similarly, 17·8 per cent had fewer bedrooms and 30·1 per cent more bedrooms following the move. The changes in dwelling size can be explained in terms of life-cycle changes; many of those moving to smaller dwellings may have been leaving the parental home to set up an independent household, and others may have been older people whose needs for space diminished as their children left home. Increase in house size may be accounted for by growth in family size and by increasing ability to pay for a larger dwelling (see Chapter 8).

Amenities

The majority of households (65·9 per cent) had a garage provided with the accommodation. This contrasts with the 35 per cent of households with a garage reported in the 1966 Sample Census,[14] although this difference should be seen in the light of the rapid increase in garage provision between 1966 and 1972. Garages were more frequently available in High Wycombe, and less frequently in Chatham, than in the other SMLAs.

A garden was available to 84·2 per cent of migrant households; 5·4 per cent had other types of outside space, including shared gardens, and 10·5 per cent had no outside space. In Northampton, 18 per cent of households lacked outside space, reflecting the high proportion of flats there. Cullingworth's survey showed 69 per cent of all households with exclusive use of a garden and 24 per cent entirely without.[15] Again, the lapse of time makes the difference between our labour migrants and Cullingworth's sample rather less clear-cut. The high rates of provision of these amenities may in any case be explained by the high income and socio-economic status of the migrants.

Fewer of the migrant households (51·4 per cent) had garages prior to the move. The difference was greatest for migrants to Huddersfield, at least 20 per cent of whom acquired a garage as a result of the move. Only 74·2 per cent had a garden in their previous residence; the discrepancy here was greatest for migrants to Chatham, 36 per cent of whom had not possessed one before the move. Thus, the evidence of these two amenities, the garden and the garage, confirms that labour migrants improved their housing situation upon moving.

G

Housing tenure

It has already been suggested (Chapters 1 and 5) that labour migrants may show a different tenure pattern from the population as a whole, if only because accommodation in local authority housing is usually dependent on the household's length of residence in the area. The constraints on movement into dwellings of other tenures are less direct, but dwellings of different tenures vary in the ease with which migrants may move into them.

Table 7.23

A. *Present tenure of labour migrant households*

Tenure	Chatham No.	%	High Wycombe No.	%	Hudders- field No.	%	North- ampton No.	%	Total No.	%
Owner occupier with mortgage	61	48·4	102	57·3	47	61·8	93	54·4	303	55·0
Owner occupier without mortgage	6	4·8	9	5·1	3	4·0	7	4·1	25	4·5
Local authority tenant	9	7·1	2	1·1	9	11·8	5	2·9	25	4·5
Rents privately furnished	18	14·3	20	11·2	4	5·3	28	16·4	70	12·7
Rents privately unfurnished	6	4·8	8	4·5	6	7·9	18	10·5	38	6·9
Rent free, with parents, in-laws, housekeeper	16	12·7	14	7·9	4	5·3	7	4·1	41	7·4
Tied cottage, goes with the job, etc.	6	4·8	18	10·1	1	1·3	9	5·3	34	6·2
Lodger	4	3·2	5	2·8	2	2·6	4	2·3	15	2·7
Total	126		178		76		171		551	

B. *Previous tenure of labour migrant households*

Tenure	Chatham No.	%	High Wycombe No.	%	Hudders- field No.	%	North- ampton No.	%	Total No.	%
Owner occupier with mortgage	31	24·6	78	43·8	31	40·8	53	31·0	193	35·0
Owner occupier without mortgage	2	1·6	8	4·5	3	4·0	5	2·9	18	3·3
Local authority tenant	14	11·1	7	3·9	8	10·5	12	7·0	41	7·4
Rents privately furnished	18	14·3	27	15·2	13	17·1	27	15·8	85	15·4
Rents privately unfurnished	18	14·3	12	6·7	8	10·5	14	8·2	52	9·4
Rent free, with parents, in-laws, housekeeper	28	22·2	21	11·8	5	6·6	36	21·1	90	16·3
Tied cottage, goes with the job, etc.	8	6·4	13	7·3	6	7·9	17	9·9	44	8·0
Lodger	7	5·6	12	6·7	2	2·6	7	4·1	28	5·1
Total	126		178		76		171		551	

The survey data (Table 7.23 and Figs. 7.15 and 7.16) showed a preponderance of owner-occupiers among the migrant households (55·0 per cent were owners with a mortgage, and 4·5 per cent were owners without a mortgage). Those renting their home from the local authority constituted only 4·5 per cent of the sample; 6·9 per cent rented unfurnished accommodation and 12·7 per cent furnished accommodation from private landlords; 16·3 per cent lived in accommodation of other tenures, including 7·4 per cent living rent-free.

These figures showed a very great divergence from those for all households in the four SMLAs, as recorded in the 1966 Sample Census (Table 7.24, Fig. 7.15).[16] Although the proportion of owner-occupiers in the whole population is similar to the proportion in the survey, there were far more local authority tenants (22·3 per cent) and renters of private unfurnished accommodation (13·6 per cent) recorded in the census. On the other hand, only 2·5 per cent of the population as a whole were tenants of private-rented furnished accommodation. These results confirm the difficulties of access to the local authority and private unfurnished renting sectors of the housing market, discussed in Chapter 1.

A comparison of our survey findings with data from the 1971 Family Expenditure Survey for England and Wales[17] (Table 7.25) reinforces these points. It also shows that migrant households were more likely than others to be living rent-free. In the owner-occupier sector, a very much higher proportion of migrant than non-migrant households held mortgages; this is only to be expected, as most migrants were comparatively young and were unlikely to have completed mortgage payments on a previous house. They would, therefore, have lacked the capital to buy a new house outright, especially if it were larger and more expensive.

The variation in tenure patterns between SMLAs was extensive. In particular, the proportions moving into local authority houses varied from 11·8 per cent (Huddersfield) and 7·1 per cent (Chatham) to 2.9 per cent (Northampton) and 1.1 per cent (High Wycombe), although the proportion of total local authority stock within the SMLAs was similar. Some light is cast on these differences by Hadjifotiou and Robinson, who examined housing availability of different tenures in the four areas. They concluded that 'labour migrant households moving to any of the authorities in the High Wycombe labour market area would find council housing difficult to obtain quickly'.[18] Local authorities in the Chatham area had accepted a larger number of exchanges and transfers to local authority housing, and private-rented dwellings were particularly scarce. The High Wycombe area contained a large number of people living in tied accommodation, including 'gardeners, estate managers, chauffeurs and butlers, who

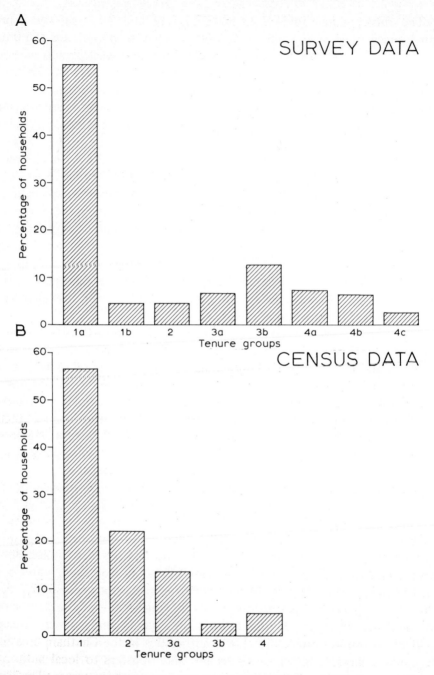

Fig. 7.15   A. Present tenure of labour migrant households
B. Tenure of all households in the four sample SMLAs, 1966. (Percentages
are derived as in Fig. 7.11A.)

182

Tenure groups: 1   owner-occupier
                 (a)   with mortgage
                 (b)   without mortgage

                   2   local authority tenant

                   3   rents privately
                 (a)   furnished
                 (b)   unfurnished

                   4   other tenures
                 (a)   rent free, with parents, in-laws, housekeeper
                 (b)   tied cottage, goes with job, etc.
                 (c)   lodger

are employed by the large land-owners in the area'. [19]

Many households changed tenure upon moving (Table 7.23 and Fig. 7.17). The figures for owner-occupation were especially striking. Only 35·0 per cent of migrant households had been owners with a mortgage, and 3·3 per cent owners without a mortgage. In total, then, the percentage of owner-occupiers before moving was lower than for the population as a whole. The proportion of local authority tenants, 7·4 per cent, was again much lower than that recorded by the census, but well above that for the present tenure of migrants. The figures for other types of tenure were all higher for labour migrants' previous accommodation than for their present accommodation, the difference being greatest for those living rent-free, many of whom may have been living with their parents.

If the statistics on the tenure of migrants' previous accommodation are compared to tenure figures for the population as a whole, we may infer differences in the propensity to become labour migrants between people in different tenure categories. It seems clear, that owner-occupiers were less likely than average to move. However, this generalisation refers entirely to those owning their dwellings outright; in contrast, those purchasing their dwellings were rather more mobile than average.

People renting from the local authority were much less likely to be labour migrants than average (7·4 per cent of labour migrants compared to 28·5 per cent of respondents in the Family Expenditure Survey). Those renting unfurnished accommodation privately were less likely to move than average, but the difference (9·4 per cent of the sample, compared to 15·6 per cent) was much smaller. Those in privately-rented furnished accommodation were far more likely to be labour migrants (15·4 per cent of the sample, but only 3·8 per cent of the Family Expenditure Survey

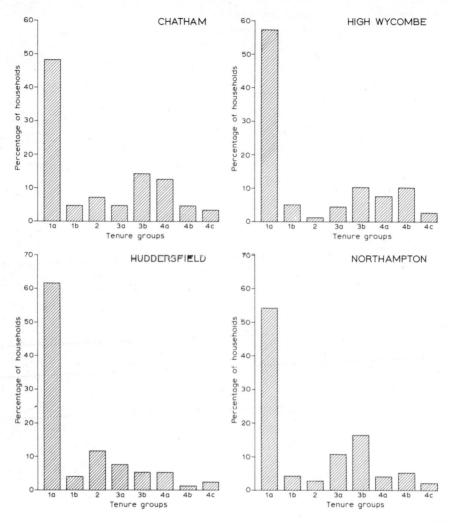

Fig. 7.16 Present tenures of labour migrant households by SMLAs. (Key as in Fig. 7.15.)

respondents). People in the other tenures also seemed to have a higher mobility rate than is typical for the entire population. This does not agree completely with Woolf's findings,[20] which referred to short-distance moves as well as labour migration; households moving from local authority and unfurnished privately-rented accommodation were much better represented in her sample.

Table 7.24

Tenure in SMLAs

Tenure	Chatham	High Wycombe	Hudders-field	North-ampton	Total
	%	%	%	%	%
Owner-occupier	56·6	59·1	55·7	53·7	56·7
Local authority tenant	22·5	20·3	24·1	22·2	22·3
Private tenant (unfurnished)	14·4	11·3	13·0	18·8	13·6
Private tenant (furnished)	2·2	2·6	2·9	2·2	2·5
Other tenures	4·3	6·6	4·3	3·1	4·9
Total on which figures are based	7,028	6,775	5,320	6,803	

Source: Housing Tables, 1966 Sample Census.
The percentages for the 'Total' column are produced by combining the figures for the SMLAs in proportion to their representation in the survey.

Table 7.25

Tenure of dwellings. England and Wales, 1971

	No.	%
In process of purchase by occupier	1,849	29·0
Owned outright	1,297	20·3
Local authority rented unfurnished	1,819	28·5
Rented unfurnished (other)	996	15·6
Rented furnished	239	3·8
Rent free	176	2·8
Total	6,376	

Source: Family Expenditure Survey, 1971, Table 58, p. 116.

A large proportion of migrants (45·7 per cent) moved between dwellings of the same tenure (see Table 7.26). Owner-occupiers with a mortgage both before and after the move constituted 30·7 per cent of the sample. Most of the much smaller number owning without a mortgage were able to remain in the same category, although some took out a mortgage after the move. It was less common for those who had been renting to transfer to accommodation with the same tenure. Only one-third of those who had been local authority tenants were still local authority tenants after the move, but rather more became owner-occupiers. Of those who had been renting unfurnished accommodation privately, more than half became owner-occupiers and only one-seventh did not change

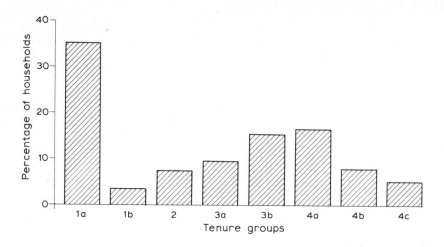

Fig. 7.17   Previous tenure of labour migrant households. (Key as in Fig. 7.15.)

their tenure. Tenants of private furnished accommodation were also most likely to become owner-occupiers (40 per cent), although a quarter of this group did remain in the same tenure. Another 15 per cent moved to rent-free accommodation. Among those who had been living rent-free, over 40 per cent became owner-occupiers, and over one-quarter moved to privately rented furnished accommodation, only one-tenth staying in the same tenure category. Households that had been living in 'tied accommodation' (housing that 'went with the job') were most likely to move to tied accommodation, although over half changed tenure, most frequently to become owner-occupiers.

The results indicate a strong tendency for households in almost all tenure groups to become owner-occupiers after the move. Renters of private accommodation and those living rent-free were the most likely to become new owner-occupiers. The largest group of local authority tenants (over half) had been local authority tenants before moving, and others had previously rented private accommodation. Those renting unfurnished private accommodation had come from many different previous tenures. There was a considerable amount of movement in both directions between private-rented furnished accommodation and rent-free tenures. Finally, lodgers were most likely to have come from rent-free accommodation, and were most likely to move to privately-rented furnished accommodation.

These figures illustrate the effect of movements through the life-cycle,

186

Table 7.26

Changes in tenure on move

Previous tenure	Present tenure							
	Owner with mortgage	Owner without mortgage	LA tenant	Rents privately furnished	Rents privately unfurnished	Rent free	Tied accommodation	Lodger
Owner occupier with mortgage	30·7	0·9	0·2	0·9	1·3	0·4	0·7	—
Owner occupier without mortgage	1·3	1·8	—	0·2	—	—	—	–
Local authority tenant	2·5	0·7	2·4	0·2	0·5	0·4	0·4	0·4
Rents privately furnished	6·4	0·2	0·4	3·8	1·6	2·4	0·5	0·2
Rents privately unfurnished	5·3	0·5	0·7	0·5	1·3	0·4	0·5	0·2
Rent free, with parents, in-laws, housekeeper	6·5	0·4	0·4	4·5	1·1	1·6	0·7	1·1
Tied cottage, goes with the job, etc.	2·0	—	0·5	0·7	0·5	0·9	3·3	—
Lodger	0·4	—	—	1·8	0·5	1·5	—	0·9

G 2

on the tenure status of migrant households, together with the desire for the greater security implied by owner-occupation. Most of those moving from rent-free status were presumably beginning their existence as separate households. The main currents of movement from rent-free accommodation were into furnished flats, direct into owner-occupied houses and, in smaller proportions, to unfurnished flats or to lodgings. Those in lodgings were most likely to move to furnished accommodation, and people in furnished accommodation were most likely to become owner-occupiers, although others moved to unfurnished accommodation. Households in this last tenure were again most likely to become owner-occupiers. All moves were not in these directions, however; there was a considerable flow, for example, of renters of furnished accommodation and of lodgers back to rent-free housing. There was also some movement out of owner-occupied tenure (over 10 per cent of owner-occupiers), mainly to unfurnished or furnished privately-rented accommodation.

In contrast to Woolf's findings (see Chapter 5), the figures also showed, for all tenures except owner-occupation and tied accommodation, a low proportion of people remaining in their original tenure. Local authority tenure emerged not only as comparatively uncommon among labour migrants, but also as a tenure which was difficult to enter. In this connection, it may be noteworthy that all but four of those who became local authority tenants for the first time were in-migrants to Huddersfield, where it was easier to get a local authority house.

These findings confirm and amplify those reported on the flows between different tenures in Chapter 5. It should be remembered that the flows reported here refer to labour migration only, and are thus not directly comparable to those studied in the other surveys which included many short-distance movers. This explains the low proportion moving from private renting to local authority housing. Movement within the owner-occupier sector was much greater than any other flow, movement between private-rented dwellings was considerably greater than movement between local authority dwellings. The largest flow between tenures was from private renting to owner-occupation; some way behind came the flows from local authority renting to owner-occupation and from owner-occupation to private renting. Movement from private to local authority renting and from local authority to private renting was much less frequent, and only one person in the sample moved from owner-occupation to a local authority house.

The distances moved by labour migrants to owner-occupied property followed roughly the same pattern as the distances moved by the whole sample. Labour migrants in other tenure categories, however, differed considerably

188

from the overall trends. Those moving to local authority dwellings had mostly moved a relatively short distance, as had those moving to private-rented unfurnished accommodation and to tied accommodation. Migrants moving to private-rented furnished accommodation were most likely to have moved a long distance: 58 per cent moved over 100 miles (160 km).

If the previous tenure of labour migrants is compared to the distance of their moves, a similar picture emerges. In this case, owner-occupiers moved longer distances than average, over three-quarters migrating more than 50 miles (80 km). This proportion was almost as high for those in private-rented furnished accommodation.

The relationship between tenure and income of labour migrants was marked by a tendency for those earning in the upper ranges to be owner-occupiers (Table 7.27). Those earning less than £80 per month were more strongly represented in the private-rented furnished sector than elsewhere. The range of incomes among local authority tenants was relatively small, and was above that of private tenants in furnished accommodation, similar to that of tenants of private unfurnished accommodation, and below that of most owner-occupiers. These results are similar to those reported by Cullingworth. [21]

A comparison with the data presented by Cullingworth for a sample of all households shows two main differences. First, among labour migrants, owner-occupiers were far more concentrated in the upper-income brackets. Second, there was a rather higher proportion of low-income people in furnished rented accommodation. Both these results seem to be in accord with what one might expect — the upper-income proportion related to the rapid increase in the cost of houses, the low-income proportion in furnished accommodation associated with the difficulties for in-migrants in obtaining local authority housing.

Labour migrants in the managerial and professional socio-economic groups (1—4) were more likely than those in the other groups to own their housing (78 per cent did so). Intermediate and junior non-manual workers (5—6) were also predominantly owner-occupiers, although the proportion of owners was only 54 per cent. Manual workers had rather lower owner-ship rates (44 per cent). Agricultural workers and personal service workers were, predictably, the two largest groups in tied accommodation, but members of many other socio-economic groups lived in such accommodation. Intermediate non-manual workers were the largest group in lodgings. Among those renting, manual workers were especially likely to be in local authority tenure. Junior non-manual workers were also strongly represent-ed in local authority tenures, but were also found in private-rented (especially unfurnished) accommodation. Intermediate non-manual and

Table 7.27

Present tenure by present net monthly income of labour migrant

Present tenure	Less than £40	£40 – £60	£60 – £80	£80 – £120	£120 – £240	£240 – £400	Over £400	Student	Unemployed	No information
Owner occupier with mortgage	0·2	1·1	2·0	11·8	26·5	9·6	1·5	–	0·2	2·2
Owner occupier without mortgage	–	0·2	0·5	1·5	1·3	–	0·9	–	–	0·2
Local authority tenant	–	0·2	0·7	2·4	0·9	–	–	–	0·4	–
Rents privately furnished	0·2	1·5	4·5	4·2	2·0	0·2	–	0·2	–	–
Rents privately unfurnished	0·5	1·1	1·3	1·6	1·6	0·2	0·2	–	–	0·4
Rent free, with parents, in-laws, housekeeper	0·5	1·3	1·6	2·2	0·7	–	–	–	0·7	0·4
Tied cottage, goes with the job, etc.	1·1	0·7	1·5	1·8	0·9	–	0·2	–	–	–
Lodger	–	0·4	1·1	0·5	0·4	–	–	–	0·4	–

professional workers were more likely to rent furnished accommodation.

Household type also bore a strong relationship to tenure for migrant families. Of the three most frequently occurring types of household, couples with all children under 15 years were heavily concentrated in the owner-occupier sector (77 per cent); couples with no children were slightly less heavily concentrated (72 per cent), and single adults were predominantly (62 per cent) in rented accommodation. In all categories except single adults and 'others', the majority of households were owner-occupiers. The rent-free tenures were mainly filled by single adults and 'others'; these

PRESENT MONTHLY HOUSING COSTS

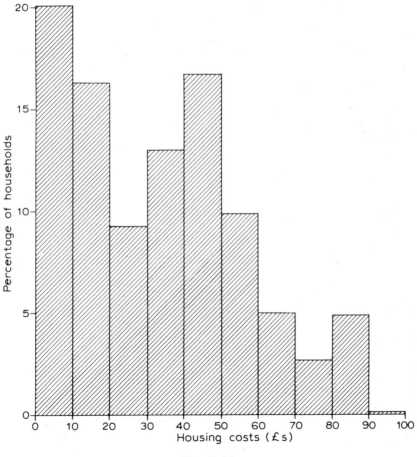

Fig. 7.18

two categories constituted all the migrant households in lodgings. Couples with young children were most likely to rent from the local authority; those in private-rented accommodation were more likely to be in un-furnished than furnished dwellings. Couples with no children were some-what more likely to be in furnished accommodation than unfurnished, and single adults much more so; indeed, 46 per cent of such single migrant households were in private-rented furnished accommodation.

Housing costs

Figure 7.18 shows the variation in housing costs among labour migrant

Table 7.28

A. *Present monthly housing costs of labour migrant households*

	Chatham		High Wycombe		Huddersfield		Northampton		Total	
	No.	%	No.	%	No.	%	No.	%	No.	%
Less than £10	29	23·0	37	20·8	15	19·7	30	17·5	111	20·2
£10 – £20	20	15·9	23	12·9	13	17·1	34	19·9	90	16·3
£20 – £30	12	9·5	12	6·7	9	11·8	18	10·5	51	9·3
£30 – £40	18	14·3	5	2·8	13	17·1	36	21·1	72	13·1
£40 – £50	30	23·8	14	7·9	20	26·3	28	16·4	92	16·7
£50 – £60	10	7·9	26	14·6	4	5·3	15	8·8	55	10·0
£60 – £70	0	–	23	12·9	1	1·3	4	2·3	28	5·1
£70 – £80	1	0·8	11	6·2	0	–	3	1·8	15	2·7
£80 – £90	3	2·4	22	12·4	0	–	2	1·2	27	4·9
£90 – £100	0	–	1	0·6	0	–	0	–	1	0·2
Over £100	0	–	0	–	0	–	0	–	0	–
No information	3	2·4	4	2·3	1	1·3	1	0·6	9	1·6
Total	126		178		76		171		551	

B. *Previous monthly housing costs of labour migrant households*

	No.	%	No.	%	No.	%	No.	%	No.	%
Less than £10	47	37·3	46	25·8	17	22·4	60	35·1	170	30·9
£10 – £20	30	23·8	31	17·4	22	29·0	34	19·9	117	21·2
£20 – £30	22	17·5	18	10·1	11	14·5	23	13·5	74	13·4
£30 – £40	18	14·3	28	15·7	15	19·7	26	15·2	87	15·8
£40 – £50	4	3·2	21	11·8	7	9·2	15	8·8	47	8·5
£50 – £60	1	0·8	16	9·0	2	2·6	2	1·2	21	3·8
£60 – £70	1	0·8	6	7·4	0	–	6	3·5	13	2·4
£70 – £80	2	1·6	3	1·7	0	–	2	1·2	7	1·3
£80 – £90	0	–	4	2·3	0	–	1	0·6	5	0·9
£90 – £100	0	–	0	–	0	–	0	–	0	–
Over £100	0	–	1	0·6	0	–	0	–	1	0·2
No information	1	0·8	4	2·3	2	2·6	2	1·2	9	1·6
Total	126		178		76		171		551	

192

PREVIOUS MONTHLY HOUSING COSTS

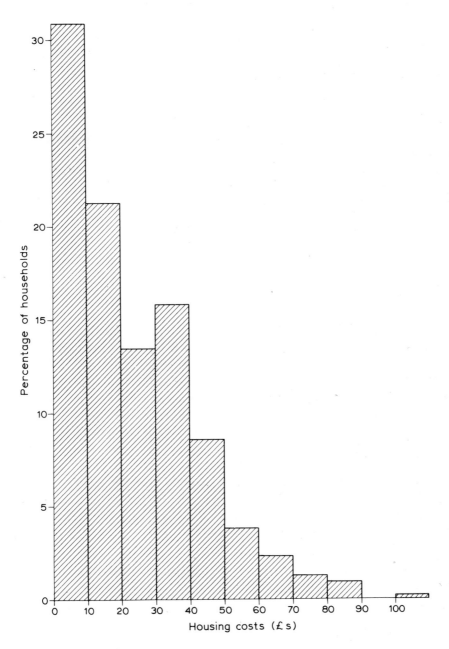

Fig. 7.19

households (see also Table 7.28). There was a great variation in expenditure, from the 20·2 per cent paying less than £10 per month to the 5·1 per cent paying more than £80 per month. The differences between the SMLAs were also sizeable; thus 69·0 per cent of migrant households in Northampton paid under £40 per month, compared with 65·7 per cent in Huddersfield, 62·7 per cent in Chatham, and only 43·2 per cent in High Wycombe. Assuming costs were evenly distributed within each £10 range, the mean monthly housing cost was £33·6, with the means for the SMLAs being £42·2 for High Wycombe, £30·1 for Northampton, £29·3 for Chatham and £28·5 for Huddersfield.

A comparison with the housing costs paid by labour migrants before moving (Table 7.28 and Fig. 7.19) shows that they had increased substantially. In particular, the proportion paying over £40 per month rose from 18·7 per cent to 43·2 per cent. The change was particularly great in Chatham, where the proportion rose from 7 per cent to 36 per cent; in High Wycombe previous housing costs, like present costs, were considerably higher than average, suggesting that many migrants to High Wycombe were accustomed to paying large amounts for accommodation. The mean monthly housing cost before the move was £23·4, and the means for in-migrants to the SMLAs were £18·5 for Chatham, £21·5 for Northampton, £22·1 for Huddersfield and £28·8 for High Wycombe. Average housing costs rose least for migrants to Huddersfield, and most for those moving to Chatham and High Wycombe, but the increase was substantial in all areas.

The study of individual migrant households confirms this trend; 57·9 per cent were in a higher housing-cost category following the move, while 23·7 per cent were in the same category and only 15·5 per cent were in a lower one. The present accommodation was more expensive by £30 per month or more for 20·8 per cent of migrants. In High Wycombe, 11 per cent were paying £50 per month or more in excess of their previous housing costs. In contrast, Huddersfield had the lowest proportion of labour migrants (47 per cent) whose housing costs had risen into a higher category.

Additional information is revealed by an examination of cross-tabulations of tenure and housing cost (Table 7.29), which shows that most households with high housing costs after moving were owner-occupiers with a mortgage (over 90 per cent of those paying over £40 per month). No local authority tenants paid more than £40 per month; there was a big range in housing costs for private-rented accommodation, the median for both furnished and unfurnished dwellings being around £20 per month. The mean housing costs for each type of tenure were as follows: £48·5 for owners with a mortgage, £13·6 for local authority tenants, £23·8 for

194

Table 7.29

Present housing costs by tenure

Present housing costs per month	Present tenure							
	Owner with mortgage	Owner without mortgage	LA tenant	Rents privately furnished	Rents privately unfurnished	Rent free	Tied accommodation	Lodger
Less than £10	0·3	60·0	24·0	8·6	18·4	92·7	97·1	33·3
£10 – £20	7·6	36·0	60·0	41·4	28·9	4·9	–	20·0
£20 – £30	4·3	–	12·0	25·7	21·1	2·4	–	46·7
£30 – £40	17·5	–	4·0	11·4	23·7	–	–	–
£40 – £50	29·4	–	–	2·9	2·6	–	–	–
£50 – £60	15·8	–	–	7·1	2·6	–	2·9	–
£60 – £70	9·2	–	–	–	–	–	–	–
£70 – £80	4·6	–	–	1·4	2·6	–	–	–
£80 – £90	8·9	–	–	–	–	–	–	–
£90 – £100	0·3	–	–	–	–	–	–	–
No information	1·9	4·0	–	1·4	2·6	–	–	–

The figures are percentages of households in each tenure group paying the stated housing costs.

private renters of furnished accommodation, £21·9 for private renters of unfurnished accommodation, and £16·5 for those in lodgings.

Just as there was a considerable range in the amount of money spent on housing by migrant households, so there were wide divergences in the proportion of total income that these costs comprised (Fig. 7.20 and Table 7.30). After migration the proportion of households paying less than 5 per cent of their household income for housing costs was 16·0 per cent (including those obtaining their accommodation rent-free), and 5·1 per cent paid more than 40 per cent of their household income. The mean percentage of household income spent on housing costs was 29·5. This figure is far higher than those quoted by Pennance and Gray (see Chapter 5). A high proportion of households in High Wycombe (38·8 per cent) spent over 25 per cent of their income on housing, whereas a comparatively low proportion (15·8 per cent) in Huddersfield spent more than 25 per cent.

A comparison of housing costs with the socio-economic group of the labour migrant indicates that managerial and professional workers paid considerably more for their housing than did manual workers. There was a

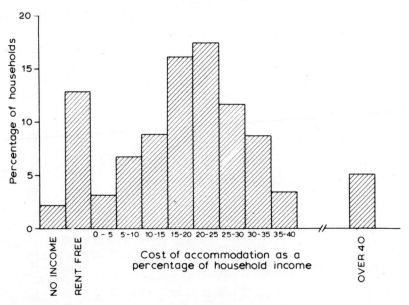

HOUSING COSTS AS A PROPORTION OF INCOME

Fig. 7.20

Table 7.30
Cost of present accommodation as a proportion of household income

Housing costs as a percentage of income	Chatham No.	%	High Wycombe No.	%	Hudders-field No.	%	North-ampton No.	%	Total No.	%
Household has no income	1	0·8	2	1·1	5	6·6	4	2·3	12	2·2
Rent free	22	17·5	30	16·9	3	4·0	16	9·4	71	12·9
Less than 5%	3	2·4	4	2·3	4	5·3	6	3·5	17	3·1
5% – 10%	5	4·0	8	4·5	6	7·9	18	10·5	37	6·7
10% – 15%	11	8·7	6	3·4	13	17·1	19	11·1	49	8·9
15% – 20%	23	18·3	22	12·4	16	21·1	28	16·4	89	16·2
20% – 25%	22	17·5	28	15·7	14	18·4	31	18·1	95	17·2
25% – 30%	14	11·1	26	14·6	6	7·9	18	10·5	64	11·6
30% – 35%	9	7·1	20	11·2	2	2·6	17	9·9	48	8·7
35% – 40%	3	2·4	10	5·6	2	2·6	4	2·3	19	3·5
Over 40%	8	6·4	13	7·3	2	2·6	5	2·9	28	5·1
No information	5	4·0	9	5·1	3	4·0	5	2·9	22	4·0
Total	126		178		76		171		551	

steady decline in amount paid, ranging from the employers and managers (71 per cent of whom paid over £30 per month) through professional workers (70 per cent), intermediate non-manual workers (53 per cent), junior non-manual workers (45 per cent), and skilled manual workers (34 per cent), to semi-skilled and unskilled manual workers (only 23 per cent of whom paid over £30 per month for housing).

Both houses and flats could use up very variable proportions of a migrant household's income. The survey results suggest, however, that people in flats were more likely than people in houses to spend a low proportion of their household income on accommodation (33 per cent of flat-dwellers and 27 per cent of house-dwellers spent under 15 per cent of their income on housing). At the same time some flat-dwellers were also likely to spend high proportions on accommodation (30 per cent of flat-dwellers compared with only 17 per cent of house-dwellers spent over 30 per cent of household income on accommodation).

Owner-occupiers

The majority of labour migrants in our sample were owner-occupiers. Residential mobility is a rather different process for those who must buy their homes; and in this section we consider features specific to this tenure category.

Table 7.31 and Figure 7.21 show the market values of the housing purchased by the 328 owner-occupiers in the sample.[22] This market value ranged from under £3,000 for 5 per cent to over £15,000 for a similar

Table 7.31

Market value of present accommodation when bought

Value	Chatham		High Wycombe		Hudders-field		North-ampton		Total	
	No.	%	No.	%	No.	%	No.	%	No.	%
Under £3,000	7	10	–		6	12	5	5	18	5
£3,000 – £4,500	7	10	2	2	17	34	24	24	50	15
£4,500 – £6,000	32	48	7	6	14	28	37	37	90	27
£6,000 – £7,500	11	16	26	23	3	6	18	18	58	18
£7,500 – £9,000	5	7	26	23	4	8	5	5	40	12
£9,000 – £12,000	4	6	18	16	4	8	8	8	34	10
£12,000 – £15,000	–		15	14	1	2	2	2	18	5
Over £15,000	1	1	14	13	–		1	1	16	5
Total	67		111		50		100		328	

The figures are percentages of the number of owner-occupiers recorded in each SMLA, not of the total number of labour migrants.

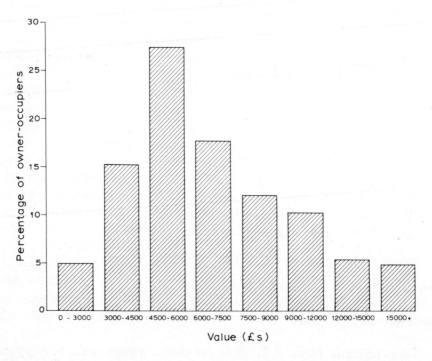

Fig. 7.21 Market value at time of purchase of present accommodation of labour migrant households. (The percentages refer to owner-occupiers only).

proportion. More houses were priced in the £4,500 − £6,000 price range (27 per cent of the total) than in any other price range. Houses were far more expensive in High Wycombe than in the other SMLAs (42 per cent there paid over £9,000); of the others, houses in Huddersfield seemed to be slightly cheaper. The average house price was £7,100, but SMLA averages ranged from £10,000 at High Wycombe to £5,800 at Northampton, £5,700 at Chatham and £5,200 at Huddersfield. Thus in High Wycombe the average price paid was almost twice that in the other three areas.

Those labour migrants who were owner-occupiers both before and after the move tended to realise slightly less from the sale of their previous accommodation than they paid for their new home. The average house price realised was £6,400, but was higher, at £7,300, for migrants to High Wycombe. For migrants to Northampton, the selling price of previous accommodation, averaging £6,000, was actually higher than the mean purchase price for their new accommodation, and the average selling prices in Chatham and Huddersfield were £5,200 and £4,800 respectively. Of those labour migrants who were owner-occupiers before and after the move, almost all going to High Wycombe found that their new accommodation had a higher market value than the old, but those moving to the other SMLAs were as likely to find these values comparable. In a few cases, especially at Northampton, the new house was cheaper than the old.

The monthly mortgage payment made by owner-occupiers was usually between £20 and £50 (62·1 per cent of households fell within this range). Some households, especially in Huddersfield, paid less, and the majority of households, especially in High Wycombe paid over £50 (22 per cent paid over £70 per month). These payments were considerably higher than those made by labour migrants for their previous accommodation, when 74·4 per cent paid less than £40 per month.

Most owners with a mortgage on their present accommodation had paid a deposit of up to 20 per cent of the price of the house; 25·0 per cent paid under 10 per cent of the price and 30·8 per cent paid between 10 and 20 per cent. Another large group, 24·7 per cent, paid between 20 and 40 per cent, and 3·0 per cent paid over 60 per cent of the purchase price as deposit. Very few labour migrants had a 100 per cent mortgage. Deposits tended to form a lower proportion of house price at Chatham than elsewhere, and a higher proportion at High Wycombe than elsewhere.

Other tenures

The proportions of households paying different levels of rent are shown in Table 7.32 and Figure 7.22. Interpretation of these figures is made more difficult by the fact that rates and other services are sometimes included

Table 7.32

Rent paid by households in all types of rented accommodation

Rent	Chatham		High Wycombe		Hudders-field		North-ampton		Total	
	No.	%	No.	%	No.	%	No.	%	No.	%
Rent free	23	39	31	46	4	15	17	24	75	34
Under £10	2	3	4	6	8	31	7	10	21	9
£10 – £20	16	27	14	21	7	27	22	31	59	26
£20 – £30	9	15	9	13	5	19	18	25	41	18
£30 – £40	5	8	4	6	1	4	3	4	13	6
£40 – £50	2	3	2	3	–		2	3	6	3
£50 – £60	–		2	3	–		2	3	4	2
Total	57		66		25		71		219	

The percentages are proportions of those households in rented accommodation.

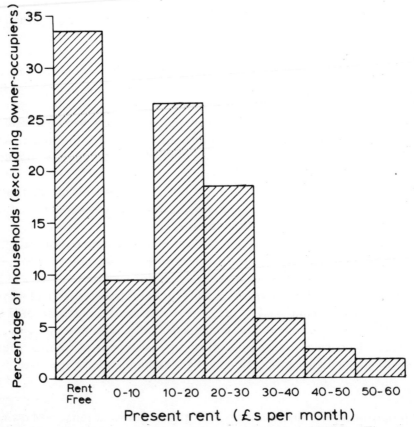

Fig. 7.22   Monthly rent paid by labour migrant households. (The percentages are calculated excluding owner-occupiers).

in the rent. Most households, excluding those living rent-free, paid between £10 and £20 per month (26 per cent of non-owning households) or between £20 and £30 (18 per cent). Migrants to Huddersfield were most likely to have the lowest rents (31 per cent paid under £10 per month); the 10 per cent of households paying over £30 per month were evenly distributed among the four SMLAs.

Rents paid by non-owning households in their previous accommodation were little different from those paid following the moves; in-migrants to Huddersfield were more likely to have paid higher rents prior to the move. Before the move, 4 per cent of households paid over £60 per month rent; such high rents may have proved an incentive to mobility, for no members of the sample paid this amount after the move. Thus, although housing costs for owner-occupiers increased after moving, this was not the case for those in other tenures.

Conclusion

In this chapter we have presented a large body of information about our sample of labour migrant households, their personal circumstances, their jobs and their housing, both before and after the move. No two of these households were subject to exactly the same constraints and inducements to move. Nevertheless, it may be helpful to attempt a classification of the sample, in order to link together our findings on the various attributes considered.

A large number of labour migrants (41 per cent) were in the managerial and professional socio-economic groups; many of these were in the higher income categories, and many travelled to work by car or train, often over fairly long distances (especially from Chatham and High Wycombe). They were likely to be relatively young, probably in the 25–34 and 35–44 age groups, married men, probably with two or three children under 15; their wives were probably not working. The move was likely to have been associated with an increase in income, to have covered 50 miles (80 km) or more, and not been their first long-distance move. Most of these migrants were likely to have been owner-occupiers with a mortgage both before and after the move; their houses were probably detached and built since the war. After paying 10 to 20 per cent of the purchase price as a deposit, £30 to £60 a month was spent on mortgage payments, rather more than they had paid for their previous houses; migrants such as these were more plentiful in High Wycombe than in the other SMLAs studied.

A second group of labour migrants consisted of less wealthy families, headed by intermediate or junior non-manual workers or manual, especially skilled workers. They were also likely to be married and most probably were aged between 25 and 34; many had some formal qualification for their work. Their moves were also likely to have led to an increase in income; for some, a change in socio-economic group may have resulted. This group had less of a record of previous mobility, and on average their moves were over relatively short distances. These migrants may have moved into owner-occupied housing, but were more likely to have become tenants, often of private unfurnished accommodation. Some were local authority tenants, and rather more gave up a council house upon moving. Most paid relatively little for their housing.

A third group of younger migrants, usually single or married without children, can be distinguished. These migrants, equally likely to be male or female, were mostly under 25, often with a good education and of professional or intermediate non-manual status. Many were starting out as independent households, often on leaving home or college. A smaller number were junior non-manual or manual workers, with less education. This third group was likely to be found in furnished accommodation rented from private landlords, although a few were in lodgings; often single migrants shared their accommodation with other single adults. Housing costs were usually high, but were shared between several people.

Many labour migrants do not fit into any of these moulds. Some moved in response to personal or economic circumstances so specific that their experiences are hard to generalise. Others had features in common with all three groups. More light is shed on the labour migrant households and their motivations in Chapters 8 and 9.

The survey findings bring out the importance of three themes in labour migration. The operation of the family life-cycle can be seen to underlie many of the moves reported in the survey. In particular, a large number of moves were made to launch an individual or a couple as an independent household; the fact that these moves also involved job changes may be incidental or may be explicable in terms of the national job market in which many students and others compete. A majority of moves seem to have been made primarily for job reasons, but the resultant move of home was also used as an opportunity to adjust housing to changes in family needs. This, in conjunction with the increase in income brought by the move for many people, led to a tendency for households to move to housing larger and more expensive than their previous accommodation.

A second theme is that of social mobility in combination with residential mobility. The first group of migrants discussed above was strongly career-directed. These migrants were in high-status occupations, in which mobility between jobs and between areas of the country may be a means of speeding advancement to the top of the career ladder, and may sometimes be essential for survival within a competitive work environment. Many of the third group also moved to pursue and further their careers; many had training and education which enabled them to compete for employment in any part of the country. Other workers had taken advantage of the move to increase their income, to take higher-status jobs or to become owner-occupiers.

Finally, a third theme, particularly relevant to the subject of this study, is the differential effect of the operation of the housing market on the selection of labour migrants. The small number of manual workers in the sample suggests that other sections of the population found mobility easier. The tenure and housing findings of the study indicate a reason: the great majority of migrants either possessed the financial resources to become owner-occupiers or belonged to families small enough to make furnished flats satisfactory for them. Local authority dwellings into which manual workers with families might normally be expected to move were grossly under-represented in the sample. One cannot infer a direct cause and effect relationship from the data presented in this chapter, but these findings at least point to the influence on labour migration of residential qualifications for local authority housing.

Notes

[1] At a number of places in this chapter, means are calculated on the basis of a set of categories, one or more of which may be open-ended. The following convention has been adopted: observations within an open-ended range are taken to average the sum of the lower limit of the category and the width of the preceding category. In the present case, the number of such observations is small, but in other cases considerable error may be introduced into the calculation of means.

[2] M. Woolf, *The Housing Survey in England and Wales: 1964*, HMSO, London 1967, p. 150.

[3] Ibid.

[4] A.I. Harris and R. Clausen, *Labour Mobility in Great Britain: 1953–63*, HMSO, London 1967, p. 104.

[5] *Survey of Personal Incomes: 1969–70*, HMSO, London 1972, p. 116.

[6] J.B. Cullingworth, *English Housing Trends*, Occasional Papers on Social Administration, no. 13, London 1965, p. 67.

[7] *Sample Census 1966, England and Wales: Workplace and Transport Tables*, HMSO, London 1968, pp. 366–584.

[8] Harris and Clausen, op. cit., pp. 116 and 121.

[9] N. Hadjifotiou and H. Robinson, 'Employment and housing conditions in four selected labour market areas in England and Wales', Housing and Labour Mobility Study, Department of Geography, University College London, *Working Paper* No. 5, 1972.

[10] Woolf, op. cit., p. 144.

[11] Ibid., p. 143.

[12] Hadjifotiou and Robinson, op. cit.

[13] Woolf, op. cit., p. 51.

[14] *Sample Census 1966, England and Wales: Housing Tables.*

[15] Cullingworth, op. cit., p. 21.

[16] *Sample Census 1966, England and Wales: Housing Tables.*

[17] Department of Employment, *Family Expenditure Survey: Report for 1971*, HMSO, London 1972, p. 116.

[18] Hadjifotiou and Robinson, op.cit., p. 41.

[19] Ibid., p. 40.

[20] Woolf, op. cit., p. 106.

[21] Cullingworth, op. cit., p. 70.

[22] It should be remembered that most of these houses were bought and sold in 1971; house price levels have risen sharply since that time, and these figures no longer reflect current conditions.

8 The Causes and Consequences of Labour Migration

Labour migration is a major upheaval for any household. Not only does it involve a change of employment for the head and possibly other members of the household, but it also presents them with the prospect of finding new accommodation in an area some distance away, during a relatively short time after the new job has been found. To these difficulties may be added the cost and personal or family upheaval of actually moving to a new area and establishing new social contacts, schooling arrangements, shopping habits and general patterns of daily life. With so many factors to be taken into account, it is obvious that some households are in a better situation to cope with the changes than others, and that each individual move is likely to entail a detailed sequence of events with unique elements. There are common influences at work, however, inherent in the motives for moving and in the ability of different income and socio-economic groups to deal with the problems which arise. The effects of these common influences at a very generalised level were discussed in Chapter 4, but it proved difficult, from the analysis of census data, to establish clear associations between the structure of labour migration and specific influences which might be expected to impinge upon individual households. The purpose of the questionnaire survey of labour migrant households was to outline the nature of these common influences and to explore the most significant factors which affect labour migrant behaviour.

Characteristics of the labour migrants interviewed have already been discussed in Chapter 7. Here, and in the next chapter, the process of labour migration will be examined in detail. For our purposes, two approaches to this examination are required. The first considers all aspects of the decision to move and its consequences, including the reasons why the individuals or families decided to make this important change, how they varied in the ways in which they approached the moves, how their lives changed as a result of migrating, what their view of the success of the changes was and, after moving, what they expected in the future. Here the influence of housing is likely to be only partial and must be placed in the context of other likely changes. The second approach will be pursued in Chapter 9, and explores the difficulties brought about by the search for accommodation itself, in order to analyse most directly the influence of housing market conditions on the ease of labour migratioñ. The survey cannot provide information on those who did not move at all because of housing or other difficulties: to a large extent these experiences are not amenable to the method of large-scale survey that we have undertaken. It can, however, indicate the types of workers who find the most difficulty when moving to new areas, as opposed to those who can move with relative ease.

This chapter will first examine the primary reasons which respondents gave for moving and will analyse the outcomes of the moves for those with different intentions. Then the consequences of the moves will be reviewed in terms of the principal changes noted by migrants and their satisfaction with life in the new area.

The reasons for moving

Although the questionnaire survey examined the experience of those who had changed their jobs in association with a recent move into the four sample labour market areas, it would be mistaken to assume that the acquisition of new jobs provides the only reason for such moves (Table 8.1). In fact, the survey identified a surprising range of unprompted reasons for labour migration and only half of the sample households moved specifically for employment reasons (including the setting-up of businesses). Several other primary reasons shared approximately equal significance; 'returning to an area of former residence' (suggesting a range

Table 8.1
Reasons for move to new labour markets

	Chatham		High Wycombe		Hudders-field		North-ampton		Total	
	No.	%	No.	%	No.	%	No.	%	No.	%
Job reason	52	41·3	95	53·4	39	51·3	86	50·3	272	49·4
Setting up business	3	2·4	4	2·3	4	5·3	2	1·2	13	2·4
Housing reasons	19	15·1	9	5·1	3	4·0	31	18·1	62	11·3
'Home town'	21	16·7	18	10·1	16	21·1	19	11·1	74	13·4
'Liked area'	6	4·8	17	9·6	2	2·6	11	6·4	36	6·5
Personal reasons	10	7·9	10	5·6	2	7·9	7	4·1	33	6·0
Travelling time	15	11·9	22	12·4	3	4·0	14	8·2	54	9·8
Other	–	–	12	6·8	3	4·0	1	0·6	7	1·3
Total	126		178		76		171		551	

of social and sentimental ties and constituting 13·4 per cent of the sample), the search for housing (11·3 per cent) and the desire to reduce the cost and time of travelling to work (9·8 per cent). More varied 'personal reasons' (including simply 'liking the area') made up another group of motivations (12·5 per cent).

The attraction of employment was significantly lower in Chatham than in the other three areas, although those moving to find housing and those returning there as an area of former residence were relatively numerous. In all these respects it differed from High Wycombe, where employment opportunities and the character of the area itself were the main attractions. Huddersfield attracted the highest proportion of those moving back to it as a 'home town' area, while Northampton seems to have been favoured because of the availability of housing. Journey-to-work time improvements were also most in evidence as reasons for moving to High Wycombe and Chatham.

It is very likely that the expectations and behaviour of labour migrants would be strongly affected by their reasons for making the changes. Those who moved primarily in search of new employment (about half the sample households) might be expected to be more concerned with income improvements, and perhaps with bettering their status as a result of the migration, compared with other households. In general, 'job-motivated' movements may reveal a relatively consistent and radical set of changes in the life-style of the household (such moves would include unemployed workers moving to new jobs).

The other reasons for moving must still have been influenced by job opportunities but are less easily summarized. A high proportion of those who said that they were moving primarily to return to an area which they already knew (where family and other contacts were already established), those who were mainly looking for a different type of accommodation, those who were seeking to reduce their journeys to work, and those who were simply moving to a new area because they liked it, must have been in occupations which are in general demand. Teachers, garage mechanics and building trade workers are examples of this type of worker with considerable freedom to move to new areas for employment, if other incentives become strong enough. The unemployed and those moving to their first jobs may also have this freedom. All of these reasons for migrating might be regarded as 'environmental improvement' reasons, based on a desire to improve the household's general living environment relative to its previous conditions rather than specifically to enhance its economic prospects.

Reasons for moving and income changes

Information was acquired both about the incomes of the labour migrants and of their households, before and after the moves. There were only minor differences in the structure of these two measures of income and their changes as a result of the moves, so that emphasis will be placed in what follows upon the income of the head of household alone. In total, the personal incomes of labour migrants grew as a result of their moves: incomes of less than £60 per month declined as a proportion of the sample, from 12 per cent to 9 per cent, while those of over £120 per month grew from 34 per cent to 47 per cent. To some extent, these changes reflect the general rise in incomes over the eighteen-month period during which the moves took place, (October 1970 to March 1972). There was also a significant element of movement to first jobs by students and to new jobs by the unemployed, so that their share of the sample fell from 9 per cent to less than 2 per cent as a result of the labour migration.

Figure 8.1 shows changes of income classified by reasons for moving. Although the income structure of the job-motivated movers was similar to that of the whole sample of labour migrants, there were some significant differences between them; for example, there is no evidence that 'job motivation' implied any special need to move away from poor economic circumstances (although some might have suffered redundancy if they had not moved). In fact, rather the contrary seems to be true, since most job-motivated migrants enjoyed higher incomes than average before they moved: 36 per cent had incomes of between £120 and £400, compared with the sample average of 31 per cent. Job-motivated moves also included a higher than average proportion of students going to new jobs and a smaller proportion with the highest incomes, of over £400 per month.

In a complementary fashion, the migrants who were not primarily job-motivated included a larger proportion than average of both low-income groups (less than £60 per month) and high-income groups (greater than £400 per month), as well as fewer students and more unemployed. This pattern, however, combines several facets. For example, those moving to reduce their travel times to work, often into High Wycombe and Chatham, included a large proportion with medium-high incomes, although some lower-income migrants also moved to Chatham for this reason. Many of those whose chief motivation was a return to a former area of residence, on the other hand, were among the less well-off (earning less than £60 per month) and unemployed, and Huddersfield featured markedly as a destination for this type of move. There is also some evidence of this reason for moving among the small sample of high earners (more than £240 per

208

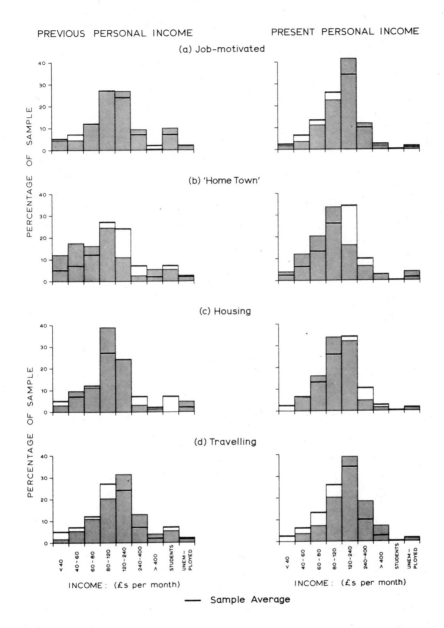

PREVIOUS PERSONAL INCOME   PRESENT PERSONAL INCOME

(a) Job-motivated

(b) 'Home Town'

(c) Housing

(d) Travelling

INCOME : (£s per month)   INCOME : (£s per month)

—— Sample Average

Fig. 8.1   Previous and present income structures of labour migrant groups compared with income structures of total sample. Labour migrants are grouped according to their motives for moving: (a) moving for employment reasons; (b) returning to an area of former residence; (c) moving for housing reasons; (d) moving to reduce cost and time of travelling to work.

209

month). Finally, the search for better accommodation was the main motivation for a high proportion of medium-income households (earning
£80–120 per month).

Perhaps of greater significance for the study of labour migration are the
contrasting results of the moves on incomes. Job-motivated movers tended
to improve their personal incomes more markedly than others (their share
of medium-high incomes, between £120 and £400 per month, growing
from 44 to 54 per cent), while there was little general improvement in the
structure of incomes for those moving for 'environmental improvement'
reasons. Both before and after the moves, 57 per cent of the incomes of
these labour migrants were below £120 per month. Afterwards, this percentage was about 10 per cent greater than the sample average and 18 per
cent greater than the average for job-motivated movers. To some extent,
these proportions were influenced by the relatively large numbers of
students and unemployed in the sample before migration, who moved for
a job and increased their incomes in doing so.

The bias towards low incomes was greatest among those returning to a
former area of residence (of whom 70 per cent earned less than £120 per
month both before and after the moves) and to a lesser extent among
those moving for housing reasons (of whom 63 per cent earned less than
£120 per month before and 56 per cent after the moves). Those seeking a
reduction in travel time were not typical of the other 'environmental
improvement' migrants, since they earned higher incomes than any other
group, both before and after their migration to a new labour market area.

Thus, in income terms, the expected pattern of 'spiralism' among job-
motivated migrants (see Chapter 5) is broadly confirmed by the results of
our sample survey. It contrasts with the experience of those, normally with
lower incomes in any case, who moved for other reasons and appeared to
gain little improvement in their incomes. A third group consists of those
high-income migrants who moved with the specific aim of reducing their
travel times to work.

Reasons for moving and socio-economic changes

The evidence for a strong relative upward movement in the income and
status of job-motivated movers is further strengthened by an examination
of socio-economic structure before migration in relation to reasons for
moving (Fig. 8.2a). A dichotomy emerged between socio-economic groups
(SEGs) 1–5 (employers, managers, professional workers and 'intermediate
non-manual' workers) and the others (SEGs 6–20). The higher-status occupation groups displayed a greater than average propensity to move for

210

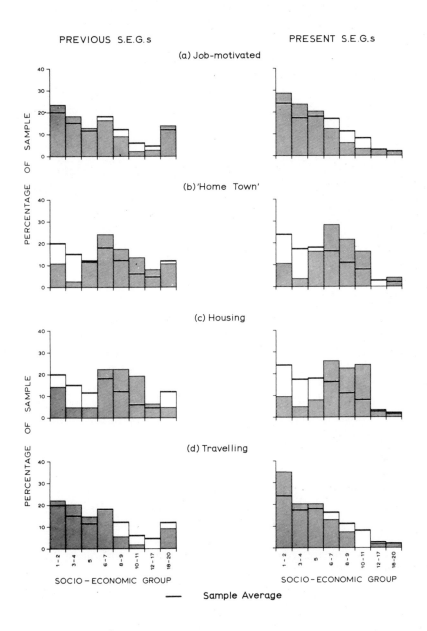

PREVIOUS S.E.G.s   PRESENT S.E.G.s

(a) Job-motivated

(b) 'Home Town'

(c) Housing

(d) Travelling

SOCIO – ECONOMIC GROUP   SOCIO – ECONOMIC GROUP

—— Sample Average

Fig. 8.2 Previous and present socio-economic structures of labour migrant groups compared with socio-economic structures of total sample. (Labour migrant groups are defined as in Fig. 8.1).

H

211

reasons of job-improvement (they made up 55 per cent of job-motivated movers, compared with 47 per cent of the whole sample). On the other hand, skilled manual workers (SEGs 8 and 9), semi-skilled and unskilled manual workers (SEGs 10 and 11) and other workers (SEGs 12–17) together included a much lower proportion of job-motivated movers than their share of the whole sample (14 per cent, compared with 23 per cent) would lead one to expect. Those not employed (SEGs 18–20) contributed only a slightly larger proportion than their overall share to job-motivated migration (14 per cent, compared with 12 per cent).

Amongst the 'environmental improvement' migrants, only those moving to reduce their travelling to work (Fig. 8.2d) were comparable with the job-motivated migrants. Before the moves, 57 per cent of this group was in SEGs 1–5, and afterwards no less than 76 per cent, compared with a sample average of 59 per cent in these SEGs. On the other hand, migration to an area of previous residence (Fig. 8.2b) or primarily to satisfy housing need (Fig. 8.2c) was particularly important for semi-skilled and unskilled manual workers (SEGs 10–11), skilled manual workers (SEGs 8–9), and junior non-manual and clerical workers (SEGs 6–7). Before migration, although these socio-economic groups represented only 37 per cent of the sample population, they comprised 56 per cent of the total 'home-town' movers and 64 per cent of those who moved for housing reasons.

Labour migration seems to have had the effect of polarising the socio-economic structures of the differently motivated groups still further. After movement, the predominance of SEGs 1–5 had increased amongst the job-motivated movers (72 per cent, compared with the sample average of 59 per cent), and a notably reduced proportion remained in SEGs 6–9 (junior non-manual and skilled manual) (Fig. 8.2a). Labour migration for job reasons was therefore a very positive agent of spiralism for the middle-classes, with the subsidiary function of providing opportunities for some unemployed workers. In contrast, the proportions of SEGs 6–11 (junior non-manual and all manual workers) grew markedly as a result of labour migration among those primarily moving either back to their 'home towns' or for housing reasons (Fig. 8.2b and c). Although the sample average proportion in SEGs 6–11 was only 36 per cent after the moves, it was 66 per cent of those returning to an area of previous residence, and no less than 77 per cent of housing-motivated movers.

From these data, it seems that the primary motivations of labour migrants are significant in distinguishing between those who benefit in terms of income and status (especially middle-class spiralists) and those who, in not seeking such gains, tend to preserve a manner of life which is generally

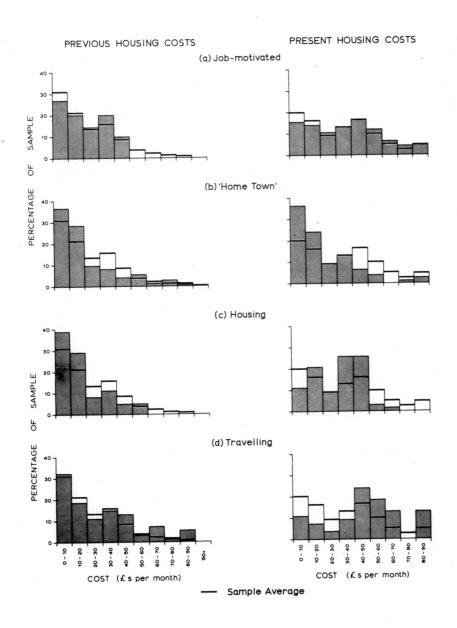

PREVIOUS HOUSING COSTS   PRESENT HOUSING COSTS

(a) Job-motivated

(b) 'Home Town'

(c) Housing

(d) Travelling

COST (£ s per month)   COST (£ s per month)

—— Sample Average

Fig. 8.3   Previous and present housing costs of labour migrant groups
compared with housing costs of total sample. (Labour migrant groups are
defined as in Fig. 8.1).

213

poorer in material terms. This analysis cannot specify the degree to which this contrast is a matter of choice or of necessity.

Reasons for moving and housing costs

A major aspect of the housing changes which resulted from labour migration was the increased cost of housing. In general, there was no significant difference before migration between the housing costs of job-motivated movers and the rest of the sample. About 80 per cent of all households spent less than £40 per month on housing, with potential job-motivated movers forming a higher proportion of those spending £30-40 per month and a lower proportion of the larger number who paid less than £10 (Fig. 8.3a). After the moves, the expenditure on accommodation by all the migrants increased sharply, so that only 59 per cent were spending less than £40 per month. Those moving mainly for job reasons, however, were now spending rather more on housing, with only 53 per cent having an outlay of less than £40 per month. Thus, to offset the higher earnings after the move of the job-motivated migrants, higher housing costs were also incurred, with 45 per cent spending more than £40 per month after moving, compared with 17 per cent doing so before.

The housing costs of the groups moving for various 'environmental' reasons both before and after the moves, display marked contrasts. In general, those moving back to an area which they already knew (Fig. 8.3b) or for housing reasons (Fig. 8.3c) had markedly low housing costs before migration (65 per cent of the former group and 68 per cent of the latter were spending less than £20 per month on housing, compared with 52 per cent sample average). In fact, no household migrating primarily in search of new housing had spent more than £60 per month on accommodation before the move. After moving, these two groups changed their housing cost profiles in opposite directions. The 'home-town' movers virtually retained their share of low-cost accommodation; 60 per cent were paying less than £20 per month after the moves, and most noticeably, the proportion paying virtually nothing for housing (36 per cent paid less than £10 per month) stayed at the same high level. Evidently, a significant section of these 'home-town' movers were living with relatives or in similar rent-free circumstances; only 15 per cent of them paid more than £40 per month, compared with the sample average of 39 per cent. In contrast, the proportion of households moving specifically for housing reasons and paying the lowest category of housing costs declined greatly. Those paying less than £10 per month fell from 39 to 11 per cent, while those paying between £30 and £50 per month rose from 16 to 51 per cent.

214

Most labour migrants increased their housing costs as a result of the moves, whether for jobs, reduced travel times to work, or for housing, although the income and socio-economic status of the last group did not allow them to pay the highest levels of housing cost. Those migrants returning to a former area of residence, however, retained low housing costs, no doubt because of their connections with the destination area. The predominance of single adults in this group, compared with the others, gives some indication of the reasons for this unusual situation.

The 'environmental improvement' migrants who paid the highest housing costs after migrating were those moving for travel-to-work reasons. In having a very high proportion paying more than £40 per month for housing after the moves (68 per cent compared with the sample average of 39 per cent), this group was more comparable with the job-motivated migrants than with the other 'environmental improvers'.

In the light of this analysis, it is to be expected that the net effect of labour migration on the share of household incomes being spent on housing was to lay a much lighter burden on the 'home-town' movers, compared with any other group. This must largely explain why this group is so well-represented in our sample; the financial benefits to be derived from such moves are clearly considerable, with 46 per cent of these 'home-town' migrants spending less than 15 per cent of their incomes on housing

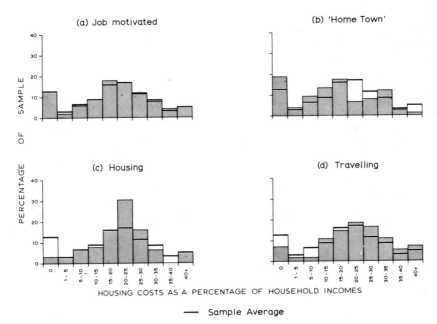

Fig. 8.4 (Labour migrant groups are defined as in Fig. 8.1).

after the moves, compared with an average of 32 per cent for the whole sample (Fig. 8.4b). On the other hand, the cost of housing increased most for those who moved for housing reasons (Fig. 8.4c). Only 21 per cent of the housing-motivated migrants were spending less than 15 per cent of their incomes on accommodation after the moves, compared with 30 per cent of the job-motivated migrants and 22 per cent of those movers, generally with high incomes, who were mainly concerned to reduce travel times. Although housing-motivated migrants were not prominent among those spending the highest proportions of their incomes on housing, nevertheless the burden of actual housing costs as a result of labour migration still seems to have been the heaviest for this group.

On balance, in spite of their increased absolute levels of housing expenditure, the proportion of the incomes of job-motivated migrants spent on housing after their moves was only marginally greater than for other labour migrants; 48 per cent spent 15–30 per cent of their household incomes on housing, compared with the sample average of 45 per cent. It appears, therefore, that even in a time of high housing costs, the job-motivated movers were able to keep up with the increase through the earnings benefits of mobility.

Reasons for moving and contrasts between sample SMLAs

In examining the reasons for labour migration, the complex relationships between family goals, incomes, social class and geographical location are well reflected in the experiences of respondents from the four sample areas. It is clear that the four SMLAs experienced different types of in-migration, reflecting their varied economic structures and prosperity.

In particular, an interesting contrast emerged between High Wycombe and Chatham. High Wycombe has already been described in Chapter 6 as an area from which attractive jobs for managerial and professional workers can be obtained; an area whose in-migrants are actively engaged in middle-class spiralism. Chatham offers a clear social contrast, since a high proportion of its respondents were in junior non-manual and manual groups. Both SMLAs contained an above-average proportion of respondents who moved in for travel reasons to reduce their journeys to work; but there the similarity ends. High Wycombe attracted a high proportion of migrants moving for job reasons, while Chatham included a distinctively low proportion of these among its respondents. A low proportion of migrants in High Wycombe moved in for housing reasons, but a high proportion in Chatham. In High Wycombe few migrants were returning to former areas of residence, but many were moving in because they 'liked the area'. The reverse situation existed in Chatham.

Similarly, Northampton and Huddersfield showed some contrast in the reasons why people moved into them. Although both SMLAs received similar proportions of job-motivated movers, Northampton emerged as the most attractive place for those primarily seeking housing, while Huddersfield was the least attractive of the four in this respect. On the other hand, Huddersfield was popular as a place to return to, while Northampton was not. In addition, Huddersfield appealed to some people as a place in which to bring up their children (the only SMLA of the four studied where this factor appeared to be significant), although few people actually admitted to liking the area!

Reasons for moving and the significance of housing choice

From the experience of households in the sample survey, it seems clear that housing has a varying level of significance for labour migrants with different motivations. Three broad groups of migrants can be identified.

The first group consists of those moving for job-motivated reasons. For them the search for accommodation follows an earlier decision to change job, and will often take place in the context of a rise in income. Therefore, many of these migrants will be able to afford a more expensive house.

For a second group the search for better housing is itself a prime reason for moving. We have seen that those who move for this reason are normally employed in fairly generally available occupations, especially in the manual and lower-paid non-manual jobs. However, they have to be prepared to pay a higher proportion of their incomes for accommodation after moving.

A third group gives priority to improvements in their general living environment, but the primary motivation varies. This group ranges from low-paid or even unemployed, unmarried workers returning to their home town to live with relatives, to well-off families moving within the southeast to an area where house and job opportunities are expected to be closer together. For a variety of reasons the members of this third group find the search for accommodation to be of subsidiary importance, although the availability of suitable accommodation is obviously necessary for the moves to be possible.

Generally speaking, the common element amongst the varied types of household in this group is that their acquisition of accommodation is a by-product of other decisions to move. Their attitudes to the search for accommodation are therefore heavily influenced by their income and status before moving, since the move itself did not produce any notable change in their material circumstances.

217

The consequences of labour migration

The balance of loss and gain

In the first half of this chapter, the material outcome of labour migration has been examined, using income, occupational status and housing costs as indices of change. The main reasons for migration, stated retrospectively by the migrants, have provided a framework for this analysis, and the varying significance of housing choice has been emphasised for households with different purposes in migrating. The rest of the chapter will be concerned with the results of the moves, as perceived by the respondents at the time of the interview.

The labour migrants were asked (Question 46) whether there was anything they felt they had gained as a result of the moves. The results are presented in Table 8.2. About 40 per cent said that they had derived benefits mainly associated with employment (22 per cent with increased incomes, 9 per cent with 'a better job' and another 10 per cent thought they were gaining valuable work experience). This response was considerably less frequent in Huddersfield than in the other three areas, all of which had similar proportions. Another 31 per cent were most impressed by the improvements either in their social life or in their living environment. This group was especially prevalent in Huddersfield. Reduced travel times to

Table 8.2
Gains resulting from moving

	Percentage of migrants				
	Chatham	High Wycombe	Hudders-field	North-ampton	Total
Improvement:					
Job	7·9	7·9	7·9	10·5	8·7
Income	25·4	24·7	9·2	22·2	22·0
'Experience'	8·7	9·0	11·8	9·9	9·6
All employment	42·0	41·6	28·9	42·6	40·3
Recreation	0	1·7	0	2·3	1·3
'Social life'	19·8	14·6	19·7	17·0	17·2
Environment	6·4	12·9	10·5	8·2	9·6
Standard of living	0·8	0·6	5·3	3·5	2·2
Schools	0	1·1	1·3	0·6	0·7
All 'Social and environmental'	27·0	30·9	36·8	31·6	31·0
Travel time	11·1	10·7	14·5	14·0	12·3
Housing	7·9	5·1	6·6	8·2	6·9
No improvement:	8·7	10·1	13·2	2·3	7·8

Table 8.3

Main reasons for moving of labour migrant households
compared with assessed main gains from moving

Reasons for moving	%	%	Gains from moving
Job and business	52	40	Income, better job, experience
'Home town', liked area, 'personal'	25	31	Social life, environment, recreation, schooling, standard of living
Travel times reduced	10	12	Travel times reduced
Improved housing	11	7	Better housing
		8	No gain

work were mentioned by 12 per cent, and improved housing by only
7 per cent. Only 8 per cent considered that they had received no benefits
from the change, although it will be shown below that a larger proportion
than this had missed some features of their former area of residence.

On balance, the gains are generally in line with the reasons given for
moving by the migrants (Table 8.3). It is clear that more migrants gave
employment benefits as reasons for moving than considered them as resultant gains (52 per cent compared with 40 per cent). In contrast, social
and environmental improvements, concerned with rather more intangible
aspects of family life-style, feature more prominently in the final assessment of migration. Many of these improvements are incidental to the
general process of finding new jobs and housing, and they cannot be
properly anticipated before the move has taken place. Afterwards,
however, they may be seen as comprising important benefits of migration, if only because of their unexpected nature. The same may be said of
improvements in travel time to work, although some sample households
deliberately sought this benefit. Improved accommodation may be
analogous to the employment motivation, since it can be anticipated
fairly precisely before the event and may be taken for granted as a benefit
in retrospect.

Thus the difference between the percentages of the sample population
seeking and achieving various benefits may indicate the relative degree to
which some aims may be precisely anticipated in advance, while others are
less clearly definable and can only emerge later.

Although 90 per cent of the sample population were able to see some
gains from migration, about 70 per cent also missed something from their
former lives. These regrets almost entirely concerned broad social and

H2

Table 8.4

Aspects missed from previous area of residence

	Percentage of migrants				
	Chatham	High Wycombe	Hudders-field	North-ampton	Total
Friends and relatives	18·3	13·4	22·4	20·5	18·0
Environment	28·6	25·9	28·9	15·4	23·8
Recreation facilities	11·9	11·2	7·9	14·0	11·8
Entertainment and shopping	13·5	9·6	7·9	16·4	12·3
Missed nothing	23·0	27·5	26·3	26·9	26·1
Other	4·7	12·4	6·6	6·8	8·0

environmental characteristics of the former situation, rather than any specific employment or housing factors (Table 8.4). Most frequently mentioned was a range of environmental conditions, including 'missing the city', 'the country', and 'the sea'. These constituted 24 per cent of the replies for the sample as a whole, but represented a much lower proportion in Northampton than in the other three SMLAs. Following these in importance was the loss of contact with friends and relatives (22 per cent in Huddersfield, in spite of its 'good image' as a town with some social life, and lowest in High Wycombe). Entertainment and shopping were about equal in importance to recreational facilities (both about 12 per cent). In both cases these amenities were missed least in Huddersfield and most in Northampton. Over one-quarter missed nothing from their old area of residence, and this sentiment was most in evidence in High Wycombe, least in Chatham.

In an attempt to summarise the subjective assessment by migrants of the results of moving, they were asked (Question 47b) whether, on balance, they were more or less happy since moving. Two-thirds of the migrants claimed to be happier than before and only 13 per cent were less so. Most prominent among the satisfied labour migrants were those in owner-occupied housing and rent-free accommodation, those with either low or high incomes and in the 25—34 age group. Least happy were households in rented property of all types, the middle-aged and middle-income groups, and those in the more senior clerical and other non-manual jobs (SEGs 5 and 6).

Perceived changes in social life

It is clear that factors other than a new job or the achievement of satisfactory accommodation are important in evaluating the success of labour migration. The acquisition of new social ties and the general acclimatisation of households to the new environment provide stimuli and opportunities which are difficult to anticipate.

In fact, 85 per cent of the sample labour migrants had expected a change in their social life, although only 70 per cent judged that they had experienced such a change. Young manual and junior non-manual workers, with little experience of migration, most often expected change, although small (two-person), middle-income households, in non-manual occupations tended to have noted a change more frequently.

Some contrasts in the social life found in the four sample areas seem also to have affected these patterns and were reflected in the answers to Question 43a. The balance of replies was most complimentary to Huddersfield and least complimentary to High Wycombe. The more detailed comments suggested a contrast between Huddersfield and Chatham. A high proportion of migrants in the former area thought that they had a better social life and entertained more (the number must have included many of those returning to it as a former place of residence), although a lower proportion than average (perhaps reflecting those in-migrants without pre-established ties in the town) were involved in clubs and other activities. Such amenities were more commonly mentioned in Chatham, but fewer labour migrants there than in Huddersfield thought that they had a better social life. The contrast seems to reflect the more informal family ties of migrants to Huddersfield and the relatively impersonal, communal facilities that tend to be recognised by labour migrants to Chatham. The responses from Northampton showed a relatively high expectation of a changed social life when moving to the town, but criticised its lack of amenities. The weight of opinion from High Wycombe, however, shows a marked alienation of labour migrants, with the most frequent mention in all of the SMLAs of missed contacts with relatives and friends, of the unfriendliness of the people in the area and of the relative lack of family or home entertainment compared with past experience.

This picture can be given further detail through an examination of the 54 per cent of the sample who already knew people in the area before moving in (Question 45a and b). Although High Wycombe contained the highest proportion of these, many said contacts there were with friends (47 per cent), rather than with relatives. Chatham, on the other hand, had the highest proportion of local contacts with relatives (17 per cent). More significant, perhaps, was the fact that only 20 per cent of the sample admitted to being strongly influenced by the presence of friends or relatives in the destination area, and this was highest in Huddersfield and lowest in Northampton. In general, single adults and young families in the

Table 8.5
Percentage of each socio-economic group enjoying various gains from moving

	SEGs (after moving)								
	1–2	3–4	5	6–7	8–9	10–11	12–17	18–20	Total
Improvements:									
Housing	3	2	5	9*	10*	18*			7
Job/Income/ Experience	40	46*	59*	26	41	25	(40)		40
Social life	15	13	13	24*	30*	23*			17
Environment	19*	6	7	11*	2	10			10
Travel time	14*	18*	8	20*	5	9			12
No improvements	19*	6	7	11*	2	10	(20)	(30)	10

*Greater than average.
Percentages based on very small sample shown in brackets.

junior non-manual and skilled manual socio-economic groups were most influenced by the presence of friends and relatives, while managerial and professional groups, especially childless couples or young families, were least influenced. Thus, the priorities which migrants had with the destination area broadly explain their reactions to the four SMLAs.

Perceived benefits of migration, by housing tenure and socio-economic groups

Housing benefits may be put into perspective by viewing them in the context of a wider 'net advantage'. For example, housing gains were most important, in the context of all the possible benefits, for those moving into owner-occupied property, but those moving to private-rented accommodation most frequently failed to see any general improvement at all in their life-styles as a result of the moves. On the other hand, income improvements were the most important benefits mentioned by those moving to local authority housing, rent-free and tied accommodation. These are the ways in which accommodation seems to exert an influence on the general success of labour migration. More generally, however, the benefits of change can be most comprehensively related to socio-economic characteristics. In essence, employment (including income) improvements were distinctively concentrated in the professional and senior non-manual groups (SEGs 3–5) (Table 8.5). A second group, consisting largely of manual workers (SEGs 8–11) and junior non-manual workers (SEGs 6–7),

Table 8.6

Percentage of each income group enjoying various gains from moving

| | Income groups (£s per month) | | | | | | | |
	<40	40–60	60–80	80–120	120–240	240–400	>400	Total
Improvements:								
Housing	–	14*	7	8*	6	4	–	7
Job/Income/ Experience	–	25	48*	41*	39	49*	(40)	40
Social life	(32)	28*	19*	19*	17	8	–	17
Environment	–	–	7	8	11*	15*	(20)	10
Travel time	–	9	5	10	18*	15*	(20)	12
No improvements	–	17*	10*	8	5	6	–	8

*Greater than average.
Percentages based on a very small sample shown in brackets.

appear to gain most either in housing or in their social lives. Finally, improvements in their living environment or in shortened travel times seem to have been most noted by managerial and by some junior non-manual and clerical workers.

These summary distinctions can be given perspective by analysis according to incomes (Table 8.6). All groups seemed to have gained to some extent in their employment (either through income improvement or through better prospects), except for the lowest paid (less than £60 per month). The highest paid were most specifically aware of improved levels of income (many of these were in the managerial groups). All income groups seemed to have enjoyed some improvement in social life, except for the highest paid (greater than £120 per month), and this benefit was especially valued by the lower-income groups. In addition, the poorer workers either tended to appreciate better accommodation or could see little improvement in their circumstances after migrating. Those who appreciated a better living environment or travel-to-work improvements, on the other hand, were generally the higher paid.

Expectations for the future

The discussion in this chapter about the motives for labour migration and the satisfaction derived from it may, finally, be extended to an investigation of the prospects for future moves, as envisaged by the migrants themselves. The question in the survey about whether labour migrants expect to be living and working in the area in five years' time (Question 50) is not an ideal indicator of any real future changes. Attitudes and personal circumstances are too volatile for this to be so. The question does, however, provide an extrapolation into the future by the migrants in the sample of their recent experience. As might therefore be anticipated, the answers to it reinforce the impressions built up so far about the nature of labour migration.

Only 40 per cent of the respondents expected to be living in the present labour market area five years later, 45 per cent expected to move and 15 per cent were unable to answer. The reasons for the likely future moves repeat the types of priorities that have already been discussed at length. Just over a quarter of those who expected to move within five years gave employment reasons for their expectation; for example, getting a better job, gaining further experience, moving as a result of reorganisation by their present employer or setting up their own business. 10 per cent of responses (which included some 'double-reason' replies) were from those who intended to move to another area or environment, and another 7 per cent thought that they would move for family or educational reasons. Only 3 per cent of those who expected to move within five years felt that the search for better housing would cause them to move. A high proportion of migrants to Huddersfield expected to have to move again for employment improvements, although relatively few felt that other reasons would cause them to leave. 'Environmental reasons' were more likely to cause people to move from Chatham, family reasons from Northampton and housing problems from High Wycombe.

High-income earners more commonly expected to undertake future moves in search of better jobs, to broaden their work experience or to comply with the changing needs of their present employer. Housing and environmental improvements remain the preoccupation of the low-middle income groups (£80–120 per month) while 'personal' reasons were most likely to cause lower-income households (less than £80 per month) to move again. In terms of socio-economic groups, this means that prospects of better employment are likely to cause managerial, professional, senior administrative and senior clerical workers to move, that housing prospects are more critical for the skilled-manual workers, and that environmental and personal reasons will be viewed as more important by the semi- and unskilled manual workers, as well as by some of the junior non-manual groups.

If attitudes about the future are related to the apparent success of the recent migrations, further evidence emerges which reinforces the conclusion that migration experience is very much a by-product of the general living experience of households in different occupation and income groups. Those, for example, who had obtained the type of accommodation that they were seeking were most likely to anticipate future employment changes. Others, who had experienced more difficulty in the housing search, were either hoping to move on to gain further working experience (which might explain why they were willing to accept current accommodation that was less than satisfactory) or preferred some other area in any case.

Viewed in terms of the total balance of satisfaction, households which were happier since moving were also likely to move in the future for job reasons, no doubt having been encouraged by their recent experience. Those who thought that they were less happy tended to feel that they would be moving for personal reasons to some other area where they would prefer to live. This confirms the earlier impression that failure of labour migration to improve the lives of households was associated with personal and family ties.

Conclusion

The first half of this chapter discussed the reasons given by labour migrants for their moves, and related them to income, socio-economic group and housing costs. Housing choice was seen to have a threefold significance, depending on whether or not it was overshadowed by other primary motivations and upon the financial and social gains which can be anticipated from the moves. Even though reasons for moving are diverse, the consequences of the changes seem to be even more varied in the retrospective judgement of labour migrants. Clearly, it is not easy to predict the level of, or reasons for, general satisfaction in a labour migrant household simply from the reasons given for moving. New living circumstances generate different attitudes to work, social life, environment and housing, which are probably impossible to anticipate in advance. But it seems that housing, in its widest sense, including the social and environmental context of a dwelling, becomes very important, especially when marked improvements in income or job prospects have not followed the move. It is clear from the second part of this chapter that different groups make different evaluations from their new situations after migrating. There is also, very often, the consolation that the household can move on again in the foreseeable future, a prospect which some groups are better equipped to deal with than others. In this way, migration experience appears to be a facet of the more general economic and social mobility of a household.

Thus, the conclusions of this chapter confirm the situation which was anticipated on *a priori* grounds in Chapter 2.

It is, thus, impossible to identify the specific influence of housing availability upon labour migration, simply because access to housing opportunities is so dependent upon the whole range of other influences on migration. This chapter has identified two ways in which housing may be critical in influencing the mobility of labour and has hinted at a third. Firstly, there is a small minority of people who move specifically to improve their housing. Not only was this motivation stated by about 10 per cent of the sample migrants, but a slightly smaller number also felt, in retrospect, that this had been the main improvement. Presumably, these migrants might not have moved if suitable accommodation had not been available, and there may be larger numbers, outside the scope of our survey, who were deterred from moving by the housing situation, especially in south-eastern England.

Secondly, as was pointed out in Chapter 2, 'housing' has a wider significance than the simple physical attributes of accommodation. The whole social and environmental context of a dwelling affects householders' attitudes towards the area in which they live. This chapter has demonstrated that our sample migrants were extremely sensitive to the 'context' of the neighbourhood into which they had moved. White-collar workers gave emphasis to environmental factors, while manual workers ware particularly concerned with social contacts after moving. As we saw earlier, these factors increased in significance when the move was being assessed after the event.

Thirdly, the search for suitable accommodation is a formidable, if not traumatic, experience for many householders, yet the evidence of this chapter suggests that those who have successfully been through such an experience are liable to discount its difficulties when they later assess the general success of the move to a new area. Nevertheless, even the successful households in our sample survey had some distressing stories to relate about their experiences. These indicate the considerable resources that are required, both of finance and information, when moving home and job. The next chapter explores some of the problems and difficulties involved in the search by labour migrants for a new home.

9 The Search for Accommodation

Finance, information and time are required during the process of labour migration. In the majority of cases that we examined the labour migrants had jobs, or were students moving to their first jobs, so that the most direct constraint on moving to a new area, lack of finance resulting from unemployment, did not apply too strongly. In certain circumstances Government aid is available to help workers in such straits, but as was seen in Chapter 1, the number so helped has been small and it is not surprising that few of these appeared in our survey. If the migrant depends upon his own income and savings, this may impose severe constraints on the capacity of his household to move, but it emerged clearly from the survey that many employers expect to pay considerable sums to attract qualified employees of various types to new locations. The expenses involved in the search and negotiations for accommodation and the costs of actually moving were often paid by employers. Such aid, however, is not normally available for poorly qualified workers.

The importance of the availability of information is more difficult to measure than the effects of financial barriers, but migrants can be classified according to the type of information about local housing availability that they used and the variety of sources tapped during the search. Finally, the time factor may be crucial. How much time can a labour migrant take off to search for housing? Are weekends and holidays available for the search? How far away from the present location is the new area? Is a period of temporary accommodation necessary and, if so, will it include just the labour migrant or his whole family? Obviously, time also involves money, especially if temporary accommodation is used or days have to be taken off work.

There is no doubt that some potential labour migrants are deterred from moving because of these difficulties. Such people are extremely difficult to identify, and a survey of why they did not move would be likely to find that the reasons given included personal, social and environmental factors, as well as the difficulties of the housing market. In other words, the manipulation of the available resources of finance, information and time would depend very much on the general circumstances of each household.

Perhaps the most effective way to open an examination of the relation-

227

ship between the search procedure and the resources available to households is to consider a few case studies, not because they are representative of identifiable groups, but because they illustrate ways in which different households deal with similar situations.

Some examples of labour migrant households

Perhaps the 'model' labour migrant, experiencing little difficulty in moving, is best exemplified by migrant A: a development engineer, about forty years old, who moved with his wife and two teenage sons in August 1971. The move, from Guildford to Chatham, was made in response to company requirements, as development work was decentralised from its headquarters to individual factories. As a highly-valued employee, the migrant received full compensation for the expense of moving, including removal and legal expenses and a disturbance allowance. The problem of obtaining suitable accommodation was minimal, once the migrant realised how much his four-bedroom, detached bungalow in Guildford was really worth, and a three-bedroom bungalow in the same price range was obtained in Chatham. Although the housing search lasted about two months, it was facilitated by the relative proximity of the two areas, and the former dwelling was sold quickly once an acceptable new home had been found. All sources of information about housing in Chatham were employed, including estate agents, friends, newspapers and personally touring the district, and a wide area of Kent was searched. When the right house was found, it was available for immediate occupation and was situated in a pleasant area. Difficulty was experienced in finding a suitable school for the two boys, but this had been overcome through direct contact with a headmaster. In this case, although the housing situation was far from easy in August 1971 when the move was made, the labour migrant had been able to obtain the support he needed, both in financial terms and in the sources of information available to him, to make a relatively smooth transition to the new area.

Another type of occupation which appears to command resources when making moves around the country is found in the case of migrant B, a deputy bank manager, moving with promotion from Coventry to Northampton, accompanied by his wife and two young children. His employer not only provided help with legal and estate agent's fees and with the removal expenses, but also gave financial assistance in buying the house. As a result, the mortgage repayments of this labour migrant were very low in relation to the value of the property. While searching for a house, the migrant stayed in a hotel for a month, returning to Coventry at weekends. The new property was actually found through a bank customer who was selling — again illustrating a peculiar occupational advantage! In general, people in such occupations as banking expect to move frequently to gain promotion, and are more prepared for the problems that are likely to arise, but the customary help from the employer is a factor which should not be underestimated in such managerial and professional jobs. Again, in this case, schooling problems were a particular preoccupation in making the move.

Even quite well-off families experience difficulties, however, particularly in an area like High Wycombe. Labour migrant C, for example, with a wife and three young sons, had lived in a four-bedroomed, detached house in Derbyshire, before he obtained a new job as deputy company secretary in a firm with several plants in the western London and Home Counties area. The three-bedroomed house which he finally obtained in High Wycombe cost around £14,000, involving mortgage repayments of over £70 per month, compared with £30–40 in Derbyshire. The search for the new house embraced most of Hertfordshire, Middlesex and south Buckinghamshire, and information came from local newspapers and estate agents, who seemed uninterested in selling houses during the summer of 1971. Finally, the migrant drove down from Derbyshire for several consecutive weekends, to scour the area and chase potential housing as soon as it was advertised. Even when this led to a suitable property becoming available to him, he was 'gazumped' (the price being raised after informal agreement), and was finally successful only because an estate agent 'took pity on him' and told him of another house which was about to come up for sale. This 'was the only one on the market that was any good at all', even though it was too small and the garden was too big. Although his job prospects were better in the south-east, this migrant was understandably aggrieved about the problems of living in the region, especially as his journey to work was now 50 minutes instead of 10 minutes, and this has had a bad effect on his social life.

In these circumstances, the position of less well-off families was often very difficult. One striking case was that of a disabled precision toolmaker (migrant D) who had obtained a job in Chatham and moved there from Grantham, in Lincolnshire, with the aid of a Department of Employment grant. His wife was employed, so that their combined income was appreciable. Unfortunately for them, mortgage levels are determined very largely by the husband's income. Earning about £100 per month, he was unable to buy a suitable property in the Chatham area and flats were considered to be of poor quality. Thus, although the job situation was good, the couple were living in a bed-sitting room obtained through an estate agent, and the

229

prospects of obtaining better permanent accommodation seemed very depressing. In this case, therefore, they were planning to leave the area as soon as possible.

As we have seen in the last chapter, manual workers migrate for personal or social reasons more commonly than other workers, as evidenced by the large proportion moving back to a 'home town'. An example is an electrical fitter in his late thirties (migrant E) who moved with his wife and two daughters from Portsmouth to Huddersfield. The reasons for moving were a desire to live near relatives in Huddersfield, so that his wife would have some company while he was away on jobs in the building industry, and to move before the eldest daughter went to a secondary school. This case is of particular interest because it illustrates a rather different mode of information gathering compared with the middle-class cases of migrants A, B and C, and because migrant E showed considerable enterprise in searching for opportunities once the decision to move had been made. From local knowledge, it was judged that housing would not be difficult to obtain in Huddersfield, but that employment might be more difficult. The search for both was concentrated into the couple's fortnight's holiday, which was spent staying with relatives in Huddersfield. During this time they paid a deposit for a new house, but later opted for an older three-bedroomed terraced house, costing less than £3,000, because of the uncertainty of employment at that time. The employment problem was overcome by systematically contacting all likely employers in the area by telephone, after the employment exchange and the largest local employers had been unable to offer a job. This proved to be successful (an employer was contacted a day before he intended to advertise a suitable job), and the move followed without difficulty. Clearly, the housing situation in Huddersfield made this type of move much easier than would be possible in the south-east, but, in the absence of any outside financial assistance and depending entirely on savings, the couple obviously used the advantages of their contacts in the area to the full, both in instigating the move and in searching for a house and a job.

Two categories of household are relatively prominent in the special nature of their accommodation problems. The first type includes young married couples, usually moving to their first jobs. Often they have relatively little choice in the area of employment, so that they are subject to the vagaries of the housing market in a direct way. They often lack experience of the housing scene and obtain financial assistance rather less frequently than do more established families. On the other hand, they are generally more adaptable to difficult circumstances, especially if these are likely to last a relatively short time. A second group which emerges as

230

consistently dissatisfied, especially in southern Britain, includes single persons. As with the newly married couples, it is often difficult to separate housing experience from other problems, but it seems clear from many examples that the shortage of accommodation for this particular minority group in the south-east leads many to move away if this can be arranged.

These cases exemplify the types of variation that occur in the resources available to different migrants and in the use made of them. It is clear that the amount of effort required in moving may be greater in some parts of the country than elsewhere, and also that difficulties may be overcome much more easily by workers in some occupations than in others. An examination of the detailed variations in these factors, however, requires a more systematic approach to the results of the survey.

The housing aspirations of migrants

A useful index of the general success of the search for accommodation was provided by asking whether the housing finally chosen was very similar to what the labour migrant had in mind when he decided to move (Question 37). 60 per cent of respondents answered 'yes' to this question, 28 per cent were not in the accommodation that they had envisaged, while 12 per cent gave 'don't know' replies. These responses were obviously affected by the realism with which the labour migrant judged his potential in the housing market, as well as his flexibility in adapting to a variety of possible types of accommodation, but the relative 'success' of the respondents and the reasons for dissatisfaction with the moves among the minority are useful indicators of the effectiveness of the search procedure. If the sample areas are compared, Northampton and Huddersfield, with their easier housing markets, provided a higher proportion of in-migrants with housing in accord with their expectations, while Chatham appeared to be least satisfactory in this respect.

Not unexpectedly, hopes were fulfilled more often by the acquisition of self-contained houses, rather than flats, maisonettes or bungalows, and by owner-occupied property rather than rented accommodation (Table 9.1). Rent-free and tied housing was very much as expected before the moves, so that dissatisfaction was rarely expressed. The failure of rented accommodation to provide what was envisaged was particularly marked in private furnished property.

Variations in the pressure on the privately-owned housing market in the four sample areas was indicated by the relatively high fulfilment of expec-

Table 9.1

Success in obtaining accommodation hoped for before moving

	Percentage of total sample by house type	Percentage in 'hoped-for' accommodation
By house type		
Self-contained house	64	70
Bungalow	8	6
Flat/maisonette	13	9
Hostel/with relatives	12	14
Other	2	1
By housing tenure		
Owner-occupiers	60	64
Private renting (unfurnished and furnished)	20	15
Local authority	5	4
Rent-free/tied cottage	14	14
Lodging	3	3
By income		
Less than £40 per month	3	3
£40 – £60	6	5
£60 – £80	13	13
£80 – £120	26	23
£120 – £240	34	37
Over £240	13	15
Others	5	4
By household size		
No. of persons in household:		
1	8	8
2	31	22
3	22	22
4	25	23
5	8	10
6	2	2
More than 6	3	2

tations amongst owner-occupiers in Huddersfield and Northampton, compared with High Wycombe and Chatham. Households with different economic and social characteristics also displayed significant contrasts in their satisfaction with their housing. Middle-income households, with the income of the labour migrant between £80 and £120 per month, least often fulfilled their expectations, while both the lower- and higher-income groups tended to obtain the sort of accommodation that they expected. Perhaps low-income groups were more realistic in their expectations than the middle-income groups, while those with high incomes were more able to achieve their hopes. In addition, household size, as a fairly simple physical measure of need, seemed to have a small effect on the likely fulfilment of housing expectations. Nevertheless, two-person households did experience difficulty in obtaining the accommodation which they had in mind. Large families were better able to achieve their expectations in Huddersfield.

In summary, those in the higher-income groups who moved to live in self-contained, owner-occupied houses, with families of average size, were likely to achieve their housing aspirations along with those on low incomes living rent-free (often with relatives). On the other hand, rented flats and maisonettes were often regarded as less satisfactory, both small and large households found their requirements more difficult to fill, and the low- to middle-income groups were also less satisfied. These conclusions reflect the inability of the housing markets of the sample areas to deal with the minority needs of certain types of household moving into their areas, although a fairly large proportion of the labour migrants managed to find the type of accommodation that they required. In total, a higher achievement of housing expectations was found in Huddersfield and Northampton, compared with Chatham and High Wycombe. Nearly 30 per cent of the households moving into the latter two areas were in accommodation which was not what they had intended, while less than 20 per cent of migrants to Huddersfield were in this situation.

Some further light is shed on the imperfections of the housing allocation procedure by the information collected about what they actually had in mind (Question 39a) from the 155 households in the sample which were not in the accommodation that they had hoped for. In fact, there was a wide range of replies to this question, but most dissatisfaction related either to the size or to the style of the house. About 18 per cent of the respondents wanted houses of a different size, while 28 per cent wanted either detached, semi-detached or bungalow-style houses instead of what they had. Dissatisfaction with private-rented, furnished accommodation arose mainly from its lack of privacy and from its cost. Again, a distinction can be drawn between the high-income groups, which more commonly criticised the style and size of houses, and the lower-income groups, which were more concerned with privacy.

The determination of housing choice

More detailed consideration will now be given to the processes by which households in the sample reviewed the accommodation that was available to them and made a final decision on housing choice. Among the 72 per cent of the sample living in the type of accommodation they had in mind, an inquiry was made into their reasons for choosing a particular district within the labour market area (Question 38a). Rather surprisingly, many had opted for what they regarded as the only suitable accommodation available (28 per cent of the total number of households surveyed and 32 per cent of the responses, allowing for those which gave more than one reason for their choice). In these cases, therefore, the choice of district was determined by the character of the particular accommodation required. Only 11 per cent of the whole sample had been able to obtain suitable housing in a district of their choice, and only a further 11 per cent had specifically chosen their accommodation from a number of suitable alternatives. Those living with relatives or choosing to live in an area near to their work made up smaller but still significant groups.

Limitations of housing choice were most frequently given as reasons for moving to a particular district in High Wycombe (34 per cent of households and 41 per cent of responses), and least frequently in Huddersfield (17 per cent of households). 'Liking the area' was most often cited as a determinant of choice in High Wycombe, and least often in Chatham, while the available choice of individual houses seemed to be greatest in Northampton and Huddersfield, and least in High Wycombe. This absence of effective choice in High Wycombe was not usually due to any lack of searching. Here, only one third of the sample households had confined their search to the local labour market area, compared with 57 per cent in Huddersfield and 47 per cent in Northampton. This partly reflects the relatively shorter journeys to work which are tolerable outside the south-east, but it also emphasises the general limitations of choice in High Wycombe as a result of the high pressure of demand. In considering the areas of search, it is also clear that rented property (especially private furnished accommodation) was sought largely within the labour market area where employment was located, by migrants with relatively low incomes. Other groups were more wide-ranging in their search, especially for owner-occupied property. Thus the contrasts in search procedure between

234

labour market areas also reflect the socio-economic differences between the labour migrant populations moving into them.

About one-third of the 28 per cent of respondents who did not find the type of accommodation they had in mind went to what they believed to be 'the only suitable accommodation available'. Financial limitations determined the choice for another quarter of them, either because they were attracted by property that was good value for the money or because it was all that was available at the price. Price limitations were most often quoted in High Wycombe and, not surprisingly, least often in Huddersfield.

In summary, the answers to these questions about the determinants of housing choice outline a variety of constraints for those seeking accommodation in a tight market situation. As a result of their selection of homes from the alternatives actually available to them in the area where they searched, only about 40 per cent of the sample arrived at the accommodation they had envisaged. Another 30 per cent obtained broadly the types of accommodation they hoped for, but with little real choice; about one-third of these were moving to live with relatives and, presumably, did not regard housing choice as a matter of importance. As we have already noted, 28 per cent of the sample did not obtain the type of accommodation that they had anticipated. In general, the lower-income groups (less than £80 per month) and manual workers were most constrained in their choices and had to accept what was available, while the middle–higher income groups as a whole displayed a variety of choice according to area, house-type and location in relation to schools and work. Even when the accommodation obtained was not what they originally had in mind, a proportion were able to console themselves that their choice was based on a 'good value for money' criterion.

Sources of information about accommodation

The crucial link between a general survey of housing prospects in an area and the choice for households of particular accommodation is information about local conditions. In a situation where a speedy decision may be essential, a labour migrant's final choice of where to live may be strongly affected by the aid which he receives from formal channels of information, such as estate agents, and the degree to which he uses other, more informal, sources such as the local knowledge of friends, relatives or future employers. As we have seen, the pressure to make a quick decision after finding something acceptable was quite strong in High Wycombe and

Chatham, where the general atmosphere of the housing market in 1971 must have exerted a marked effect on decisions taken during the study period.

Two questions were asked of labour migrants about the sources of information used in their search for accommodation. The first (Question 38d) inquired into the principal methods used to gain general information about housing in the prospective labour market area. A combination of means emerged, interestingly differentiated between income and socio-economic groups. In the sample as a whole (Table 9.2), about equal proportions (19 to 21 per cent) used local newspaper advertisements, gained information from friends and relatives and searched the area themselves. Only 13 per cent relied upon estate agents to provide general information and 10 per cent used work or business contacts in the area. Manual workers (SEGs 8−11), the lower-paid (less than £80 per month) and those with little previous migration experience, tended to rely more upon informal channels, such as relatives and friends and a personal search of the area, while higher-income, managerial, professional and non-manual groups (SEGs 1−6), often with greater experience of moving, as well as using informal means, such as touring the area, tended to employ estate agents and newspapers more often.

Table 9.2

Information sources about housing

	Primary information sources		Sources used to discover final accommodation	
	Number	%	Number	%
Estate agents/flat agency	73	13·3	218	39·6
Newspaper advertisements	115	20·9	74	13·4
Friends and relatives	109	19·8	119	21·6
By going around the district	103	18·7	26	4·7
Saw it accidentally	10	1·8	14	2·5
Local authority	16	2·9	14	2·5
At work	24	4·4	14	2·5
Citizen's Advice Bureau	6	1·1	—	—
Business contacts	34	6·2	50	9·1
Other	11	2·0	20	3·6
No information/not applicable	52	9·4	3	0·5

Totals exceed 551 households because some respondents cited more than one information source.

It appears that those who failed to obtain what they had in mind (often in the middle-income groups and living especially in High Wycombe), tended to rely more than others upon newspapers and travelling around the area. In contrast, labour migrants who accepted the advice of friends and relatives (often to share accommodation with them), or work contacts (especially in Huddersfield) more often obtained the type of accommodation that they had anticipated.

The second question about the supply of information in the search for accommodation (Question 38e) focused on the means by which labour migrants discovered the accommodation they eventually accepted. A rather different picture emerges from that above, most strikingly through the high proportion of the sample (40 per cent) obtaining the critical information from estate agents. This proportion was particularly high amongst those who settled for something other than they had in mind (44 per cent). Thus, in spite of the variety of search procedures employed, many labour migrants finally resorted to estate agents to find something that was satisfactory, if not always ideal. This may be compared with the much less frequent use of estate agents by intra-urban migrants, noted by Herbert (see Chapter 5). The role of personal contacts with friends, relatives and at work remained important in the final choice of accommodation (about 35 per cent of the sample in all). Accommodation was found less frequently through newspaper advertisements than their use would lead one to expect. However, those who found their accommodation through newspaper advertisements were more likely to have obtained what they wanted. Going around the district was also relatively unsuccessful as a basis for finding specific types of suitable accommodation.

In summary, although migrants sought accommodation in a new area through a variety of channels of communication and some were successful through informal means, in the final analysis estate agents provided a relatively high proportion of accommodation, even if not at first resort. Yet, perhaps it is more remarkable that over half the labour migrants in the sample obtained their accommodation independently of estate agents. The well-off tended to use estate agents more frequently, and the fact that they were more critical in the type of accommodation that they expected to obtain may explain the relatively high proportion of estate agents' customers who were not able to obtain the sort of accommodation they had in mind. Those, often in lower-income groups, who obtained accommodation through friends and relatives and other personal contacts were likely to be less demanding and less likely to criticise what they got, especially if they were living with friends or relatives.

237

The problems of moving

Analysis of the open-ended question about the general difficulties of carrying out the actual move to the new job and accommodation (Question 28) showed that a considerable proportion of the 551 respondents mentioned more than one difficulty. As a result, there were 671 responses to this question. These are summarised in Table 9.3. In fact, 30 per cent of the respondents claimed to have experienced no real difficulties in moving to a new area, a proportion that was about the same in the four labour market areas. This figure is consistent with the evidence discussed above of relative satisfaction with the result of moving, and with the choice of accommodation available. About 45 per cent of the sample responses mentioned various types of housing problems, strong evidence in itself of the influence of housing market factors on the process of labour migration. 26 per cent of responses mentioned personal and family problems which were consequences of the moves. Relatively few migrants (5 per cent) had difficulties with employment, since obtaining a satisfactory job was the main precondition for making a move in the first place.

Among housing difficulties, the main group of problems arose from the need to acquire temporary accommodation during the course of the move to a new area. This was necessary either during the search for accommodation or during the period before final occupation when the house was being purchased or its building completed. Temporary accommodation

Table 9.3

Problems involved in the move

Problem	Chatham	High Wycombe	Huddersfield	Northampton	Total
No difficulties	34·9	29·8	32·9	28·1	30·1
Housing difficulties	43·7	47·8	39·5	45·0	44·8
Of which:					
Needed temporary accommodation	16·7	21·9	15·8	18·7	18·9
Timing difficulties	11·9	9·0	6·6	10·5	9·8
Technical difficulties	15·1	16·9	17·1	15·8	16·1
Personal difficulties	18·3	30·3	31·6	25·1	26·1
General upheaval	11·9	14·6	9·2	18·1	14·3
Employment difficulties	6·3	2·8	6·6	5·9	5·1

Figures do not add up to 100 per cent because some people gave more than one reason.

238

was often required for quite a long period (see below), with the need often extending into the first weeks or even months after the labour migrant had taken up local employment. 19 per cent of the sample responses mentioned temporary accommodation problems (many more actually went into temporary accommodation) and this proportion was similar in the four labour market areas, although more people in High Wycombe were concerned with this matter and rather fewer in Huddersfield.

A further 10 per cent of the responses mentioned difficulties associated with the timing of the moves. The most important of these was finding suitable housing at the right moment (most acute in Chatham and least in Huddersfield). Another type of problem, experienced by about 16 per cent of the sample, was associated with the technical difficulties of moving to a new area, including the disposal of old accommodation, or having to wait for possession while the previous occupants found new housing. Both of these difficulties were most important for those moving into Huddersfield. Other less common reasons in this group included problems which arose during the legal transfer of the new accommodation, where arrangements had to be renegotiated after falling through, or there were problems of obtaining mortgages. In summary, most of the housing difficulties were concerned with timing, the disposing of former residences, getting mortgages, and especially in acquiring temporary accommodation while these other procedures were taking place.

The more varied 'personal' difficulties during the moves to a new labour market area are fairly clear-cut for individual households, although they undoubtedly overlap with the problems of acquiring accommodation already discussed. The main personal difficulties reported arose from the need to travel back and forth for some time between the old and new areas of residence, a problem which was most acute in Huddersfield and least so in Chatham. After this, complications in personal and family circumstances during the period of the move were important; births and deaths are important events in normal times, but may create more problems if a major change of accommodation is taking place. A period of separation of the labour migrant from his family during the period of transfer also often caused personal anxiety and difficulty. 14 per cent of the sample experienced problems concerned with the general upheavals of moving, not specific to housing or personal problems, and no doubt some of the 30 per cent who did not recognise any great difficulties also suffered in this way to some degree, without regarding it as being of great significance.

Temporary accommodation

The need for temporary accommodation was most evident among families moving into owner-occupied housing, but was also significant for those going to rented, furnished accommodation. In the former case, no doubt because of the complexity of the operation and the time needed for its completion, movement involved more disturbance than was the rule for other forms of tenure. The greater period of time needed to find private-rented furnished accommodation seems to highlight its shortage and poor range, compared with other types of renting.

Temporary accommodation was sought by 65 per cent of the migrant sample during the moves, most commonly for a period of one to three months. More than 20 per cent of the labour migrants stayed in such accommodation for over three months, however, and only 12 per cent did so for less than one month. Migrants to Huddersfield seem to have used temporary accommodation most often, while those to Northampton did so least. Managerial and professional workers, seeking owner-occupied housing, were the most frequent users of temporary accommodation, in contrast to manual workers (Table 9.4). Those in their thirties and forties were led by family commitments and the cost of moving to use temporary accommodation more often than younger people. Again, a combination of attributes, including age, family structure, type of housing being sought and past experience of labour migration, seems to explain the use of this interim form of accommodation. For example, 60 to 70 per cent of the high-income households (above £120 per month) used temporary accommodation, while the proportion of income groups below this drops rapid-

Table 9.4

Proportions of labour migrants taking temporary accommodation, classified by socio-economic group, income and age

Socio-economic group	%	Income (per month)	%	Age	%
Managerial and employers (1–2)	66·7	Less than £40	35·7	15–19	55·6
Professional (3–4)	64·6	£40 – £60	40·0	20–24	46·4
Intermediate non-manual (5)	50·0	£60 – £80	47·9	25–34	57·7
Junior non-manual and personal service (6–7)	47·5	£80 – £120	57·3	35–44	62·3
Skilled manual (8–9)	47·5	£120 – £240	63·5	45–59	61·0
Semi- and unskilled manual (10–11)	45·5	£240 – £400	56·4	60–64	28·5
Others	60·0	Over £400	66·7		

240

ly. Similarly, those with some experience of past moves used temporary accommodation, but the 'immobile' group had a very low tendency to do so. There is also some tendency for both the lower income groups, and the less mobile (often the same people) to stay in temporary accommodation for a shorter period than the others.

Hotels and boarding houses were most commonly used but staying with relatives was also important, especially in Chatham and Huddersfield. Other minor alternatives included renting houses and flats and staying with friends. The mobile, high-income workers in managerial, professional and non-manual groups, tended to stay in hotels and boarding houses, while the less mobile, lower-income groups more often shared with relatives. The same pattern emerged with different age groups: those over 25 years old more often stayed in hotels and boarding houses, while younger labour migrants were more likely to stay with relatives.

Assistance during the course of labour migration

This account of the difficulties of moving has pointed to the common need for some sort of assistance for households taking part in labour migration. In fact, quite a high proportion of the sample population, 47 per cent, did receive some form of help. This proportion was highest in High Wycombe and lowest in Chatham. Help seems to have been available more often to those in highly-paid, prestigious jobs, moving to owner-occupied housing.

The form of assistance usually consisted either of monetary expenses to

Table 9.5

Proportions of labour migrants receiving assistance,
classified by socio-economic group, income and age

Socio-economic group	%	Income (per month)	%	Age	%
Managerial and employers (1–2)	66·7	Less than £40	28·6	15–19	33·3
Professional (3–4)	58·3	£40 – £60	20·0	20–24	25·4
Intermediate non-manual (5)	44·4	£60 – £80	30·1	25–34	51·0
Junior non-manual and personal service (6–7)	33·3	£80 – £120	28·0	35–44	60·7
Skilled manual (8–9)	24·6	£120 – £240	67·2	45–59	54·5
Semi- and unskilled manual (10–11)	31·8	£240 – £400	74·6	60–64	14·3
Others	53·3	Over £400	53·3		

cover the cost of moving, or more broadly assessed 'disturbance allowances'. Another important type of help affected the provision of temporary accommodation, which may have been provided free of charge or supported through financial aid. A third category of support provided for legal expenses or estate agents' fees in obtaining the new accommodation.

Two-thirds of the managerial socio-economic groups (SEGs 1 and 2) obtained some form of assistance, 58 per cent of the professional groups (SEGs 3–4) and about 44 per cent of the 'intermediate non-manual' group (SEG 5) (Table 9.5). Only one-quarter of the skilled manual workers and one-third of the unskilled and semi-skilled manual workers received any help. In terms of income groups, the proportions of the sample receiving assistance increased with income and it was also higher for those in the 35–44 age groups, as opposed to younger migrants of less than 25. It is also clear that those with high customary levels of mobility received assistance more often than those with less experience of moving, including the young and manual workers. Thus, as in so many aspects of the labour mobility problem, moving was facilitated for some by a combination of influences: status, income, age, past experience and also aid in making the changes. It is clear that all these factors act together in differentiating between those who find mobility easy and those for whom it is a matter of difficulty.

If the four sample areas are compared, the only significant contrast in the type of assistance available to the sample households was that in High Wycombe help was more readily available to the lower income, non-manual workers than elsewhere, while in Huddersfield more of the higher-income, employer and managerial groups seem to have benefited. This pattern may indicate an awareness by employers of the difficulties of attracting the different types of workers to their respective areas.

By far the largest proportion of the sample labour migrants who received assistance obtained it from their present employers; 85 per cent were aided in this way and no doubt many were moving from one area to another without changing their employers. The proportion of employer support rose to 92 per cent in Northampton. In contrast, official sources of aid were of very little importance. Only 4 per cent received any form of Department of Employment support and other Governmental sources of aid were on the whole even less frequently used. In addition, 62 per cent of the sample had also used some of their own savings to facilitate the move and this proportion was highest among the managerial and employer SEGs, presumably those who possessed spare funds for such purposes. On the other hand, semi-skilled manual workers also seemed to dip into their savings more often than average, and this may reflect the absence of

242

outside help. Certainly the labour mobility of such workers may be restricted to those who have their own finance to support a move. Of the various categories of possible aid, removal expenses were generally available to the middle-income groups (£60 − £240 per month) and the professional and intermediate non-manual groups, but a disturbance allowance tended to be more frequently available to the higher-income groups (more than £120 per month). Travelling expenses between the new and old areas were more often available to the lower-income groups (less than £60 per month), although this aid was no doubt smaller in quantity and was also less frequently available than removal expenses or disturbance allowances. Thus, the form of aid to lower income groups was also different from that available to the better-off, although there was some overlap between the categories, since some manual workers received removal expenses and some professional and managerial workers travelling expenses.

Conclusion

It is clear that in moving to a new area the search for new accommodation is a difficult experience for many labour migrants. However, the paths followed vary between different groups of migrants, and are more arduous in some areas and for some people than for others.

In general the search was successful, with a large majority obtaining the accommodation they had expected. The better-off and the poorer groups seemed to come closest to fulfilling their hopes, probably because the former had the financial resources to indulge them while the latter did not expect much in the first place. There were some diffences between the four areas in terms of satisfaction with the accommodation they found. Huddersfield and Northampton were both associated with a higher degree of satisfaction than High Wycombe and Chatham, partly a reflection of the easier housing markets, with more choice open to migrants, in the northern areas.

Although over two-thirds of migrants professed satisfaction with their new accommodation, a variety of constraints operated on their choices, so that only 40 per cent of them actually were able to choose from a range of acceptable alternatives. Thus, a majority of migrants obtained accommodation that was either not satisfactory or was what they believed to be the only acceptable dwelling available. There were, however, marked differences between income groups, with poorer migrants being most constrained in their choices and having to accept what was there, much more often than those who were more affluent. Thus, the evidence here suggests that, in moving to a new area, migrants in the lower socio-economic groups are much more narrowly confined in the type of housing available to them than are the other groups. If they are small households, the difficulties faced will be compounded.

Clearly, in a situation where choice of new accommodation is limited for most migrants, the sources of information to guide them to what is available become critical. Most people found some accommodation, often temporary, before starting the new job but the sources and search procedures used were different depending upon individual circumstances. Formal channels of information, such as estate agents, were used particularly by the higher socio-economic groups, while informal sources, such as friends and relatives, appealed more to the lower status groups.

Consideration of the problems involved in moving suggests that housing constitutes the single most important set of difficulties, although not experienced by a majority of migrants. It is not possible to specify one particular type of housing difficulty as being paramount, although the need to find temporary accommodation, often for quite long periods, exercised many migrants. Labour migration, it seems, necessitates for a majority of those involved, a period in some interim form of accommodation, the finding of which is itself a source of real difficulty. Thus, an important element in successful labour migration is the provision of this short-term accommodation while the search for a permanent home goes on.

Yet perhaps the most surprising finding in this analysis of the search for accommodation is the extensive nature of the assistance received by migrants. Almost half had some financial help, with 85 per cent of this coming from the new employer. The amount of Department of Employment sponsored movement among our sample migrants was minimal. The aid received was also strongly correlated with income and socio-economic group. Higher-income, higher-status migrants received most aid, while manual workers received much less. Thus, it can be argued that those workers whose career hierarchies necessitate frequent movement, the higher socio-economic groups, find migration easier because they receive help in surmounting many of the barriers, especially of cost, that are in their way. In contrast, other groups, to whom migration might be attractive for many reasons but whose career patterns do not depend upon it, are constrained by the lack of this hidden subsidisation.

10 Conclusion

This book has been an introductory study of the largely uncharted relationship between labour migration and housing. By concentrating its attention upon those who have successfully moved, it is open to criticism that perhaps the greatest effect of housing as a barrier to migration is felt by those people not surveyed — that is, those who were prevented from moving for some reason primarily connected with their housing. There are serious methodological difficulties in questioning people about something they have not done. Perhaps one answer, for some future study, would be to concentrate attention on a group of people who have all been given the opportunity to move. Such a case might be the employees of a firm moving its operation and wishing to take all or part of its labour force to a new location. A comparative survey of those who took the opportunity to move and those who refused might provide a clearer understanding of the role of housing factors in the migration process.[1] But even then the issue would be clouded by the availability of aid from the company to those employees invited to move, smoothing over the various housing difficulties we know would normally arise.

The information we have obtained from those who did succeed in moving does allow us to measure the importance of various aspects of housing as they affect the migration of different groups in the labour force. Because these people have succeeded in moving, we have been able to assess the means they used to overcome various housing barriers during the migration process. What has emerged from our study is a convergence of evidence to produce a remarkably coherent picture of the nature of labour migration in England and Wales and its relationship to the availability and characteristics of housing. The main spatial patterns of labour migration and the types of labour involved in the flows have both been identified.

It has been suggested in Chapter 2 that there are good reasons to expect that, on the basis of employment alone, labour migration would predominantly be between the largest employment centres, and that higher-status socio-economic groups would be the most mobile. The first of these points was confirmed in Chapter 4, where analysis of the actual flows of labour showed three main types of migration pattern, hierarchically arranged according to the sizes of the employment nodes linked. As far as the second point is concerned, we should expect that a high proportion of the migrants in the longer-distance flow patterns centred on London and on the provincial cities would be the high-status groups in the population. As these flow patterns account for a majority of the labour migration in England and Wales, it is reasonable to suppose that a high proportion of labour migrants would be in the high-status groups, and that they would tend to move over longer distances. The survey results confirm that this is indeed the case. We should expect the pattern of mainly short-distance flows, based on regional systems, to contain a higher proportion of lower-status groups. Again the survey evidence is confirmatory. Thus, we can suggest the existence of different types of labour migration identified through an association of spatial and social characteristics.

The survey results have not only provided a clearer identification of the groups which migrate, but have also shown the principal constraints operating upon them. The nature of these constraints varies according to the characteristics of the local labour and housing market to which the migrant intends moving. The four areas studied were chosen on the basis of their contrasting migration, employment and housing conditions, and these contrasts were apparent in the survey results. It is easier to move to some parts of the country than to others; for example, migrants had less trouble moving to Northampton and Huddersfield than to High Wycombe and Chatham. Perhaps more important, different types of migrants move to different types of areas; it seems that the socio-economic character of the migrants to an area will reflect the existing socio-economic composition of that area. Good evidence of this is provided in Chatham and High Wycombe, which have different socio-economic compositions and have attracted different types of migrants. Because the characteristics of migrants vary from place to place, the housing problem also varies accordingly.

The majority of labour migrants are middle class, in the 25—44 age group, and have middle—high incomes. They are professional and managerial workers in a career structure that encourages movement. Their occupational status frequently entitles them to financial and other forms of aid which make migration easier. They move within a housing market that is especially geared to their requirements. They can get mortgages more readily than other people, and as owner-occupiers they can use the services of estate agents, the best organised channel of information about housing open to migrants. Hence, there is an accumulation of factors — high earnings, migration aid, ability to gain mortgages, information sources — in favour of this high-status group, enabling its members to move relatively freely.

246

The rest of the labour migrants fall into several minority groups, none as well defined as the high-status group discussed above. Their very heterogeneity makes it difficult to generalise about the resources they can command, their housing needs and the problems they experience. These groups include the lower-paid white-collar workers, the young (including students), manual workers, single people, and a small number of unemployed. Many young people, especially students taking their first job, are often just entering career hierarchies which will entail subsequent mobility. At this stage they take whatever accommodation is available — usually rented and often unsatisfactory — but are willing to put up with it as an interim expedient. The lower-paid white-collar and manual groups form a much smaller proportion of the labour migrant population than they do of the total population. Although there is no evidence that obtaining accommodation is such a formidable barrier for these people that it will itself prevent their migration, it does seem that getting another house is more difficult for them than for most labour migrants. They operate in all sectors of the housing market, but are more likely to rent than to be owner-occupiers. If they are owner-occupiers, they are likely to live in cheaper homes.

However, the lack of mobility of manual workers and of lower-paid white-collar workers is probably because they do not want to move rather than because they cannot move. Not only are they more likely to obtain alternative employment locally, but they may put a higher value on social ties within a local area. Their propensity to move is therefore lower. When they do move long distances it tends to be to areas which are familiar to them through pre-existing ties.

The small number of unemployed among the migrants makes it difficult to say much about them as a group. What is perhaps most interesting is the very small proportion of the total amount of labour migration that they account for. This indicates that, despite theories of labour migration suggesting that labour will move from areas of unemployment to areas of labour shortage, the type of labour migration that predominates at present will not solve regional differences in labour supply and demand.

There is no clear evidence that housing on its own inhibits labour migration; housing has emerged as just one type of barrier among several others and the ability to surmount these barriers depends on the resources, especially of finance and information, available to potential migrants. The exact role of housing in labour migration remains elusive, for 'housing' can be several things to a migrant. Most obviously, it can be the building itself — whether or not it is detached, how many bedrooms it has, how much it costs, and so on. In fact, only a minority of labour migrants moved specifically for reasons connected with the physical nature of the accommodation, or felt afterwards that a better housing situation was the primary benefit from moving. To other migrants the environmental and social context of the dwelling was important. Liking the new area or missing something from the old became of particular concern if improved earnings had not followed the move; social contacts were valued especially highly by lower-paid white-collar and manual workers. Hence moves were often judged, both prospectively and retrospectively, by the environmental and social context of the dwelling rather than by the dwelling itself. Housing may also act as a barrier to migration because of the problem of searching for a new dwelling. As indicated in Chapter 9, some groups clearly found the search much more of a problem than others, as reflected in the sources of information used. If it is necessary to rent a dwelling, for example, there is no readily accessible 'clearing-house' for information, which functions for the private-renting or local authority sectors as estate agents do for owner-occupiers.

It is inadequate to talk in general terms of housing as a barrier to mobility. Problems in finding accommodation crop up in different ways for different groups of migrants, and it is important to distinguish between the various aspects of housing supply and housing requirements as they affect mobility. It is also misleading to assume simply that tenure either prevents or increases mobility. Tenure is certainly important: the small number of local authority tenants in our sample is good evidence of the difficulties for labour migrants in moving into dwellings of this tenure. Our results also demonstrate the significance of the private-rented furnished sector in articulating movement. Yet clearly, at the level of individual households engaged in labour migration, tenure cannot be considered in isolation from other attributes of the housing stock and from the migrants' requirements.

Despite the elusive nature of the precise role of housing, we can suggest that it is the characteristics of housing in the destination area rather than at the origin that most influence labour migration. At the origin the constraints imposed by housing relate to the disposal of the existing accommodation, a problem not found unduly onerous by most of our sample of migrants. In the destination area, migrants must find housing that is acceptable to them and to which they can obtain access. Each area has a stock of available housing of various sizes, types, tenures, locations and prices. Different migrants require, according to their household size, incomes and aspirations, very specific types of housing. Those who want accommodation of the sort that is readily available to them at their chosen destinations are more likely to move than others. This may be because of

248

the ease of getting information about house vacancies, the necessity of fulfilling various qualifications, or the ability to raise the money to enter a particular tenure group. Thus, it is the combination of housing characteristics and migrant characteristics, rather than housing factors viewed in isolation, that influences the migration of labour.

Note

[1] M. Mann, *Workers on the Move: the Sociology of Relocation*, Cambridge 1973, presents an interesting study of this kind.

Appendix 1

Method of classification used for Standard Metropolitan Labour Areas

The aim of the classification of SMLAs was to indicate the degree of similarity between them in terms of their pattern of migration between 1965 and 1966, and of the housing and employment conditions operating at the time. Having chosen the variables to be included in the classification (see Chapter 3), a similarity measure was required to indicate the closeness of the relationship between every pair of SMLAs in terms of the chosen attributes. Then a grouping strategy was needed that would produce the most efficient and significant grouping of similar SMLAs.[1]

Similarity measure.   Spence and Taylor have discussed a number of classification procedures available for different purposes and types of data.[2] The similarity classification of SMLAs should reflect such features as the size of migration flows, additions to the housing stock and unemployment levels in the various SMLAs, thus necessitating the use of a distance measure. It was decided to use 'squared Euclidean distance' as a measure of similarity; the distance between two points, *i* and *j*, is

$$d_{ij} = \sqrt{\sum_{z=1}^{n} (X_{iz} - X_{jz})^2}$$

Each SMLA is represented by a point in *n*-dimensional space (11 dimensions in this case), where each dimension corresponds to one of the variables. Distances between the ith and j^{th} SMLA are computed by squaring the difference between their values on each variable (X), and taking the square root of the sum of this value for all 11 variables. The variables were transformed to unit variance, so that each was given equal weight in the distance computation.

Grouping strategy. A hierarchical technique was used to produce groupings of the SMLAs. At each stage in this process two units are combined to form one new unit; thus the total number of classes is reduced by one, until the desired number is attained. Ward's method was used for grouping, in which the two units combined are those whose union resulted in the minimum increment to the pooled within-group sum of squares. Their centroid is then computed, and distances recalculated from this point to each of the remaining units. The techniques used are available as options of the CLUSTAN 1A program package.[3]

Notes

[1] A full discussion of some of the options available is found in N. Hadjifotiou, 'The multivariate classification of local labour market areas', Housing and Labour Mobility Study, Department of Geography, University College London, *Working Paper* no. 2, 1972.

[2] N.A. Spence and P.J. Taylor, 'Quantitative methods in regional taxonomy' *Progress in Geography: International Reviews of Current Research* 2, London 1970, pp. 13–15.

[3] D. Wishart, 'CLUSTAN 1A', mimeographed booklet, Computing Laboratory, University of St. Andrews, 1969.

Appendix 2

Questionnaire used during survey of sample of labour migrant households

Dataplan   R.9358
(Division of Marplan Ltd.)
Fourth Floor
Park House
22 Park Street
Croydon
Surrey
CR9 1TS

'Phone 01-686-3051   CONFIDENTIAL

Job No.	Card No.	Area	Serial No.
COL.1-2	COL.3-7	COL.8	COL. 9-12

HOUSE VISITED   Col.13

PRE 1919	1	WIFE PRESENT	5
1919 - 38	2	WIFE NOT PRESENT	6
POST WORLD WAR 2	3		

HOUSING AND LABOUR MOBILITY STUDY

1st Date Time Result CALL	2nd Date Time Result CALL	3rd Date Time Result CALL	Area ....

I am from ....(Market Research Firm). We are conducting some interviews for a Research Group in University College London. They are interested to find out how much influence the availability of housing in certain areas of the country has on peoples willingness to move to those areas for employment.

I understand that you have recently moved to ....(Labour Market) and taken a new job, and it would be of very great help to us if you could tell us something of your experiences both of finding a job and suitable accommodation.

I have a questionnaire which usually takes about an hour to complete, and we should very much appreciate your help. Your name and address do not appear on the questionnaire, and information given will be completely confidential.

Q.1.   Who in your household actually changed place of employment and therefore address (or vice-versa) ?   Col.13.

Head of Household	7	
Wife	8	See Note Below
Both	9	

CONDUCT THE INTERVIEW WITH THE LABOUR MIGRANT IE. THE PERSON CODED ABOVE. IF 'BOTH' CODED TAKE THE HEAD OF HOUSEHOLD.

BUT DO NOT INTERVIEW:-

a) PEOPLE WHO MOVED INTO THIS LABOUR MARKET AREA ON RETIREMENT AND ARE STILL RETIRED.

b) PEOPLE WHO MOVED INTO THIS LABOUR MARKET AREA ON RETIREMENT BUT WHO HAVE SUBSEQUENTLY TAKEN A JOB, IF THEY ARE MALE OVER 65 AND FEMALE OVER 60 YEARS.

c) PEOPLE CURRENTLY IN THE SERVICES

d) FULL-TIME STUDENTS

c) WOMEN WHO HAVE MOVED TO A NEW LABOUR MARKET ON MARRIAGE, PROVIDING THE HUSBAND IS NOT A LABOUR MIGRANT

TIME INTERVIEW STARTED	

254

Q.2. ASK THE LABOUR MIGRANT

Who else lives in this house and what is their relationship to you ?

PERSON	1	2	3	4	5	6	7	8	9	10	
RELATIONSHIP COL.	14	15	16	17	18	19	20	21	22	23	RECORD FULL DETAILS FOR ALL MEMBERS OF THE HOUSEHOLD.
Labour Migrant	1	1	1	1	1	1	1	1	1	1	
Spouse	2	2	2	2	2	2	2	2	2	2	
Parent	3	3	3	3	3	3	3	3	3	3	
Child	4	4	4	4	4	4	4	4	4	4	
Grandparent	5	5	5	5	5	5	5	5	5	5	
Grandchild	6	6	6	6	6	6	6	6	6	6	
Brother/Sister	7	7	7	7	7	7	7	7	7	7	
Other Adult Relation	8	8	8	8	8	8	8	8	8	8	
Other Child Relation	9	9	9	9	9	9	9	9	9	9	
Other Adult not Relation	0	0	0	0	0	0	0	0	0	0	
Other Child not Relation	A	A	A	A	A	A	A	A	A	A	
SEX COL.	24	25	26	27	28	29	30	31	32	33	
Male	1	1	1	1	1	1	1	1	1	1	SEX
Female	2	2	2	2	2	2	2	2	2	2	
AGE 0 – 4	3	3	3	3	3	3	3	3	3	3	AGE GROUP
5 – 14	4	4	4	4	4	4	4	4	4	4	
15 – 19	5	5	5	5	5	5	5	5	5	5	
20 – 24	6	6	6	6	6	6	6	6	6	6	
25 – 34	7	7	7	7	7	7	7	7	7	7	
35 – 44	8	8	8	8	8	8	8	8	8	8	
45 – 59	9	9	9	9	9	9	9	9	9	9	
60 – 64	0	0	0	0	0	0	0	0	0	0	
65 +	A	A	A	A	A	A	A	A	A	A	
MARITAL STATUS COL.	34	35	36	37	38	39	40	41	42	43	Is he(she) married, single, widowed etc. ?
Married	1	1	1	1	1	1	1	1	1	1	
Single	2	2	2	2	2	2	2	2	2	2	
Widowed	3	3	3	3	3	3	3	3	3	3	
Divorced/Separated	4	4	4	4	4	4	4	4	4	4	
WORKING STATUS Full-time	5	5	5	5	5	5	5	5	5	5	Is he(she) working or not?
Part-time	6	6	6	6	6	6	6	6	6	6	
Unemployed	7	7	7	7	7	7	7	7	7	7	
Sick	8	8	8	8	8	8	8	8	8	8	
Retired	8	9	9	9	9	9	9	9	9	9	
Not-working/pre-school	0	0	0	0	0	0	0	0	0	0	
15+ in full time education	A	A	A	A	A	A	A	A	A	A	
Under 15 at school	B	B	B	B	B	B	B	B	B	B	

Q.2.

PERSON	1	2	3	4	5	6	7	8	9	10
What type of firm/ organisation does he/she work for ?										
What exactly does he/she do ? (SPECIFY)										
Does this require special qualifications? (TICK) (SPECIFY)										
Internal (eg. Banks) Certificates										
H.N.C. (Higher National Certificates)										
Diploma										
Degree Other										

OFFICE
USE
ONLY

COL.44

Col.45.

Q.2 continued

PERSON	1	2	3	4	5	6	7	8	9	10		
COL.	46	47	48	49	50	51	52	53	54	55		
Which other educational qualifications (if any) are held?												REPHRASE THIS QUESTION – "What educational qualifications"etc. TO THOSE NOT CURRENTLY IN EMPLOYMENT
C.S.E.	1	1	1	1	1	1	1	1	1	1		
'O' Level	2	2	2	2	2	2	2	2	2	2		
'A' Level	3	3	3	3	3	3	3	3	3	3		
H.N.C.	4	4	4	4	4	4	4	4	4	4		
DIPLOMA	5	5	5	5	5	5	5	5	5	5		
DEGREE	6	6	6	6	6	6	6	6	6	6		
OTHERS (Specify)												
COL.	56	57	58	59	60	61	62	63	64	65	Skip	Card 1 Code
AGE ON LEAVING SCHOOL 13 years	1	1	1	1	1	1	1	1	1	1		
14 years	2	2	2	2	2	2	2	2	2	2		
15 years	3	3	3	3	3	3	3	3	3	3		
16 years	4	4	4	4	4	4	4	4	4	4		
17 years	5	5	5	5	5	5	5	5	5	5		
18 years	6	6	6	6	6	6	6	6	6	6		
19 or over	7	7	7	7	7	7	7	7	7	7	Q.3a.	

Q.3a)   Would you say your accomodation here is

A self-contained house	1	Q.3b.
A bungalow	2	Q.3c.
A flat or maisonette or (Huddersfield only) Under dwelling	3	Q.3d.
Other type e.g. hostel, living with parents-in-law, etc.	4	Q.4.
Others (specify)	9	Q.4.

Col.66 (right margin, Q.3a)

Col.67 (right margin, Q.3b)

Q.3b)   Is it detached/semi-detached or terrace/town house ?

detached house	1	Q.4.
semi-detached	2	Q.4.
terraced/town house	3	Q.4.

Q.3c)   Is it detached/semi-detached or terraced ?

detached bungalow	4	Q.4.
semi-detached bungalow	5	Q.4.
terraced bungalow	6	Q.4.

Q.3d)   Is it self-contained or with shared facilities ?

self-contained flat	7	Q.4.
flat with shared facilities	8	Q.4.

257

COL.68				Skip	Card 1 Code
L.R.		B.R.			

Q.4. a) How many living rooms do you have ?

b) How many bedrooms do you have ?
c) Is this a single bedsitter ?
d) Are any rooms used both as living rooms and bedrooms ?

					Skip	Card 1 Code
1	1	1	7			
2	2	2	8			
3	3	3	9			
4	4	4	0			
5+	5	5+	A			

YES	
NO	

Single Bedsitter   B

Rooms are used as both living and bedrooms

WRITE IN DETAILS ....

....   Q.5.

Q.5. Have you any outside space of your own with this accommodation?   Col.69

Garden   1

Other

Specify:.........   Q.6.

Q.6. Is there a garage provided with this accommodation ?

Yes   A

No   B   Q.7a.

Q.7a. Do you own or rent this house or flat ?

Own   1   Q.7b.   Col.70

Rent   2   Q.7c.

Other e.g.
Rent Free
(Specify) ....   Q.10a.

Q.7b. With mortgage or without mortgage ?

With   6   Q.8a.

Without   7   Q.8a.

Q.7c. Is that from the local authority, privately furnished or privately unfurnished ?

From Local Authority   9   Q.9a.

Privately furnished   0   Q.9a.

Privately unfurnished   A   Q.9a.

INTERVIEWERS NOTE:

THOSE WHO OWN, ABOVE, GO TO Q.8a.

THOSE WHO RENT ABOVE, GO TO Q.9a.

THOSE WHO ARE OTHER, GO TO Q.10a.

258

		Skip	Card 1 Code

OWNER OCCUPIERS

Q.8a. What was the market value of your house at the time you bought it ? (Probe - Building Society Valuation)

Col.71

£ - 0 to under 3,000	1	
3,000 to under 4,500	2	
4,500 to under 6,000	3	
6,000 to under 7,500	4	
7,500 to under 9,000	5	
9,000 to under 12,000	6	
12,000 to under 15,000	7	
15,000 and over	8	Q.8b.

Q.8b. Is your property free-hold or leasehold ?

Freehold	0	Q.8d.
Leasehold	A	Q.8c.

Q.8c. If leasehold, how much do you pay in ground rent per annum ?

Col.72

Per Annum - £ 0 - £ 50	1	
£ 50 to under £100	2	
£100 to under £200	3	
£200 and over	4	Q.8d.

Q.8d. How much do you pay in rates including water rates, per annum ?

Per Annum - £ 0 to under £ 50	6	
£ 50 to under £100	7	
£100 to under £150	8	
£150 and over	9	Q.8e.

Q.8e. Have you any other regular fixed payments to make, e.g. maintenance ?

Col.73

Yes	1	Q.8f.
No	2	Q.8h.

Q.8f. IF YES SPECIFY AND PROMPT IF NECESSARY.

Caretaking	3	
Gardening	4	
Other - Specify		Q.8g.

Q.8g. IF YES How much does this cost per annum ?

Per Annum - Under £ 50	9	SEE NOTE BELOW.
£ 50 to under £100	0	
£100 and over	A	

Q.8h. TO OWNER OCCUPIERS WITH MORTGAGES (Coded 6 Question 7b)
How much is your regular mortgage payment per month ? (N.B. TO INTERVIEWER - where payment is made as part of an insurance policy and the exact figure is not known, try to get approx.)

Col.74

Per Month - Less than £20	1	
£20 to under £30	2	
£30 to under £40	3	
£40 to under £50	4	
£50 to under £60	5	
£60 to under £70	6	
£70 and over	7	Q.8j.

OWNER OCCUPIERS WITHOUT MORTGAGE - SKIP TO Q.11.

			Skip	Card 1 Code

Q.8j.   What was the amount you paid in deposit .... and what % of the cost of your house did this form ?

				Col.75
	Less than 10%	1		
	10% to under 20%	2		
	20% to under 40%	3		
	40% to under 60%	4		
	60% and over	5	Q.11.	

RENTED FROM LOCAL AUTHORITY OR PRIVATELY

Q.9a.   Does your monthly payment of rent include payment for rates ? (including water rates).

				Col.76
	Yes	1	Q.9b.	
	No	2	Q.9c.	

Q.9b.   If Yes - How much do you pay per month for rent and rates including water rates combined ?

Per Month - Under £10	3	
£10 to under £20	4	
£20 to under £30	5	
£30 to under £40	6	
£40 to under £50	7	
£50 to under £60	8	
£60 to under £70	9	
£70 and over	0	Q.9d.

Q.9c.   If No - How much do you pay per month in rent ?

			Col.77
Per Month - Under £10	1		
£10 to under £20	2		
£20 to under £30	3		
£30 to under £40	4		
£40 to under £50	5		
£50 to under £60	6		
£60 to under £70	7		
£70 and over	8		

How much do you pay in rates including water rates per annum ?

Per Annum - Under £50	9	
£50 to under £100	0	
£100 to under £150	A	
£150 and over	B	Q.9d.

Q.9d.   Are any services included in your rent, e.g. heating ?

				Col.78
	Yes	1	Q.9e.	
	No	2	Q.11.	

Q.9e.   If Yes, please specify: FOR EACH NOT MENTIONED SPONTANEOUSLY ASK HOW ABOUT HEATING, REPAIRS ETC.

Heating	3	
Repairs	4	
Cleaning/Caretaking	5	
Other - Specify		
....		
....		Q.11.

260

Q.10a. Is this accommodation rent free ?

		Skip	Card 2 Code
Yes	1	Q.10b.	Col.14
No	2	Q.10d.	

Q.10b. Are you required to undertake any services instead of rent ?

None	3	
General domestic duties	4	
Cleaning only	5	
Caretaking	6	
Other - Specify		
....		Q.10c.

Q.10c. Are you required to make other fixed payments e.g. maintenance, rates etc. PLEASE SPECIFY.

Repairs	1	Col.15
Maintenance	2	
ALL ANSWERING Q.10b. and	Other - Specify	
c. NOW SKIP TO Q.11.	....	Q.11.

Q.10d. How much do you pay in rent per month ?

Less than £10	1		Col.16
£10 to under £20	2		
£20 to under £30	3		
£30 to under £40	4		
£40 to under £50	5		
£50 to under £60	6		
£60 to under £70	7	SEE NOTE	
£70 and over	8	BELOW.	

ALL ANSWERING NO at Q.10a. NOW ASK Q.10e. and f. and g.

Q.10e. What services, if any are included in this payment ?

(FOR EACH NOT MENTIONED ASK HOW ABOUT ....)

Heating	1	Col.17
Meals	2	
Cleaning/Caretaking	3	
Repairs	4	
Maintenance	5	
Other - Specify		
....		Q.10f.

Q.10f. Have you any other fixed payments to make not included in your rent ? e.g. Maintenance, rates.

Yes	1	Q.10g.	Col.18
No	2	Q.11.	

Q.10g. What are these ? (SPECIFY)

Maintenance	4	
Rates	5	
Other - Specify		
....		Q.11.

Q.11. Could you please tell me within which group your average NET
INCOME falls. By NET INCOME I mean your income less deductions
for Tax, and including overtime and bonus, where these are
regular occurrences. Please include any earnings from part-time
employment. (SHOW CARD A)

FOR THOSE UNCERTAIN e.g. SELF-EMPLOYED OR ONLY RECENTLY IN
EMPLOYMENT Could you please tell me what you think your income
will be per month ?

(INTERVIEWER: Where income
is given per week,
multiply by 4 to record
monthly figure and insert
in appropriate box.)

Monthly Income –	Col.19 L.M.	Col.20 Spouse
Less than £40	1	1
£ 40 to under £ 60	2	2
£ 60 to under £ 80	3	3
£ 80 to under £120	4	4
£120 to under £240	5	5
£240 to under £400	6	6
£400 and over	7	7

Q.12a.

Q.12a. Do you have a fixed place of work ?

Yes   1   Q.12c.   Col.21

No   2   Q.12b.

Q.12b. FOR THOSE WHO DO NOT HAVE A FIXED PLACE OF WORK E.G. SALESMEN,
BUILDING LABOURERS, OR THOSE WHOSE TIME IS DIVIDED BETWEEN
OFFICE WORK AND TRAVELLING.

In which area are you working at present ....

How far is that from here ?

0 – 25 miles   3

26 – 50 miles   4

51 – 100 miles   5

Over 100 miles   6

Scotland, Ireland &
Channel Isles   7

Abroad (Outside UK)   8   Q.12c.

Q.12c. How do you usually travel to work and how long does it take ?

Time	Car	Bus	Train	Walk	Cycle	Other	Total
	Col.22.		Col.23.		Col.24.		Col.25.
0 – 15 mins	1	6	1	6	1	6	1
16 – 30 mins	2	7	2	7	2	7	2
31 – 60 mins	3	8	3	8	3	8	3
Over 60 mins+	4	9	4	9	4	9	4

DO NOT OMIT TO CODE TOTAL JOURNEY.   Q.12d.

Q.12d. How much does it cost you per week ?

Weekly – Up to 50p   1   Col.26

50p to £1   2

Over £1 to £2   3

Over £2 to £4   4

Over £4   5

Nothing   6   Q.13.

262

		Skip	Card 2 Code

Q.13.   Where did you live before you moved here ?

PRECISE DETAILS.

.... Town/Village

.... Area/County.

How many miles from here is that ?

0 - 25 miles	1	Col.27
26 - 50 miles	2	
51 - 100 miles	3	
Over 100 miles	4	
Scotland, Ireland and Channel Isles	5	
Abroad (outside UK)	6	Q.14.

Q.14.   What date did you move here ?

.... Month .... Year

Less than 6 months ago	1		Col.28
6 months to 1 year ago	2		
More than 1 year ago	3	Q.15a.	

As we are interested to find out about the changes that take place when people move, I should like to ask you about your house and work when you lived in ....
(FILL IN FROM Q.13.) particularly in the last six months of your stay there.

Q.15a.   Were there any members of your household at ....
who did not move here with you and have not since joined you ?

RECORD IN GRID
OVERLEAF.

Yes	1	Q.15a,	Col.29
No	2	Q.15b.	

RECORD IN GRID OVERLEAF.

263

Q.15a. Members of household who did not move here with L.M.

Person	1	2	3	4	5	6
Relationship	Col.30	Col.31	Col.32	Col.33	Col.34	Col.35
Spouse	1	1	1	1	1	1
Parent	2	2	2	2	2	2
Child	3	3	3	3	3	3
Grandparent	4	4	4	4	4	4
Grandchild	5	5	5	5	5	5
Brother/Sister	6	6	6	6	6	6
Other Adult Relation	7	7	7	7	7	7
Other Child Relation	8	8	8	8	8	8
Other Adult Not Relation	9	9	9	9	9	9
Other Child Not Relation	0	0	0	0	0	0
Sex	Col.36	Col.37	Col.38	Col.39	Col.40	Col 41
Male	1	1	1	1	1	1
Female	2	2	2	2	2	2
Age						
0 - 4	3	3	3	3	3	3
5 - 14	4	4	4	4	4	4
15 - 19	5	5	5	5	5	5
20 - 24	6	6	6	6	6	6
25 - 34	7	7	7	7	7	7
35 - 44	8	8	8	8	8	8
45 - 59	9	9	9	9	9	9
60 - 64	0	0	0	0	0	0
65 +	A	A	A	A	A	A
Marital Status	Col.42	Col.43	Col.44	Col.45	Col.46	Col.47
Married	1	1	1	1	1	1
Single	2	2	2	2	2	2
Widowed	3	3	3	3	3	3
Divorced/Separated	4	4	4	4	4	4
Working Status						
Full-time	5	5	5	5	5	5
Part-time	6	6	6	6	6	6
Unemployed	7	7	7	7	7	7
Sick	8	8	8	8	8	8
Retired	9	9	9	9	9	9
Not-working/Pre School	0	0	0	0	0	0
15+ in full-time education	A	A	A	A	A	A
Under 15 at school	B	B	B	B	B	B

Col.48

Col.49

Skip
Q.15b.

Q.15b. Which members of your present household, **who were** not resident **at your previous address** have joined you since you moved here? (including e.g. new births, lodgers etc)

SEE
NOTE
BELOW.

Col.50

WRITE IN PERSON(S) NUMBER ....
INTERVIEWER: PLEASE CHECK THAT DETAILS OF THESE PERSONS HAVE
        BEEN RECORDED ON PAGE 2.

Q.15d.

Col.51

Q.15c. For the members of your household who moved here from your previous address i.e. excluding those listed in Q.15b. could you please give the following information, referring to the LAST SIX MONTHS AT YOUR PREVIOUS ADDRESS.

Person	1	2	3	4	5	6	7	8	9	10
Relationship	Col 52	Col 53	Col 54	Col 55	Col 56	Col 57	Col 58	Col 59	Col 60	Col 61
Labour Migrant	1	1	1	1	1	1	1	1	1	1
Spouse	2	2	2	2	2	2	2	2	2	2
Parent	3	3	3	3	3	3	3	3	3	3
Child	4	4	4	4	4	4	4	4	4	4
Grandparent	5	5	5	5	5	5	5	5	5	5
Grandchild	6	6	6	6	6	6	6	6	6	6
Brother/Sister	7	7	7	7	7	7	7	7	7	7
Other Adult Relation	8	8	8	8	8	8	8	8	8	8
Other Child Relation	9	9	9	9	9	9	9	9	9	9
Other Adult Not Relation	0	0	0	0	0	0	0	0	0	0
Other Child Not Relation	A	A	A	A	A	A	A	A	A	A
Marital Status	Col 62	Col 63	Col 64	Col 65	Col 66	Col 67	Col 68	Col 69	Col 70	Col 71
Married	1	1	1	1	1	1	1	1	1	1
Single	2	2	2	2	2	2	2	2	2	2
Widowed	3	3	3	3	3	3	3	3	3	3
Divorced/Separated	4	4	4	4	4	4	4	4	4	4
Working Status										
Full-time	5	5	5	5	5	5	5	5	5	5
Part-time	6	6	6	6	6	6	6	6	6	6
Unemployed	7	7	7	7	7	7	7	7	7	7
Sick	8	8	8	8	8	8	8	8	8	8
Retired	9	9	9	9	9	9	9	9	9	9
Not-working/Pre school	0	0	0	0	0	0	0	0	0	0
15+ in full-time education	A	A	A	A	A	A	A	A	A	A
Under 15 at school	B	B	B	B	B	B	B	B	B	B

CONTINUED ON NEXT PAGE

Q.15c. (cont'd)

Card 2
Code

PERSON	1	2	3	4	5	6	7	8	9	10
What type of firm does he/she work for ?										
What exactly does he/she do ? SPECIFY										
Does this require special qualifications ? (TICK)										
Internal (eg. Banks) Certificates										
H.N.C. (Higher National Certificates)										
Diploma										
Degree Other										

Col.72.

Col.73.

Same as before   A { FOR OFFICE USE ONLY – CODING DEPARTMENT

Different   B { TRANSFER INFORMATION TO COLUMN 77 – OVERPAGE. }

266

Q.16a. Was your accommodation in .... (FILL IN FROM Q.13.) at your last address:

		Skip	
A self-contained house	1	Q.16b.	Col.74
A bungalow	2	Q.16c.	
A flat or maisonette or (Huddersfield only) Under dwelling	3	Q.16d.	
Other type e.g. hostel, living with parents-in-law etc.	4	Q.17.	
Others (specify)	9	Q.17.	

Q.16b. Was it detached/semi-detached or terrace/town house ?

Detached house	1	Q.17.	Col.75
Semi-detached	2	Q.17.	
Terraced/Town house	3	Q.17.	

Q.16c. Was it detached/semi-detached or terraced ?

Detached bungalow	4	Q.17.
Semi-detached bungalow	5	Q.17.
Terraced bungalow	6	Q.17.

Q.16c. Is it self-contained or with shared facilities ?

Self-contained flat	7	Q.17.
Flat with shared facilities	8	Q.17.

INTERVIEWER. With reference to Q.3. please code previous accommodation as:

Same as now	A	
Different	B	Q.17.

Q.17. a) How many living rooms did you have ?

b) How many bedrooms did you have ?

c) Was this a single bedsitter ?

d) Were any rooms used both as living rooms and bedrooms ?

YES	
NO	

WRITE IN DETAILS

....

Col.76			
L.R.		B.R.	
1	1	1	7
2	2	2	8
3	3	3	9
4	4	4	0
5+	5	5+	A
Single Bedsitter			B
Rooms were used as both living and bedrooms			

....

INTERVIEWER. With reference to Q.4. please code previous number and use of rooms as:

Same as now	1	
Different	2	Q.18.

Col.77

			Skip	Card 2 Code

Q.18.   Did you have any outside space of your own with this accommodation ?

				Skip	**Card 2 Code**
Q.18.	Did you have any outside space of your own with this accommodation ?				
		Garden	1		Col.78
		Other - specify			
		. . . .			
	INTERVIEWER.	With reference to Q.5. please code previous situation as:			
		Same as now	7		
		Different	8	Q.19.	
Q.19.	Was there a garage provided with this accommodation ?				
		Yes	9		
		No	0		
	INTERVIEWER.	With reference to Q.6. please code previous situation as:			
		Same as now	A		
		Different	B	Q.20a.	
Q.20a.	Did you own or rent this house or flat ?				
		Own	1	Q.20b.	Col.79.
		Rent	2	Q.20c.	
		Other e.g. Rent Free (Specify)		Q.23a.	
Q.20b.	Was it with a mortgage or without a mortgage ?				
		With	6	Q.21a.	
		Without	7	Q.21a.	
Q.20c.	Was that from the local authority, privately furnished or privately unfurnished ?				
		From Local Authority	9	Q.22a.	
		Privately furnished	0	Q.22a.	
		Privately unfurnished	A	Q.22a.	
	INTERVIEWER.	With reference to Q.7. please code tenure of previous accommodation as:			Col. 80
		Same as now	A	SEE NOTE BELOW.	
		Different	B		

INTERVIEWERS NOTE.

THOSE WHO OWNED ABOVE, GO TO Q.21a.

THOSE WHO RENTED ABOVE, GO TO Q.22a.

THOSE WHO WERE OTHER, GO TO Q.23a.

OWNER OCCUPIERS - At your previous address in ....

Q.21a. What was the market value of your house at the time you sold it?

		Skip	Card 3 Code
£ - 000 to under £ 3,000	1		Col.14
£ 3,000 to under £ 4,500	2		
£ 4,500 to under £ 6,000	3		
£ 6,000 to under £ 7,500	4		
£ 7,500 to under £ 9,000	5		
£ 9,000 to under £12,000	6		
£12,000 to under £15,000	7		
£15,000 and over	8	Q.21b.	

Q.21b. Was your property free-hold or leasehold ?

		Skip	
Freehold	0	Q.21d.	
Leasehold	A	Q.21c.	

Q.21c. If leasehold, how much did you pay in ground rent per annum ?

		Skip	Card 3 Code
Per Annum - £ 0 - £ 50	1		Col.15
£ 50 to under £100	2		
£100 to under £200	3		
£200 and over	4	Q.21d.	

Q.21d. How much did you pay in rates including water rates, per annum?

		Skip	
Per Annum - £ 0 to under £ 50	6		
£ 50 to under £100	7		
£100 to under £150	8		
£150 and over	9	Q.21e.	

Q.21e. Did you have any other regular fixed payments to make, e.g. maintenance ?

		Skip	Card 3 Code
Yes	1	Q.21f.	Col.16
No	2	Q.21h.	

Q.21f. IF YES SPECIFY AND PROMPT IF NECESSARY.

		Skip	
Caretaking	3		
Gardening	4		
Other -Specify			
....		Q.21g.	

Q.21g. IF YES How much did this cost per annum ?

		Skip	
Per Annum - Under £ 50	9		
£ 50 to under £100	0	SEE NOTE BELOW.	
£100 and over	A		

TO OWNER OCCUPIERS WITH MORTGAGES (Coded 6 Question 20b)

Q.21h. How much was your regular mortgage payment per month ? (N.B. TO INTERVIEWER - where payment was made as part of an insurance policy and the exact figure is not known, try to get approx).

		Skip	Card 3 Code
Per Month - Less than £20	1		Col.17
£20 to under £30	2		
£30 to under £40	3		
£40 to under £50	4		
£50 to under £60	5		
£60 to under £70	6		
£70 and over	7	Q.21j.	

OWNER OCCUPIERS WHO DID NOT HAVE A MORTGAGE - SKIP TO Q.24.

269

Q.21j. What was the amount you paid in deposit .... and what
% of the cost of your house did this form ?

	Less than 10%	1	
	10% to under 20%	2	
	20% to under 40%	3	
	40% to under 60%	4	
	60% and over	5	Q.24.

Q.22a. RENTED FROM LOCAL AUTHORITY OR PRIVATELY
Did your monthly payment of rent include payment for rates ?
(including water rates).

	Yes	1	Q.22b.	Col.19.
	No	2	Q.22c.	

Q.22b. If Yes - How much did you pay per month for rent and rates
including water rates combined ?

Per Month -	Under £10	3	
	£10 to under £20	4	
	£20 to under £30	5	
	£30 to under £40	6	
	£40 to under £50	7	
	£50 to under £60	8	
	£60 to under £70	9	
	£70 and over	0	Q.22d.

Q.22c. If No - How much did you pay per month in rent ?

Per Month -	Under £10	1	Col.20
	£10 to under £20	2	
	£20 to under £30	3	
	£30 to under £40	4	
	£40 to under £50	5	
	£50 to under £60	6	
	£60 to under £70	7	
	£70 and over	8	

How much did you pay in rates including water rates per annum ?

Per Annum -	Under £50	9	
	£50 to under £100	0	
	£100 to under £150	A	
	£150 and over	B	Q.22d.

Q.22d. Were there any services included in your rent, e.g. heating ?

	Yes	1	Q.22e.	Col.21.
	No	2	Q.24.	

Q.22e. If Yes, please specify: FOR EACH NOT MENTIONED SPONTANEOUSLY
ASK HOW ABOUT HEATING, REPAIRS ETC.

Heating	3	
Repairs	4	
Cleaning/Caretaking	5	
Other - Specify		
....		
....		Q.24.

			Skip	Card 3 Code
Q.23a.	Was this accommodation rent free ?			Col.22.
	Yes	1	Q.23b.	
	No	2	Q.23d.	
Q.23b.	Were you required to undertake any services instead of rent ?			
	None	3		
	General domestic duties	4		
	Cleaning only	5		
	Caretaking	6		
	Other - Specify			
	....		Q.23c.	
Q.23c.	Were you required to make other fixed payments e.g. maintenance, rates etc. PLEASE SPECIFY.			Col.23.
	Repairs	1		
	Maintenance	2		
ALL ANSWERING Q.23b. and c. NOW SKIP TO Q.24.	Other - Specify			
	....		Q.24.	
Q.23d.	How much did you pay in rent per month ?			Col.24.
	Less than £10	1		
	£10 to under £20	2		
	£20 to under £30	3		
	£30 to under £40	4		
	£40 to under £50	5		
	£50 to under £60	6	SEE NOTE BELOW.	
	£60 to under £70	7		
	£70 and over	8		
ALL ANSWERING NO at Q.23a. NOW ASK Q.23e. and f. and g.				
Q.23e.	What services, if any were included in this payment ?			Col.25.
(FOR EACH NOT MENTIONED ASK HOW ABOUT)	Heating	1		
	Meals	2		
	Cleaning/Caretaking	3		
	Repairs	4		
	Maintenance	5		
	Other - Specify			
	....		Q.23f.	
Q.23f.	Did you have any other fixed payments to make not included in your rent ? e.g. Maintenance, rates.			Col.26.
	Yes	1	Q.23g.	
	No	2	Q.24.	
Q.23g.	What were they ? (SPECIFY)			
	Maintenance	4		
	Rates	5		
	Other - Specify			
	....		Q.24.	

271

ASK ALL

Q.24.   When you were living in .... could you
please tell me within which group your average NET INCOME
fell. By NET INCOME, I mean your income less deductions for
Tax, and including overtime and bonuses, where these are
regular occurrences. Please include any earnings from part-
time employment. (SHOW CARD A)

IF INCOME WAS IRREGULAR PLEASE GIVE AN ESTIMATE OF YOUR
AVERAGE MONTHLY INCOME IN THE LAST 6 MONTHS BEFORE YOU MOVED.

(INTERVIEWER: Where income is given per week, multiply by 4 to record monthly figure and insert in appropriate box.)	Monthly Income –	Col.27 L.M.	Col.28 Spouse
	Less than £40	1	1
	£ 40 to under £ 60	2	2
	£ 60 to under £ 80	3	3
	£ 80 to under £120	4	4
	£120 to under £240	5	5
	£240 to under £400	6	6
	£400 and over	7	7

Q.25a.

Q.25a.   When you lived in .... did you have a fixed
place of work ?

Yes	1	Q.25c.
No	2	Q.25b.

Col.29

Q.25b.   FOR THOSE WHO DID NOT HAVE A FIXED PLACE OR WORK E.G. SALESMEN,
BUILDING LABOURERS, OR THOSE WHOSE TIME WAS DIVIDED BETWEEN
OFFICE WORK AND TRAVELLING.

In which area were you working.
How far was that from here ?

0 – 25 miles	3
26 – 50 miles	4
51 – 100 miles	5
Over 100 miles	6
Scotland, Ireland & Channel Isles	7
Abroad (Outside UK)	8

Q.25c.

Q.25c.   How did you usually travel to work and how long did it take ?

Time	Car	Bus	Train	Walk	Cycle	Other	Total
	Col.30		Col.31		Col.32		Col.33.
0 – 15 mins	1	6	1	6	1	6	1
16 – 30 mins	2	7	2	7	2	7	2
31 – 60 mins	3	8	3	8	3	8	3
Over 60 mins+	4	9	4	9	4	9	4

DO NOT OMIT TO CODE TOTAL JOURNEY.

Q.25d.

Q.25d.   How much did it cost you per week ?

Weekly – Up to 50p	1
50p to £1	2
Over £1 to £2	3
Over £2 to £4	4
Over £4	5
Nothing	6

Col.34

Q.26.

	Skip	Card 3 Code

PART 2

In this second part, the questions ask about how you went about looking for a job and a house and any problems you had in moving house and job at the same time.

Q.26.   Why did you decide to come to .... (present labour market) ?

Col.35.

Q.27.

Q.27.   In coming to .... you have changed both your place of work and your house. Could you describe to us, step by step the way in which this move took place, and the various procedures (eg application to a local authority for a house) which were involved.)
What was the first step you took ? (Probe did you look for a job first, or a house first ?)

Col.36.

And then what happened ?

Col.37.

CONTINUE TO PROBE.

Q.28.

Q.28.   What (if any) were the difficulties you encountered in changing your job and your house at the same time ? (PROBE FULLY)

Col.38.

Q.29.

EMPLOYMENT

Q.29.   Concerning your employment, on moving to ....
did you:

		Skip
Have A New Employer	1	Q.30a.
Have The Same Employer	2	Q.31a.
Remain/Become Self-Employed	3	Q.32a.
Remain/Become Unemployed	4	Q.33a.

Col.39.

Q.30a.   LABOUR MIGRANTS WITH NEW EMPLOYER
Why did you leave your previous employment ?

Voluntary	7
Redundancy	8
Dismissal	9
Retirement	0
Other - Specify	
....	Q.30b.

Q.30b.   What sort of job were you looking for when you left your
previous employment ?   CODE AS APPROPRIATE BUT DO NOT READ OUT.

Similar to the one I left	1
Better pay	2
Better pay and conditions	3
Job more interesting	4
More responsibility/ prospects	5
Job with less strain	6
Just a job/Any job	7
Other - Specify	
....	
....	Q.30c.

Col.40.

Q.30c.   Is your present job similar to the one you were looking for ?

Yes	A	Q.30e.
No	B	Q.30d.

Q.30d.   If No, why did you choose the particular job you are doing ?

Col.41.

Q.30e.

Q.30e.   Please name any other areas you looked for work in besides this
one ? (LIST ALL GIVEN)

Col.42.

Q.30f.

Q.30f. Why did you choose this <u>area</u> in particular ? <u>PRECODE COMMENT.</u>

Know people in the area	1
Lived in the area previously	2
Was able to find houseing here	3
Employment reasons mainly	4
Other - Specify	

....

CODE AS APPROPRIATE BUT DO <u>NOT</u> READ OUT.

Q.30g.

<u>LABOUR MIGRANTS WITH NEW EMPLOYER</u>

Q.30g. In what ways did you seek information about job? <u>DO NOT READ OUT</u>

Q.30h. How did you find the job you moved to ? <u>DO NOT READ OUT.</u>

	Q.30g Col.44.	Q.30h Col.45.
Employment Exchange	1	1
Private Employ. Agency	2	2
Local Papers	3	3
National Papers	4	4
Friends & Relatives	5	5
Chance Contact	6	6
Direct Approach	7	7
Business Contacts	8	8
Other - Specify -	....	....
	....	....
	....	....

SEE NOTE BELOW.

INTERVIEWER: Go to Questions 34 - 36.

Q.31a. <u>LABOUR MIGRANTS WITH SAME EMPLOYER</u>
Did you ask your employer to be transferred to ....
or did you move because your employer wanted you here ?

Col.46

Labour M. Choice	1	Q.31b.
Employer Choice	2	Q.31c.

Q.31b. <u>If L.M. asked Employer</u> - why did you ask your employer to
transfer you to .... ?

Col.47.

Q.34.

Q.31c. If Employer asked L.M. - why do you think your employer asked
you to move to .... ?

Col.48.

SEE NOTE BELOW.

INTERVIEWER: Go to Questions 34 - 36.

K

275

Q.32a. **SELF-EMPLOYED AFTER MOVE**
In the six months before moving to ....
were you self-employed ?

			Skip	Card 3 Code
	Yes	1	Q.32d.	Col.49.
	No	2	Q.32b.	

Q.32b. If No, why did you leave your previous employment ?

	Voluntary	3	
	Redundancy	4	
	Dismissal	5	
	Retirement	6	
	Other - Specify		
	....		Q.32c.

Q.32c. What sort of job were you looking for when you left your
previous employment ?

CODE AS APPROPRIATE BUT DO NOT READ OUT.			Col.50.
	Similar to the one I left	1	
	Better Pay	2	
	Better pay and conditions	3	
	Job more interesting	4	
	More responsibility/ prospects	5	
	Job with less strain	6	
	Just a job/Any job	7	
	Other - Specify		
	.......,...................		

What made you decide to become self-employed ?   Col.51.

	Q.32e.

Q.32d. If Yes to Q.32a. - Why did you give up your business in
.... ?   Col.52.

	Q.32e.

Q.32e. **TO ALL SELF-EMPLOYED L.M.**
Please name any other areas you looked for work in besides
this one ?   Col.53.

	Q.32f.

276

				Skip	Card 3 Code

Q.32f. Why did you choose this area in particular ? (CODE AS APPROPRIATE BUT <u>DO NOT</u> READ OUT)

Knew people in the area	1		<u>Col.54.</u>
Lived in the area previously	2		
Was able to find housing here	3		
Employment reasons mainly	4		
Other - Specify			
....		Q.32g.	

Q.32g. In deciding to set up business here, was there any information about this area which influenced your choice ? If so, please specify.

<u>Col.55.</u>

Q.34.

INTERVIEWER. Go to Questions 34 - 36.

Q.33a. <u>LABOUR MIGRANT UNEMPLOYED AFTER MOVE.</u>
In the six months before moving to ....
(Labour Market) were you unemployed ?

Yes	1	Q.33b.	<u>Col.56.</u>
No	2	Q.33c.	

Q.33b. For how long (approximately) were you unemployed ?

Less than 1 month	3	
Over 1 - 6 months	4	
Over 6 months to 1 year	5	
Over 1 year	6	Q.33c.

Q.33c. Why did you leave your previous employment ?

Voluntary	7	
Redundancy	8	
Dismissal	9	
Other - Specify		
....		Q.33d.

Q.33d. What sort of job were you looking for when you left your previous employment ? (or became unemployed) ?
CODE AS APPROPRIATE BUT <u>DO NOT</u> READ OUT.

Similar to the one I left	1	<u>Col.57.</u>
Better Pay	2	
Better pay and conditions	3	
Job more interesting	4	
More responsibility/prospects	5	
Job with less strain	6	
Just a job/Any job	7	
Other - Specify		
....		Q.33e.

Q.33e. Please name any other areas you looked for work in besides this one ?

Q.33f.

Q.33f. Why did you choose to move to this area in particular ?
CODE AS APPROPRIATE BUT <u>DO NOT</u> READ OUT.

Knew people in the area	1
Lived in the area previously	2
Was able to find housing here	3
Employment reasons mainly	4
Other - Specify	
....	

Col.59.

Q.33g.

Q.33g. In what ways did you seek information about jobs ? <u>CODE BUT DO NOT READ OUT.</u>

Employment Exchange	1
Private Employ. Agency	2
Local Papers	3
National Papers	4
Friends & Relatives	5
Chance Contacts	6
Direct Approach	7
Business Contact	8
Other - Specify	
....	

Col.60.

Q.33h.

Q.33h. What do you think are the reasons why you have not found employment ?

Col.61.

SEE NOTE BELOW.

QUESTIONS 34 - 36 TO SPOUSE, COMPARING WORK SITUATION PRESENT AND PREVIOUS GIVEN IN QUESTIONS 2 AND 15, AND RELATING TO THE PERIOD 6 MONTHS BEFORE THE MOVE TO (LABOUR MARKET) ....

INTERVIEWER. CHECK ON PRESENT AND PREVIOUS WORK SITUATION OF SPOUSE.

Col.62.

Spouse is <u>working</u> now and <u>was working</u> previously	1	Skip to Q.34.
Spouse is <u>working</u> now and was <u>not working</u> previously	2	Skip to Q.35.
Spouse is <u>not working</u> now and <u>was working</u> previously	3	Skip to Q.36.
Spouse is <u>not working</u> now and was <u>not working</u> previously	4	Skip to Q.37.

WHERE SPOUSE <u>IS</u> WORKING NOW AND WAS WORKING PREVIOUSLY.

Q.34. How does this job compare with the previous one ?

COMMENT -		
....	Pay,conditions,much the same	5
....	Better Pay	6
....	Worse Pay	7
....	Better Conditions	8
....	Worse Conditions	9
....	Friendlier	0
....	Not so Friendly	A
....	Not changed job	B

Col.63.

Q.37.

Q.35.   **WHERE SPOUSE IS WORKING NOW AND WAS NOT WORKING PREVIOUSLY**
Why have you taken a job ?

Q.37.

Q.36.   **WHERE SPOUSE IS NOT WORKING NOW BUT WAS WORKING PREVIOUSLY**

Why are you not working now ?

COMMENT -	Family Reasons	1
....	No Suitable Employment	2
....		

Col.65.

Q.37 - 48 INTERVIEWER - THE FOLLOWING QUESTIONS TO BE ASKED
OF THE LABOUR MIGRANT BUT WHERE SPOUSE HAS CONFLICTING OPINIONS
RECORD THIS ON THE LAST PAGE.

Q.37.   **HOUSING.**
Would you say that this house is very similar to the one you
had in mind when you decided to move from ....?
(fill in Town/Area).

	Yes	1	Q.38.	Col.66.
	No	2	Q.39.	
	D.K.	3	Q.38.	

INTERVIEWER: If Yes or D.K.-Skip to Q.38.
If No   -Skip to Q.39.

Q.38a.   IF YES OR D.K. TO Q.37.
In coming to the .... area why did you choose to
live in this district in particular ?   DO NOT READ OUT.

COMMENT -	Only house available	4
....	Good shopping	5
....	Good transport	6
....	Good schools	7
,.......................	Other -Specify	
....	....	

Col.67.

Q.38b.

Q.38b.   Please name any other areas, if any, outside of the
.... area, in which you considered living ?

Col.68.

Q.38c.

Q.38c.   Why did you choose the .... area ? DO NOT READ OUT

COMMENT -	Knew people in the area	1
....	Lived in the area previously	2
....	Was able to find housing here	3
....	Employment reasons mainly	4
....	Other - Specify	
....	....	

Col.69.

Col.70.

Q.38d.

		Skip	Card 3 Code

Q.38d. In what ways did you seek information about housing ?

COMMENT -   Estate Agents/Flat Agency   1   Col.71.

....   Newspaper Advertisements   2

....   Friends & Relatives   3

....   By going round District   4   Col.72.

....   Other - Specify

....   Q.38e.

Q.38e. IF 'YES' TO Q.37.
How did you find out about this house ?   Col.73.

Q.38f.

Q.38f. Why did you finally choose this house and district ?   Col.74.

Q.40a.

Q.39a. IF 'NO' TO Q.37.
Can you describe the kind of house you had in mind when you
decided to move from .... ?   Col.75.

Q.39b.

Q.39b. Please name the areas of the country in which you looked for
such a house ?   Col.76.

Q.39c.

Q.39c. Why did you choose the .... area ? (L.M.)
CODE AS APPROPRIATE BUT DO NOT READ OUT.

COMMENT -   Knew people in the area   1   Col.77.

....   Lived in the area previously 2

....   Was able to find housing   3
                                   here

....   Employment reasons mainly   4   Col.78.

....   Other - Specify

....   Q.39d.

280

Q.39d.   In what ways did you seek information about the kind of house you were originally looking for ?

Q.39e.   How did you find out about this house ?

		Q.39d.	Q.39e.
COMMENT - Q.39d.		Col.14.	Col.15.
....	Estate Agents/Flat Agency	1	1
....	Newspaper Advertisements	2	2
....	Friends and Relatives	3	3
....	By going round district	4	4
COMMENT - Q.39e.	Other - Specify	....	....
....		....	....
....		....	....
....		....	.... Q.39f.
....			

Q.39f.   Why did you finally choose this house and district even though the house was not what you originally had in mind ?

Col.16.

Q.40a.

Q.40a.   In moving from .... to .... did you receive any assistance towards the costs involved ?

Yes	1	Q.40b.	Col.17.
No	2	Q.41.	

Q.40b.   In what way(s) ?

Removal Expenses	3
Legal Expenses	4
Travel to old area	5
Accommodation short time	6
Financial assistance towards cost of accommodation	7
Other - Specify	
....	Q.40c.

Q.40c.   From whom did you receive this assistance ?

Present employer	1	Col.18.
Department of Employment	2	
Relative	3	
Friend	4	
Other - Specify		
....	Q.41.	

Q.41.   During this period, i.e. moving your house and job, did you have to use up any of your personal savings ?

Yes	9	
No	0	Q.42a.

281

Q.42a. Between leaving ...., and coming to live in your present house, did you stay in temporary (i.e. less than nine months) accommodation in either your old area or here ?

Col.19

		Skip
Yes	1	Q.42b.
No	2	Q.43.

Q.42b. <u>If Yes</u> - How long did you stay there ?

Col.20.

Less than 1 week	1	
1 week to 4 weeks	2	
Over 1 month to 3 months	3	
Over 3 months to 6 months	4	
6 - 9 months	5	
Over 9 months	6	Q.42c.

Q.42c. What type of accommodation did you occupy for this ?

Col.21.

Hotel/Boarding House	1	
Hostel	2	
Flat	3	
House	4	
Shared with Relatives	5	
Shared with friends	6	
Other - Specify		
....		Q.43.

Q.43a. <u>SOCIAL LIFE AND COMMUNITY TIES</u>
Has moving here resulted in any changes in your social life ?

Col.22.

COMMENT -	Yes	1	
....	No	2	Q.43b.
....			

Q.43b. Is this what you expected ?

COMMENT -	Yes	3	
....	No	4	Q.44.
....			

Q.44. <u>TO LABOUR MIGRANTS WITH CHILDREN</u>
To what extent, if any, has moving here affected your children ?
(a) Under 15 years. (b) 15 and over.

		Q.44a.	Q.44b.
COMMENT - Q.44a.		Col.23.	Col.24.
....	Very much	1	1
....	To some extent	2	2
....	Very little	3	3
....	Not at all	4	4
COMMENT - Q.44b.	Other - Specify	....	....
....		....	....
....		....	....
....		....	....	Q.45a.
....			

				Skip	Card 4 Code

Q.45a.   Did you know anyone in the .... area before you moved ?

	Yes	1	Q.45b.	Col.25.
	No	2	Q.45d.	

Q.45b.   If Yes. - Were they relatives or friends ?

	Relatives	3	
	Friends	4	Q.45c.

Q.45c.   To what extent, if any, did their presence in this area influence your decision to come ?

	Very much	5
	To some extent	6
	Very little	7
	Not at all	8
	Other - Specify	
	....	Q.46.

Q.45d.   If No. - Were you at all apprehensive about moving to an area in which you knew no-one ?

COMMENT -	Very apprehensive	1	Col.26.
....	A little apprehensive	2	
....	Not apprehensive	3	
....	Other - Specify		Col.27.
....	....		Q.46.

Q.46.   Is there anything you have gained by moving here ?

COMMENT -	Improvement in Housing	1	Col.28.
....	Improvement in Job Position	2	
....	Improvement in Income	3	
....	Improvement in Recreation	4	
....	Improvement in Social Life	5	Col.29.
,....................	Travelling Easier	6	
....	Other - Specify		
....	....		Q.47a.

Q.47a.   Is there anything about the old area you particularly miss ? If so what ?

COMMENT -	Friends & Relatives	1	Col.30.
....	Entertainment	2	
....	Schools for children	3	
....	Shopping facilities	4	
....	Recreation facilities	5	
....	Travelling Difficulties	6	
....	Other - Specify		
....	....		Q.47b.

Q.47b.   On balance would you say that you (i.e. the Labour Migrant) are happier or less happy since moving here ?

COMMENT -	Happier	1	Col.31.
....	Less Happy	2	
....	Don't Know	3	
....			Q.48.

K2

283

MIGRATION EXPERIENCE

INTERVIEWER - WHERE YOU ARE UNCERTAIN ABOUT THE TOWN/AREA
                   GIVEN, OBTAIN THE COUNTY FOR THAT TOWN/AREA

Q.48.   TO LABOUR MIGRANT

a)   Where were you born ? .... (Town)

                         .... (County)

b)   As far as you can remember, please list the town/areas
in which you have lived since your birth in ....
(given above) until this most recent move to
....
Give some indication of how long you lived in each
area.

STARTING WITH YOUR SCHOOL YEARS

PLACE	CODE	HOW LONG LIVED THERE

c)   Please indicate the following where applicable:-   CODE

1. Where did you live on leaving school	A
2. Where did you live during higher education	B
3. Where did you live on entering the workforce	C
4. Where did you live on marriage	D
5. The move which involved leaving the parental home	E

INTERVIEWER - PLEASE PLACE THE APPROPRIATE CODE LETTER IN THE
BOX AGAINST THE PLACES MENTIONED. IT WILL BE
POSSIBLE FOR MORE THAN ONE LETTER TO APPEAR IN
A BOX.

FOR OFFICE USE ONLY - CARD 4			
Col.32.	Col.33.	Col.34.	Col.35.

Q.49.

284

Q.49. TO SPOUSE

a) Where were you born ? .... (Town)

.... (County)

b) As far as you can remember, please list the towns/areas
in which you have lived since birth in ....
(given above) until this most recent move to
....
Give some indication how long you lived in each area.

STARTING WITH YOUR SCHOOL YEARS

PLACE	CODE	HOW LONG LIVED THERE

c) Please indicate the following where applicable:-

	CODE
1. Where did you live on leaving school	A
2. Where did you live during higher education	B
3. Where did you live on entering the workforce	C
4. Where did you live on marriage	D
5. The move which involved leaving the parental home	E

INTERVIEWER - ENTER THE CODES AS BEFORE.

FOR OFFICE USE ONLY - CARD 4			
Col.36.	Col.37.	Col.38.	Col.39.

Q.50.

285

	Skip	Card 4 Code

Q.50. Do you expect to be both living and working in
....

<table>
<tr><td>a) In two years -</td><td>Yes</td><td>1</td><td>Q.50b.</td><td>Col.40.</td></tr>
<tr><td></td><td>No</td><td>2</td><td>Q.50b.</td><td></td></tr>
<tr><td>b) In five years -</td><td>Yes</td><td>4</td><td>See Note.</td><td></td></tr>
<tr><td></td><td>No</td><td>5</td><td>Q.50c.</td><td></td></tr>
</table>

IF 'NO' TO EITHER OF THE ABOVE QUESTIONS: (LEAVE DIRECTION IN)

c) Why ?

		Col.41.
		Col.42.
	Q.51.	

Q.51. Finally, considering everything you have said, what were the
three most important reasons for moving, in order of importance?

1.

		Col.43.

2.

		Col.44.

3.

		Col.45.
	CLOSE.	

THANK INFORMANT AND CLOSE INTERVIEW.

```
TIME INTERVIEW COMPLETED
```

286

....
....
....

287

Bibliography

Bakke, E.W. (ed.), *Labor Mobility and Economic Opportunity*, New York 1964.

Barbolet, R.H., 'Housing classes and the socio-ecological system', Centre for Environmental Studies *University Working Paper* 4, 1969.

Becker, G., *Human Capital*, New York 1964.

Berry, B.J.L. (ed.), 'Comparative Factorial Ecology' *Economic Geography* 47, No. 2 (Supplement), 1971, pp. 209–367.

Blumen, I., Kogan, M. and McCarthy, P.J., *The Industrial Mobility of Labor as a Probability Process*, Ithaca, N.Y., 1955.

Bogue, D.J., *The Population of the United States*, Glencoe, Ill., 1959.

Burn, S.M., 'Local Authority Housing: Implications for Labour Mobility' M. Phil. thesis, Department of Town Planning, University College London, 1972.

Burney, E., *Housing on Trial: a Study of Immigrants and Local Government*, London 1967.

Butler, E.W., Chapin, F.S., Jr., Hemmens, G.C., Kaiser, E.J., Stegman, M.A. and Weiss, S.F., 'Moving Behavior and Residental Choice: a National Survey' *National Cooperative Highway Research Program Report* 81, Highway Research Board, 1969.

Census of Population, *Sample Census 1966, England and Wales*, HMSO, London.

Centre for Urban Studies, *Housing in Camden*, London 1967.

Chisholm, M. and Manners, G. (eds.), *Spatial Policy Problems of the British Economy*, Cambridge 1971.

Clark, B.D. and Gleave, M.B. (compilers), *Social Patterns in Cities*, Institute of British Geographers, Special Publication no. 5, 1973.

Confederation of British Industry, *C.B.I. Regional Study: Regional Development and Distribution of Industry Policy*, duplicated typescript, 1968.

Connell, J., 'Social networks in urban society' in B.D. Clark and M.B. Gleave (compilers), *Social Patterns in Cities*, Institute of British Geographers, Special Publication no. 5, 1973, pp. 41–52.

Consumers' Association, 'The cost of moving home' *Which?*, June 1973, pp. 174–6.

Cullingworth, J.B., *English Housing Trends*, Occasional Papers on Social Administration, no. 13, London 1965.

Cullingworth, J.B., *Housing and Labour Mobility*, OECD, Paris 1969.

Cullingworth, J.B., 'Housing Analysis', in S.C. Orr and J.B. Cullingworth (eds), *Regional and Urban Studies*, London 1969, pp. 149–87.

Cullingworth, J.B., *Scottish Housing in 1965*, HMSO, Edinburgh 1967.

Daniel, G.H., 'Some factors affecting the movement of labour', *Oxford Economic Papers* 3, 1940, pp. 144–79.

Department of Employment, *Family Expenditure Survey: Report for 1971*, HMSO, London 1972.

Department of the Environment, *Long Term Population Distribution in Great Britain – a Study*, Report by an Inter-departmental Study Group, HMSO, London 1971.

Department of the Environment, 'Survey of Movers 1972' (not yet published).

Dixon, W.J. (ed.), *BMD: Biomedical Computer Programs. X-series Supplement*, University of California Publications in Automatic Computation, no. 3, 1970.

Donnison, D.V., *The Government of Housing*, Harmondsworth, Middx., 1967.

Donnison, D.V., 'The movement of households in England', in D.V. Donnison, C. Cockburn, J.B. Cullingworth and A.A. Nevitt, *Essays on Housing*, Occasional Papers on Social Administration, no. 9, London 1964, pp. 42–67.

Donnison, D.V., Cockburn, C. and Corlett, T., *Housing since the Rent Act*, Occasional Papers on Social Administration, no. 3, Welwyn 1961.

Donnison, D.V., Cockburn, C., Cullingworth, J.B. and Nevitt, A.A., *Essays on Housing*, Occasional Papers on Social Administration, no. 9, London 1964.

Drewett, J.R., 'The definition of Standard Metropolitan Labour Areas', Urban Growth Study, Political and Economic Planning, *Working Paper* no. 1, 1968.

Eversley, D.E.C., 'Population changes and regional policies since the war' *Regional Studies* 5, 1971, pp. 211–28.

Fielding, A.J., 'Internal migration in England and Wales', Centre for Environmental Studies *University Working Paper* 14, 1971.

Friedlander, D. and Roshier, R.J., 'A study of internal migration in England and Wales. Part II: Recent internal migrants – their movements and characteristics', *Population Studies* 20, 1966, pp. 45–59.

Gluckman, M. (ed.), *Closed Systems and Open Minds: the limits of Naivety in Social Anthropology*, Edinburgh 1964.

Goodman, J.F.B., 'The definition and analysis of local labour markets: some empirical problems' *British Journal of Industrial Relations* 8, 1970, pp. 179–95.

Gray, P.G. and Russell, R., *The Housing Situation in 1960*, HMSO, London 1962.

Hadjifotiou, N., 'The analysis of migration between Standard Metropolitan Labour Areas in England and Wales', Housing and Labour Mobility Study, Department of Geography, University College London, *Working Paper* no. 4, 1972.

Hadjifotiou, N., 'The multivariate classification of local labour market areas', Housing and Labour Mobility Study, Department of Geography, University College London, *Working Paper* no. 2, 1971.

Hadjifotiou, N. and Robinson, H., 'Employment and housing conditions in four selected labour market areas in England and Wales', Housing and Labour Mobility Study, Department of Geography, University College London, *Working Paper* no. 5, 1972.

Hall, P., 'Spatial structure of metropolitan England and Wales', in M. Chisholm and G. Manners (eds.), *Spatial Policy Problems of the British Economy*, Cambridge 1971, pp. 96–125.

Harris, A.I. and Clausen, R., *Labour Mobility in Great Britain: 1953–63,* HMSO, London 1967.

Hart, R.A., 'A model of inter-regional migration in England and Wales', *Regional Studies* 4, 1970, pp. 279–96.

Herbert, D,T., 'Residential mobility and preference: a study of Swansea', in B.D. Clark and M.B. Gleave (compilers), *Social Patterns in Cities*, Institute of British Geographers, Special Publication no. 5, 1973, pp. 103–21.

Herbert, D.T., 'The residential mobility process: some empirical observations' *Area* 5, 1973, pp. 44–8.

Herne, R., 'Housing and labour mobility: some theoretical considerations', Housing and Labour Mobility Study, Department of Geography, University College London, *Working Paper* no. 6, 1972.

Holmans, A.E., 'A forecast of effective demand for housing in Great Britain in the 1970s', *Social Trends* 1, 1970, pp. 33–42.

Hunter, L.C. and Reid, G.L., *Urban Worker Mobility*, OECD, Paris 1968.

Jackson, J.A. (ed.), *Migration*, Cambridge 1969.

Jansen, C.J., 'Some sociological aspects of migration' in J.A. Jackson (ed.), *Migration*, Cambridge 1969, pp. 60–73.

Johnson, J.H., Salt, J. and Wood, P.A., 'Housing and the geographical mobility of labour in England and Wales: some theoretical considerations', in L.A. Kosinski and R.M. Prothero (eds.), *People on the Move* (in press).

Johnston, R.J., 'Population movements and metropolitan expansion: London, 1960–61' *Transactions, Institute of British Geographers* no. 46, 1969, pp. 69–91.

Johnston, R.J., *Urban Residential Patterns*, London 1971.

Kerr, C., 'The balkanization of labor markets', in E.W. Bakke (ed.),, *Labor Mobility and Economic Opportunity*, New York 1964.

Kosinski, L.A. and Prothero, R.M. (eds.), *People on the Move* (in press).

Ladinsky, J., 'Occupational determinents of geographic mobility among professional workers' *American Sociological Review* 32, 1967, pp. 253–64.

Lansing, J.B. and Morgan, J.N., 'The effect of geographical mobility on income' *Journal of Human Resources* 2, 1967, pp. 449–60.

Lansing, J.B. and Mueller, E., *The Geographic Mobility of Labor*, Ann Arbor, Mich., 1967.

MacKay, D.I., Boddy, D., Brack, J., Dieck, J.A. and Jones, N., *Labour Markets under Different Employment Conditions*, London 1971.

Mangalam, J.J., *Human Migration: a Guide to Migration Literature in English 1955–1962*, Lexington, Ky., 1968.

Mann, M., *Workers on the Move: the Sociology of Relocation*, Cambridge 1973.

McDonald, G.C., 'Social and geographical mobility: studies in the New Towns', Department of Geography, University College London, *Occasional Paper* no. 12, 1970.

McGinnis, R., 'A stochastic model of social mobility' *American Sociological Review* 33, 1968, pp. 712–22.

Merton, R.K., *Social Theory and Social Structure*, Glencoe, Ill., 1957.

Ministry of Housing and Local Government, *Council Housing – Purposes, Procedures and Priorities*, 9th Report, The Housing Management Sub-Committee, Central Housing Advisory Committee, HMSO, London 1969.

Moore, E.G., 'Residential Mobility in the City' *Resource Paper* 13, Commission on College Geography, Association of American Geographers, 1972.

Morgan, B.S., '"Why Families Move": a re-examination', *Professional Geographer* 25, 1973, pp. 124–9.

Morrison, P.A., 'Theoretical issues in the design of population mobility models', *Environment and Planning* 5, 1973, pp. 125–34.

North Regional Planning Committee, *Mobility and the North* (3 volumes), 1967.

Oliver, F.R., 'Inter-regional migration and unemployment, 1951–61'

Journal of the Royal Statistical Society, Series A, 127, 1964, pp. 42–75.

Organisation for Economic Co-operation and Development, *International Management Seminar on Active Manpower Policy*, OECD, Paris 1964.

Organisation for Economic Co-operation and Development, *Wages and Labour Mobility*, OECD, Paris 1965.

Orr, S.C. and Cullingworth, J.B. (eds.), *Regional and Urban Studies*, London 1969.

Pennance, F.G., and Gray, H., *Choice in Housing*, The Institute of Economic Affairs, London 1968.

Pickett, K.G., 'Aspects of migration in N.W. England 1960–61' *Town Planning Review* 38, 1967, pp. 233–44.

Richardson, H.W., Vipond, J. and Walker, J.B., *The Finance of House Purchase*, Housing Research Foundation, London 1972.

Robinson, H., 'Survey method and questionnaire design', Housing and Labour Mobility Study, Department of Geography, University College London, *Working Paper* no. 3, 1971.

Rose, A.M., 'Distance of migration and socio-economic status of migrants' *American Sociological Review* 23, 1958, pp. 420–3.

Rossi, P.H., *Why Families Move: a Study in the Social Psychology of Urban Residential Mobility*, Glencoe, Ill., 1955.

Salt, J., 'The impact of the Ford and Vauxhall plants on the employment situation of Merseyside, 1962–1965' *Tijdschrift voor Economische en Sociale Geografie* 58, 1967, pp. 255–64.

The Scottish Economy 1965 to 1970: a Plan for Expansion, Cmnd. 2864, HMSO, Edinburgh 1966.

Simmie, J.M., 'The sociology of internal migration', Centre for Environmental Studies *University Working Paper* 15, 1972.

Spence, N.A. and Taylor, P.J., 'Quantitative methods in regional taxonomy', *Progress in Geography: International Reviews of Current Research* 2, London 1970, pp. 1–64.

Stewart, M., 'Markets, choice and urban planning' *Town Planning Review* 44, 1973, pp. 201–20.

Stone, P.A., *Urban Development in Britain: Standards, Costs and Resources 1964–2004*, vol. 1 'Population Trends and Housing', Cambridge 1970.

Survey of Personal Incomes: 1969–70, HMSO, London 1972.

Tarver, J.D., 'Occupational migration differentials' *Social Forces* 43, 1964, pp. 231–41.

Taylor, R.C., 'Migration and motivation: a study in determinants and types', in J.A. Jackson (ed.), *Migration*, Cambridge 1969, pp. 99–133.

Thomas, D.S., *Research Memorandum on Migration Differentials*, Social Science Research Council Bulletin 43, New York 1938.

Thompson, W.R., *A Preface to Urban Economics*, Baltimore 1965.

US Department of Commerce: Bureau of the Census, 'Mobility of the population of the United States March 1963 to March 1964', *Current Population Reports: Population Characteristics* P-20, 141, 1965.

Van Arsdol, M.D., Jr., Sabagh, G., and Butler, E.W., 'Retrospective and subsequent metropolitan residential mobility' *Demography* 5, 1968, pp. 249–67.

Watson, W., 'Social mobility and social class in industrial communities', in M. Gluckman (ed.), *Closed Systems and Open Minds: the Limits of Naïvety in Social Anthropology*, Edinburgh 1964, pp. 129-57.

Welch, R.L., *Migration Research and Migration in Britain: a Selected Bibliography*, Occasional Paper no. 14, Centre for Urban and Regional Studies, University of Birmingham, 1971.

Wilkinson, R.K. and Gulliver, S., 'The economics of housing: a survey' *Social and Economic Administration* 5, 1971, pp. 83–99.

Willis, J., 'Population growth and movement', Centre for Environmental Studies *Working Paper* 12, 1968.

Wishart, D., 'CLUSTAN 1A' mimeographed booklet, Computing Laboratory, University of St. Andrews, 1969.

Woolf, M., *The Housing Survey in England and Wales: 1964*, HMSO, London 1967.

Index

Educational standard of migrants 105

Elasticity of labour supply 27–8

Employment characteristics of SMLAs 52–7

Employment of migrants 105

Employment Transfer Scheme (Resettlement Transfer Scheme) 12, 13

European Economic Community 1

Eversley, D.E.C. 8, 9

Factors encouraging migration, combination of 246

Friedlander, D. 105, 107

Gains from labour migration 218

Geographical mobility, index of 109–10

Geographical scale, problem of 32–3

Goodman, J. F. B. 35

Gravity model of migration 31

Gravity model approach 101

Gray, H. 109, 111

Hadjifotiou, N. 89

Harris, A. I. 5–6, 31, 103–5, 108, 112–13

Herbert, D. T. 116–17

Highly-educated workers, combination of factors influencing migration of 30

High Wycombe: conditions in, 1971 127–9; sources of migrants to 141

Households, overcrowded, distribution of 59

Household size of migrants 104

Household type of migrants 105

Houses completed in England and Wales, 1950–70 17

Housing: capital cost of 15; characteristics of 15; durability of 13; immobility of 15; rent-free 23; as a barrier to labour migration 1, 2

Housing as a barrier to migration, inadequacy of concept of 248

Housing aspirations of migrants 231–5

Housing cost 111–12; as a proportion of income 196–7; by tenure 194–5; present, of labour migrants 191–2; previous, of labour migrants 192–3

Housing characteristics of SMLAs 57–62

Housing choice, determinants of 234–5

Housing context in England and Wales 14

Housing stock, additions to 16

Housing tenure and migration 109

Housing tenure groups 18, 19

Housing tenures, England and Wales, 1971 185

Huddersfield: housing and employment conditions in, 1971 127–9; sources of labour migrants to 142

Hunter, L. C. 102–3

Industrial Selection Scheme 11, 13

Information about accommodation, sources of 116–17, 235–7

In-migrants: as a percentage of total residential population 48; major origin of 93

In-migrants to SMLAs: from other SMLAs 50–1; origins of 70

Intermediate skill groups, migration

potential of 31

Inter-regional migration in Britain 33

Inter-SMLA migration flows: analysis of 71–3; magnitude of 73–4; regional patterns of 87–96

Intra-urban population migration 32

Jansen, C. J. 107

Kerr, C. 35

Key Workers Scheme 12

Kogan, M. 108

Labour-market mechanism 27

Labour migrant households: accommodation of 172–9; age of 146; composition of 147; examples of 228–31; identification of 129–32; present tenure of 180–5; previous tenure of 180–3, 186; size of 148–51; type of 151

Labour migrants: ages of 144–5; career pattern of 103; classification of 201–3; distance moved by 138–9; distance moved by different socio-economic groups of 165; education of 151–3; future expectations of 223–5; housing aspirations of 231–5; housing tenure of 190; income of 155–6, 190; journey to work of 167–71; marital status of 144; migration experience of 166; personal characteristics of 139–71; previous tenure of 186; proportion receiving assistance 241; socio-economic group of 158–64; sex of 144; spouses of 145, 147, 157–8; unemployment of 153–5; working status of 144

Labour migrants' spouses, income of 157–8

Labour migration: barriers to 1; definition of 1, 5; long-distance affinities in 96; reasons for 206–17

Labour mobility, conflicting evidence on 2

Ladinsky, J. 107

Lansing, J. B. 103–4, 105–6, 113–14, 115

Leeds-centred migration pattern 86

Leeds in-migration, 1965–66 86

Leeds out-migration, 1965–66 87

Life cycle of migrants 102–3

Liverpool-centred migration pattern 86

Liverpool in-migration, 1965–66 84

Liverpool out-migration, 1965–66 85

Local authority accommodation, distribution of 61–2

Local authority renting 21

Local labour market: as study area 33; concept of 34–6; delimitation of 35–6, 39

Local employment exchanges, use for survey 130–1

Local unemployment rate, March 1972 10

Location readjustment, of labour force 28

London-centred migration pattern 77–9

London: in-migration, 1965–66 76; out-migration, 1965–66 78; per cent of in-migrants to SMLAs from 91; per cent of out-migra-

297

tion from SMLAs to 90

McCarthy, P. J. 108
McDonald, G. C. 109
McGinnis, R. 108
MacKay, D. I. 36
Managerial and professional workers, distribution of 55
Manual workers, distribution of 56
Manchester-centred migration pattern 82–6
Manchester: in-migration, 1965–66 82; out-migration, 1965–66 83
Marital status of migrants 104
Market research firms' surveys 130
Merton, R. K. 107
Migrants: characteristics of 101–12; education of 105; employment of 106
Migrants interviewed, number of 134
Migrants into Chatham, High Wycombe, Huddersfield, and Northampton, origins of 126
Migration: government sponsorship of 12–13; net advantage of 222–3; per cent of total residential population 45–7; rate of 8; rate of in US, 1963–64 106
Migration experience: in relation to distance moved 167; past 108
Moore, E. G. 107
Mortgage payments, monthly 199
Movement between occupations, barriers to 27–8
Movements of population, classification of 1
Moving home: consequences of 114–15; problems of 238–41; process of 115–16
Mueller, E. 103–4, 105–6, 113–15

National Coal Board, assistance to migration by 13
Natural increase, rates of 6, 8
New houses, survey of 129–30
Northampton: housing and employment conditions in 127–9; sources of labour migrants to 143
North Midlands, interlinkage in 94
North-east, interlinkage in 95
North Regional Planning Committee 112
North-west, interlinkage in the 94
Nucleus Labour Force Scheme 12

Occupational and spatial mobility, interdependence of 28–31
OECD report on labour mobility, 1965 5
Outmigrants from SMLAs: moving to other SMLAs 52; major destination of 92; per cent of total residential population 49
Owner-occupation 18, 20–1

Pennance, F. G. 109, 111
Personal difficulties in moving home 239
Political and Economic Planning 39
Population change, Britain, 1951–69 8
Primary information sources 236–7
Private-rented accommodation, distribution of 60

Questionnaire, design of 133, 135
Questionnaire survey, details of response to 132

Reasons for moving 112–15; effects of on expectations and behaviour of migrants 207; in relation to distance moved 113; in relation to housing choice 217; in relation to housing costs 213–16; in relation to income changes 208–10; in relation to resulting gains 219; in relation to socio-economic changes 210–12; SMLA contrasts in 216–17

Redistributive function of SMLAs 51

Regional system of interlinkage 94–5

Reid, G. L. 102–3

Rented accommodation, monthly cost of for migrants 200–1

Renting: local authority 21; private 22

Residential population, changes in 45–6

Richardson, H. W. 20

Roshier, R. J. 105, 107

Rossi, P. H. 112, 116–17

Sample, structure of 137

Simmie, J. M. 114–15

Social life changes on moving, perceived 220–2

Social losses from moving 220

Socio-economic group of migrants 106–7

South Wales, interlinkage in 95

Spence, N. A. 251

'Spiralism' 107, 210

SMLAs: classification map of 64; classification of 41, 44, 62-6; clustering diagram of 63; definition of 40; identification 42–3; migration characteristics of 45

Standard Metropolitan Statistical Area (USA) 39

Standard Regions 6–7; house-build-

ing in, during 1960s 16–17

Stewart, M. 2

Stone, P. A. 2

Success in obtaining 'hoped for' accommodation 232–3

Survey areas, choice of 123–6

Survey strategy 123–35

Tarver, J. D. 107

Taylor, P. J. 251

Taylor, R.C. 108

Temporary accommodation, need for 238, 240–1

Tenure changes after migration 187

Tenure groups, migration flows between 110–11

Thompson, W. R. 35

Timing problems in moving home 239

Toothill Report on the Scottish economy 2

Types of inter-SMLA flows of population 75

Unemployed male workers, distribution of 54

Unemployment, local variations in 9, 11

Unskilled workers, combination of factors influencing migration of 30

Value of housing purchased 198

Vipond, J. 20

Walker, J. B. 20

Watson, W. 107

West Midlands, interlinkage in 94

West Riding of Yorkshire, interlinkage in 95

Willis, J. 106

Woolf, M. 105, 106, 111, 114, 188